Democratization in Central a

Democratization in Central and Eastern Europe

Edited by

Mary Kaldor and Ivan Vejvoda

continuum
LONDON · NEW YORK

Continuum

The Tower Building, 11 York Road, London SE1 7NX
370 Lexington Avenue, New York, NY 10017-6503

First published 1999 by Pinter, an imprint of Cassell
Paperback edition published 2002

British Library Cataloguing-in-Publication Data
A catalogue record for this book is available from the British Library.

ISBN 1-85567-527-7 (hardback)
0-8264-5257-4 (paperback)

Library of Congress Cataloging-in-Publication Data

Democratization in Central and Eastern Europe / edited by Mary Kaldor
and Ivan Vejvoda.
    p. cm.
    Includes bibliographical references (p.   ) and index.
    ISBN 1-85567-527-7 (hardcover) – 0-8264-5257-4 (paperback)
    1. Democracy—Europe, Eastern—Case studies.   2. Europe, Eastern—
Politics and government—1989– —Case studies.   I. Kaldor, Mary.
II. Vejvoda, Ivan, 1949–

JN96.D45   1998
320.94'09171'7—dc21   97-42436
                                                                     CIP

Typeset by YHT Ltd, London
Printed and bound in Great Britain by Cromwell Press, Trowbridge, Wilts.

Contents

Contributors

Editors:

Mary Kaldor	School Professor, Centre for the Study of Global Governance, London School of Economics; formerly at Sussex European Institute, University of Sussex
Ivan Vejvoda	Executive Director, Fund for an Open Society, Belgrade, Yugoslavia; formerly at Sussex European Institute, University of Sussex

Country reports by:

András Bozóki	Central European University, Budapest, Hungary
Martin Bútora	University of Bratislava, Slovakia
Kęstutis Girnius	Vilnius, Lithuania; RFE, Prague
Zdeněk Kavan	University of Sussex
Rumyana Kolarova	University of Sofia, Bulgaria
Marcin Król	Graduate School for Social Research, Poland
Tonči Kuzmanić	University of Ljubljana, Slovenia
Alina Mungiu Pippidi	University of Bucharest, Romania
Martin Palouš	Charles University, Prague, Czech Republic
Andris Runcis	University of Riga, Latvia
Jüri Ruus	University of Tartu, Estonia

Foreword

Enlargement to include the countries of Central and Eastern Europe is a historic challenge for the European Union. It is a process that began with the political upheavals almost a decade ago and will not end until all applicants in the region are European Union members. Enlargement will enhance peace, stability and prosperity throughout Europe.

The European Commission plays an important role in the enlargement process. In July 1997 it published a comprehensive report, Agenda 2000, which contained not only opinions on the candidate countries, but also proposals on future financing and the reform of major policy areas. In preparing the opinions, the Commission assessed the applications for membership in terms of the political, economic and acquis-related criteria established by the European Council in 1993. The Commission's assessments were based on information from a number of sources including the applicant countries, member states, international organizations such as the Organization for Security and Cooperation in Europe and Council of Europe, as well as the academic world.

In this context, the study undertaken by Mary Kaldor and Ivan Vejvoda of the Sussex European Institute, together with a team of experts from the applicant countries, on the state of democracy in Central and Eastern Europe is of particular interest. I hope that its publication will stimulate a wider debate in present and future member states on how further to consolidate democracy in Europe.

Hans van den Broek
Commissioner for External Affairs, European Union

Preface to the Paperback Edition

More than a decade ago, the stirring events of 1989 opened the path of democracy and a market economy for the countries of Central and Eastern Europe (CEECs). In the ensuing and ongoing process of reform and democratization, all the countries of the region stated and reconfirmed their firm commitment to joining the European Union and other European and Atlantic organizations. The eastern enlargement of the EU was defined as a key strategic goal, and mechanisms and procedures were put in place to further this process.

This book, commissioned by the European Union in 1995, was the result of an in-depth study of the state of democracy in the CEECs prior to their engagement in the accession process. Its aim was to develop a methodology for assessing the process of democratization, which would assist the preparation of 'opinions' on eligibility for membership.

The European Commission pronounced its 'Opinions' on the candidate CEECs in 1997. During the Luxembourg summit of the European Council on 12–13 December 1997, five of the countries studied in the book – Poland, Hungary, the Czech Republic, Slovenia and Estonia (as well as Cyprus) – were invited as front-runners to begin accession negotiations in 1998. Two years later, at the Helsinki summit of the European Council on 10–11 December 1999, Bulgaria, Latvia, Lithuania, Romania and Slovakia were invited to begin negotiations in 2000 (along with Malta and the opening of the road to Europe for Turkey).

When the first draft of the manuscript was prepared in 1996, we advocated that these ten eligible CEECs should be included. This eventually occurred when the second-tier group was admitted to the EU accession negotiating table in 1999. It was clearly understood that each country would travel at its own speed and thus CEECs in the second group, if their negotiations advanced at a faster pace, could join the first group.

The key analytic point we made was that, in researching the state of these polities, a distinction should be made between formal and substantive democracy. It was concluded that all CEECs had more or less fulfilled the required conditions at the formal democratic level, i.e., the existence of institutions, rules and procedures. When we looked at the democratic political culture, however, and several of its features such as constitutional issues, human rights, political parties, the role of the media, public admin- istration, local government and civil society, it became clear that in many instances there were still clear deficiencies. These deficiencies were different in different countries and, at least in part, could be explained by burdensome historical legacies.

Since we wrote the book, all of the ten countries have gone through further alternations in power. In Slovakia, in September 1998, a coalition of parties defeated Vladimir Mečiar's ruling party. In Romania, in November 2000, Ion Iliescu's party returned to power after four years of reformist coalition government, and on 17 June 2001 the reformist government of Bulgarian Prime Minister Ivan Kostov was defeated by a newly emerged party, NMSII (National Movement for Simeon II), led by the former King, Simeon Saxco- burggotski. Although both are populist leaders, they proclaim a commitment to continuing internal reforms, the struggle against corruption and con- tinued negotiations with the EU. Most recently in the September 2001 general election in Poland, the Democratic Left Alliance (reformed or ex- communists) massively defeated the Solidarity bloc of parties in a low turn-out of 46 per cent of voters. Also in September, a former high-ranking Estonian Communist Party official Arnold Ruutel was elected President of Estonia by the electoral college.

These changes are proof of a continuing consolidation of democratic institutions and procedures. They are also testimony to the herculean difficulties these polities face in the transitional political, economic, social and judicial reform process. Voters-citizens in all CEECs have to varying degrees been dismayed by the social and economic costs they have had to pay on the path of reforming and restructuring their societies. And this explains the pendulum swings of the political parties in power after each election.

The difficulties faced by these countries are not merely a consequence of the burdens of the past. The conditionalities put forward by the international financial institutions and by the European Union have not always been tailored to the specific realities of each country. It seems rather that a single mould has been applied to all, causing greater difficulties and misunder- standings. Furthermore, the emphasis on the market and the formal aspects of democracy has led to a neglect of critical issues, in particular, the need to restructure the post-communist state. Hence, reform of public administra- tion, the streamlining of law enforcement agencies and the establishment of a truly independent judiciary all lagged behind other reforms, and this, in turn, has contributed to the continuing existence of corruption within the political and business elites, which has hindered political and economic progress.

Indeed, as we argue in the last chapter of the book, some of the difficulties faced by transitional countries are also experienced elsewhere in greater or lesser degrees. The tendency for political parties to become instruments of patronage rather than vehicles for political ideas, the disillusion with and growing apathy towards formal politics, the distrust of politicians, and growing tendencies towards populism, can be observed in many parts of the world. These phenomena can be partly explained in terms of the way in which the process known as globalization erodes the decision-making power at state level and therefore undermines the substantive character of democracy. However perfect the constitution, individual citizens cannot influence the decisions which affect their lives if the decisions which matter are taken at a European or global level. Developments since the book was written underscore this conclusion. At the same time, however, as we noted in the book, a tendency throughout East and Central Europe for the growth of civil society and for links between civil society at local levels with European and international institutions seems to have strengthened.

This book, with its individual contributions on the ten CEECs, stands today as relevant as when it first appeared. The issues that were identified at a general regional and specific country level remain in the forefront of the process of democratization. There is no doubt that the implementation of formal democratic rules and procedures is a long-term process, which requires the efforts of responsible and accountable governments. Nevertheless, our conclusions suggest that, if the process is to be sustained, international institutions, especially the European Union, have to find ways, in dialogue with civil society, to reduce the high social cost of reform. The state, political society and civil society share a common responsibility for strengthening substantive democracy in the CEECs, if a democratic political culture is to continue taking root.

Mary Kaldor
Ivan Vejvoda
October 2001

Acknowledgements

This book is based on a research project undertaken by the Sussex European Institute, University of Sussex at Brighton, in collaboration with the Forward Studies Unit of the European Commission and the Research Department of the Council of Europe. The aim of the project was to assess the process of democratization in those Central and East European countries (CEECs) eligible for membership in the European Union (EU) and the extent to which these countries met the political criteria for membership. The ten CEECs studied in this project were Estonia, Latvia, Lithuania, Poland, the Czech Republic, Slovakia, Hungary, Slovenia, Romania and Bulgaria.

We would like to thank the Forward Studies Unit of the European Commission as well as the Research Department of the Council of Europe in Strasbourg for making this project possible. Special thanks go to Fraser Cameron and Anna Michalski of the European Commission and to Francis Rosenstiel and Edith Léjard of the Council of Europe. We also want to thank the Sussex European Institute and its director Helen Wallace for providing the physical and intellectual environment conducive to accomplishing such a project, requiring as it did many transnational European links.

Our gratitude extends to all those who commented on drafts of various chapters: Helen Wallace, Martin Shaw, Antje Wiener, Zdeněk Kavan, Ulrich Sedelmeier, William Outhwaite. Thanks also to Konstanty Gebert, Paul Löser and Klaudijus Maniokas, who contributed to our first meeting in Sussex in January 1996; to Paul Lewis, Thanos Veremis, Michel Lesage, Gilles Bertrand and Vasil Hudak, who came to discuss the work in progress at Strasbourg in May 1996; and to Elémer Hankiss, who came to Sussex for our July 1996 meeting. Detailed comments on our introductory chapter were made at different stages by all the chapter-writers and additional editing help was provided by Zdeněk Kavan for the Slovak chapter and by Kestutis Girnius for the Latvian and Estonian chapters, for which we are most grateful.

A special thanks also goes to those who helped with the organization: Károly Grúber, assistant on the project; Jenny Forrest, secretary to the project; and Alasdair Young, who prepared the manuscript for the publisher, with the help of Katharina Grimme.

As is customary but also always necessary, we wish to underscore that the responsibility for the content of the chapters in this book lies entirely and exclusively with those who have written them and not with any of the institutions that sponsored the research project.

Mary Kaldor
Ivan Vejvoda

Abbreviations

AGA	Board of Shareholders (Romania)
BBB	Bulgarian Business Block
BSP	Bulgarian Socialist Party
CAP	Common Agricultural Policy (of the European Union)
CEECs	Central and East European countries
CIS	Commonwealth of Independent States
CME	Central European Media Enterprise
Comecon	Council of Mutual Economic Assistance
CPSU	Communist Party of the Soviet Union
CSCE	Conference on Security and Co-operation in Europe
CSSD	Czech Social Democratic Party
DAHR	Hungarian Alliance (Romania)
DCR	Democratic Convention of Romania
DEMOS	Democratic Opposition of Slovenia
DU	Democratic Union (Slovakia)
ECSC	European Coal and Steel Community
EDU	European Democratic Union
EMU	economic and monetary union
EU	European Union
FIDESZ	Federation of Young Democrats (since 1995: FIDESZ-MPP) (Hungary)
FIDESZ-MPP-FIDESZ	Hungarian Civic Party
FKGP	Independent Smallholders' Party
FNM	National Property Fund (Slovakia)
FSZDL	Democratic League of Independent Trade Unions (Hungary)
GDP	gross domestic product
HZDS	Movement for a Democratic Slovakia
IGC	Intergovernmental Conference
IMF	International Monetary Fund
JNA	Yugoslav People's Army
KDH	Christian Democratic Movement (Slovakia)
KDNP	Christian Democratic People's Party (Hungary)
KDU/CSL	Christian Democratic Union/Czech People's Party
KGB	Soviet state security agency

KSCM	Communist Party of Bohemia and Moravia
LCP	Lithuanian Communist Party
LDLP	Lithuanian Democratic Labour Party
LDS	Liberal Democracy of Slovenia
LNNK	Latvian National Independent Movement
LPF	Latvian Popular Front
MDF	Hungarian Democratic Forum
MDNP	Hungarian Democratic People's Party
MIEP	Hungarian Justice and Life Party
MP	Workers' Party (Hungary)
MRF	Movement for Rights and Freedoms (Bulgaria)
MSZDP	Hungarian Social Democratic Party
MSZMP	Hungarian Socialist Workers' Party
MSZOSZ	National Federation of Hungarian Trade Unions
MSZP	Hungarian Socialist Party
NACC	North Atlantic Cooperation Council
NATO	North Atlantic Treaty Organization
NGO	non-governmental organization
NPF	National Property Fund (Slovakia)
NSF	National Salvation Front (Romania)
ODA	Civic Democratic Alliance (Czech Republic)
ODS	Civic Democratic Party (Czech Republic)
OECD	Organization for Economic Co-operation and Development
OSCE	Organization for Security and Co-operation in Europe
PDSR	Party for Social Democracy of Romania
PFE	Popular Front of Estonia
PSL	Polish Peasants' Party
PU	People's Union (Bulgaria)
RCP	Romanian Communist Party
RSI	Romanian Service of Information
SDL	Party of the Democratic Left (Slovakia)
SDSS	Social Democratic Party (Slovakia)
SIS	Slovak Intelligence Service
SLD	Alliance of the Democratic Left (Poland)
SNS	Slovak National Party; Slovene National Party
SPR–RSC	Association for the Republic–Czech Republican Party
StB	Czech secret service
STV	Slovak Television
SZDSZ	Alliance of Free Democrats (Hungary)
UDF	Union of Democratic Forces (Bulgaria)
USD	Social Democratic Union (Romania)
USSR	Soviet Union (i.e. Union of Soviet Socialist Republics)
UW	Union of Freedom (Poland)
VAN	Public against Violence (Slovakia)
WEU	Western European Union
ZRS	Association of Workers of Slovakia

1

Democratization in Central and East European Countries: An Overview

MARY KALDOR AND IVAN VEJVODA

> The misery of Eastern Europe's small nations ... causes such great suspicion and irritation in Western European observers. [This] leads many people to conclude that the entire region ... should be abandoned to its fate. ... This region's inability to consolidate itself is not due to its inherently barbarian nature, but to a series of unfortunate historical processes which squeezed it off the main course of European consolidation. ... We should not give up on the idea of consolidating this region if for no other reason than for the fact that today, after 30 years of great confusion, we can clearly see the course of consolidation; after the passing of mutual hatreds, occupations, civil strife, and genocidal wars. ... We must make sure only that heavy-handed and violent attempts at solutions do not return the filthy tide toward our region. Of course consolidation can also be thwarted; after all, it is not an elemental process that irresistibly takes over a region, but a delicate, circumspect, and easily derailed human endeavour facing the forces of fear, stupidity and hatred. However, it should be emphasized that the consolidation of this region is *feasible*.
>
> István Bibó [1946] (1991 edn)

The countries of Central and Eastern Europe (CEECs) finally seem to be on the 'course of European consolidation'. Despite the optimism of the Hungarian historian István Bibó after World War II, expressed in the passage from 1946 quoted above, they were pushed off course, yet again, for more than forty years. Now the CEECs are in the seventh year of 'consolidation' and there is something to be consolidated. The political stabilization of the region and the consolidation of the newly emerged democratic regimes of the CEECs is, in spite of the many challenges they face, not only feasible but an ever-growing reality. In the search for democratic institutions, rules and procedures the main internal obstacle remains the absence of a democratic political culture, while externally the key question is the willingness of the West to provide help through this precarious phase during which the danger of a relapse into forms of totalitarianism, authoritarianism and populism lurks in the background.

Time is a crucial factor in this process of 'democratic invention' (Lefort, 1991), as is the international political and economic environment. An overwhelming but simplistic popular perception in the CEECs after 1989 was that democracy was synonymous with a 'return to Europe'. In fact, the geographical barriers imposed by Yalta were not the only ones to be overcome. The political, economic and psychological practices that evolved during the forty years of communism were going to prove a far greater impediment to an early 'return' than seemed to be the case in 1989. Moreover, the trials and tribulations of democracy in the West have a direct impact on the image and influence of democratic ideas in the CEECs.

While it is generally argued that the institutional, formal prerequisites for democracy have been broadly fulfilled in the ten CEECs under consideration, it is more difficult to assess in such a clear manner the level of consolidation of democratic behaviour, or of the fledgling democratic political culture, that has been attained. It seems that, whatever their mutual differences, all CEECs have gone beyond the point of a return to the *ancien régime*, though in some – particularly Slovakia and Romania – there have been menacing signs of a willingness on the part of the democratically elected majorities to transform themselves into a contemporary variant of what de Tocqueville (1981 edn, p. 386) called regimes of 'democratic despotism'. The question arises as to whether these particularly fragile new democratic polities will find the internal political energy and the necessary external support and pressure to overcome these difficulties. Some authors contend that we are witnessing only a 'mirage of democracy' where there is 'reason to suppose that the post-communist world finds a suitable option in a semiauthoritarian order ... [in which the CEECs] may embrace somewhat harsher and more centralised political practices than can be found in Western democracies' (Gati, 1996).

In this book we put forward the argument that the political systems which characterize the CEECs constitute a particular variant of democracy that is specific to this part of this world; we argue that it is possible to talk about a *sui generis* post-communist political model which is influenced by the legacy of communism and, at the same time, by both the strengths and the weaknesses of contemporary Western democracy. In order to develop this argument, we draw a distinction between formal and substantive democracy, which enables us to assess critically the process of democratization in terms both of formal criteria and of what we consider to be substantive features of democracy. The result is a more differentiated understanding of the process of democratization as it is experienced by individual CEECs. Our conclusions about the extent to which individual CEECs fit this model of democratization are drawn from the individual chapters which describe the state of democracy in each of the ten countries that have applied to join the European Union (EU). In this introduction we summarize our findings, and in the final chapter we put forward the concept of a European Democratic

Space as a way of consolidating democracy in the CEECs and of reinvigorating democracy in Western Europe.

In October 1992 Elémer Hankiss, a Hungarian sociologist and the first post-1989 director of Hungarian state television, commented that, if 1989 was the *annus mirabilis*, then 1990 was the *annus esperantiae*, 1991 the *annus miserabilis* and 1992 *annus desillusionis* or *realismis*. We are now four years into the awakening of the CEECs to the realities of their new situation in which the brave new democracies continue to recast their politics, economies, culture, law and education while at the same time confronting the great burden of the totalitarian past. Meanwhile the West and North are beset by questions about the 'end of politics' and of the 'democratic deficit'.

One may ask whether the seventh year of experience of new regimes in the CEECs is too soon to make meaningful assertions as to the foundations of democracy in these countries. Lijphart (1984, p. 38), for example, formulated one of the criteria for determining 'whether a political system can be called democratic – that is whether it is sufficiently close to the democratic ideal' as that 'it must be reasonably responsive to the citizens' wishes over a *long period of time*'. This criterion, persistence of democratic rule, was defined in temporal terms as 'at least thirty to thirty-five years'.[1] The CEECs have by this criterion achieved only a fifth or a quarter of the 'required' temporal experience. However precarious it may appear, we consider that it is nevertheless worthwhile to make a preliminary assessment about whether a genuine process of democratization is under way.

On formal and substantive democracy

Ever since democracy became the subject of political philosophy and political theory there have been varying definitions and usages of the term.[2] For de Tocqueville, democracy had essentially two meanings: one was as a political regime defined by the rule of the people, with all the institutional and procedural mechanisms that had been specified by earlier theorists of democracy; and the other was as a condition of society characterized by its tendency towards equality. This social, societal democratic condition, the Tocquevillian 'habits of the [democratic] heart' (much in the sense of a Hegelian *Sittlichkeit*), meant that democracy could not be reduced to its formal, institutional aspects.[3]

In this introduction we distinguish between formal (procedural) democracy and what we call substantive democracy.[4] Formal democracy is a set of rules, procedures and institutions which we attempt to define below. We consider substantive democracy as a process that has to be continually reproduced, a way of regulating power relations in such a way as to maximize the opportunities for individuals to influence the conditions in which they live, to participate in and influence debates about the key decisions that affect society.

We take it as given that the formal character of democracy is the indispensable presupposition of the democratic social condition. Attempts under various guises to represent the social condition as the pre-eminent substantive value have, through an over-emphasizing of the idea of community, led in the twentieth century to the modern political form of totalitarianism. This Orwellian image of a finally 'real' democracy, as totalizing community, has been the political form from which the CEECs have emerged. 'All those who want to replace formal democracy with so-called substantive democracy, and thereby reunify state and society in a totalising way, surrender democracy as such' (Heller, 1988, p. 131). On the other hand, the existence of formal mechanisms and procedures, which represent an *a priori* safeguard against abuses of power, is a necessary but by no means a sufficient condition for democracy in a substantive sense.

Democracy is a set of formal institutions, a way of redistributing power and a way of life. When distinguishing between formal and substantive in this chapter we separate out for analytical purposes the institutional and procedural aspects from the way they are implemented, from the practices and 'habits of the [post-communist] heart'.

Compliance with formal criteria

There have been many attempts to define the criteria for democracy. We have assembled our own list of formal criteria, adapting a set of 'procedural minimal conditions' originally drawn up by Robert Dahl (1982, p. 11):

1. *Inclusive citizenship*: exclusion from citizenship purely on the basis of race, ethnicity or gender is not permissible.
2. *Rule of law*: the government is legally constituted and the different branches of government must respect the law, with individuals and minorities protected from the 'tyranny of the majority'.
3. *Separation of powers*: the three branches of government – legislature, executive and judiciary – must be separate, with an independent judiciary capable of upholding the constitution.
4. *Elected power-holders*: members of the legislature and those who control the executive must be elected.
5. *Free and fair elections*: elected power-holders are chosen in frequent and fairly conducted elections, in which coercion is comparatively uncommon and in which practically all adults have the right to vote and to run for elective office.
6. *Freedom of expression and alternative sources of information*: citizens have a

right to express themselves on political matters, broadly defined, without the danger of severe punishment, and a right to seek out alternative sources of information; moreover, alternative sources of information exist and are protected by law.

7. *Associational autonomy*: citizens also have the right to form relatively independent associations or organizations, including independent political parties and interest groups.

8. *Civilian control over the security forces*: the armed forces and police should be politically neutral and independent of political pressures, and under the control of civilian authorities.

Table 1.1 summarizes the findings from our study about the extent to which the CEECs meet the formal criteria of democracy as defined above. The material is based on the studies presented in the following chapters addressing each of the ten applicant CEECs. By and large, we find that the ten CEECs do meet the formal criteria for democracy. They have democratically ratified constitutions. Some are already refining and amending their post-1989 constitutions so as to attain existing higher democratic standards. Constitutional courts play an important role in this sense and have proved themselves to be a major institutional democratic actor in the present transformations.

Only Estonia and Latvia do not fully meet the criterion of inclusive citizenship (see Chapters 2 and 3). In both countries substantial ethnic minorities, especially Russians, lack citizenship primarily for procedural reasons, even though the citizenship laws do not explicitly exclude minorities. In the Czech Republic (Chapter 6), Roma people do not automatically qualify for citizenship because, after the split of Czechoslovakia, they were classified as Slovaks; they have had difficulty acquiring citizenship for procedural reasons, particularly because of a clause (since removed under international pressure) that those eligible for citizenship must have no criminal record during the previous five years.

Apart from these citizenship problems, the key formal criterion of existing and guaranteed democratic civil liberties (human rights), in particular for minorities, has been met in the CEECs. However, in none of these countries is the rule of law fully implemented. Although this is a criterion that it is difficult to gauge fully with respect to an ideal-typical rule of law, it can none the less be said that as a result of weak judiciaries and/or inadequate machinery for law enforcement the individual citizen in the CEECs is, in a variety of ways (with marked differences among the countries), still grappling with the practical use of formal legal guarantees that have been enshrined in statute. Hence there exists a continued sense of individual insecurity in a number of the countries under review.[5]

Table 1.1 Formal democracy: main criteria

Criterion	Bulgaria	Czech R.	Estonia	Hungary	Latvia	Lithuania	Poland	Romania	Slovakia	Slovenia
Inclusive citizenship	A	B	C	A	C	A	A	A	A	A
Rule of law	B/C	B	B/C	B	B	B/C	B	B/C	C	A/B
Separation of powers	A	A	A	A	A	A	B	B	C	A
Elected power-holders	A	A	A	A	A	A	A	A	A	A
Free and fair elections	A	A	B	A	B	A	A	A	A	A
Freedom of expression and alternative information	A	A	A	A	A	A	A	A/B	A	A
Associational autonomy	B	A	A	A	A	A	A	A	A	A
Civilian control of the armed forces/ security services	A	A	A	A	A	A	A	A/B	B	A

Source: Interpretation from country assessments for this volume

A = Formal procedures are in place and mostly implemented
B = Formal procedures are in place, but some lack of implementation
C = Formal procedures are in place, but hindrances to implementation
D = Formal procedures not in place

The separation of powers between the legislative, executive and judicial branches is more or less in place. In Slovakia the election of a new president has been blocked as the result of a deliberate parliamentary deadlock engineered by Mečiar. In Poland, former president Wałęsa, on occasion, abused his position by interfering in the functioning of government. In Romania, former president Iliescu played a very powerful role and insisted on standing for a third period in office, although this appears to be contrary to the constitution. In the Baltic states, the weakness of the judiciary – a Soviet inheritance – makes it difficult for the judicial arm to balance the other branches of government. In Latvia the legislative branch dominates the executive branch.

Regular elections have led to the alternation in the power of divergent parties or coalitions, thus proving that the mechanisms of political competition can operate and are accepted by the political actors. In Romania, peaceful alternation has only recently taken place for the first time, as a result of the November 1996 elections.

It is clear that elections are not a sufficient condition for the existence of democracy but have to be complemented by a 'variety of competitive processes and channels for the expression of interests and values – associational as well as partisan, functional as well as territorial, collective as well as individual' (Schmitter and Karl, 1991, p. 78). These can become efficient and operational only in a free public realm where open access to a variety of sources of information can then lead to deliberation concerning the collective norms and choices that are binding on the society and backed by state coercion. In Bulgaria (see Chapter 11), associational autonomy is restricted when it is based on ethnicity.

The control of civilian authorities over the military has been largely achieved, although in some countries, especially Romania and Slovakia, the so-called dark forces, remnants of the secret police, lurk in the shadows of politics and society.

Getting under the skin of the new democracies in the CEECs

Democracy, however, is not reducible to institutions, rules and procedures; that is, to its formal aspects. It is a way of life of the individual citizen in the societies born out of the modern democratic revolutions. The 1989 transformations mark the new beginning of this process in the CEECs. How are these formal institutions, rules and procedures implemented in practice? Are the CEECs following the blueprint of an existing democratic model or have these seven years of democratization displayed tendencies towards a *sui generis* model of partially developed democracy?

The extent to which a particular society can be said to be characterized by a democratic political culture in which there is a genuine tendency for political equalization and in which the individual feels secure and able and willing to participate in political decision-making is not something that can be easily measured. We have chosen to focus here on what we see as key features of substantive democracy, which have a bearing on the deeper nature of democratic life. These features include the character of constitutions and the way in which human rights are perceived; the role of political parties and the extent to which they provide a vehicle for political participation; the role of the media and the extent to which they are capable of representing a broad political debate; whether and how far the former communist administration has been able to transform itself into a genuine public service which individuals trust; the degree to which local government is able to manage and respond to local concerns; and finally, the existence of an active civil society, in the sense of independent associations and institutions, which is able to check abuses of state power. We are aware that these features by no means constitute an exhaustive list of characteristics of substantive democracy, but our research suggests that these are the aspects that are most relevant to an assessment of substantive democracy.

Constitutional issues and human rights

The social function of constitutions has become increasingly complex because of their historical and theoretical development (Preuss, 1993). The basic function is the limitation of power both in a negative, defensive sense and in a positive sense as the 'authorizing function'. The capacity to legitimize political authority is closely related to the integrative function of modern constitutions. Constitutions, in so far as they 'incarnate the goals, aspirations, values and basic beliefs which its members commonly hold and which bind them together ... may serve as a kind of secular catechism' (Preuss, 1993, p. 7).

Overall, the legitimizing function of the new constitutions in the CEECs has fostered stability and a process of consolidation. It has provided a framework in which the workings of institutions, rules and procedures have slowly been adapting. The constitution-makers in the CEECs have demonstrated their concern for both rights and social justice, and, in spite of differences, all reveal a significant preference for a communitarian concept of constitutionalism, as opposed to a rights-based concept, thus emphasizing the 'nation' as opposed to the 'citizen'. Contemporary debates in the field of political philosophy suggest an alternative between a political concept of the 'right' or of the 'good', or between justice and community. The new constitutions of the CEECs tend to express a preference for the latter rather than the former, although neither rights nor justice is disregarded (Preuss, 1993, p. 34).

According to C. R. Sunstein (1995, p. 61), human rights

depend on public institutions, they cost money (and this is true not only for social and economic rights but for the so-called negative rights as well); government cannot protect property and life itself without resources . . . rights will not exist without a rights bearing culture, that is a culture in which ordinary people are at least sometimes willing to take serious personal risks by challenging powerful people by insisting that rights are at stake. The protection of rights will require government to act in both public and private spheres, sometimes within the family itself (to prevent domestic violence).

The problem of individual and collective (minority) rights is one of the stumbling-blocks in the CEECs. Lacking a rights-based culture, slanted towards a communitarian outlook, with a scarcity of resources and the absence of any tradition of community policing, there are persistent problems in certain countries – particularly those in which there are important minorities. This relates to the Russians living in Estonia and Latvia, the Hungarians living in Slovakia and Romania, and the Roma living in the Czech Republic, Slovakia, Hungary, Romania and Bulgaria; as well as discrimination and abuse of foreigners, especially from developing countries, who came to study or work in the CEECs during the communist period.

The legacy of social guarantees under communism has left an inclination to view human rights as equated not with individual, civic and political rights, but largely with economic and social rights, such as guarantees of work; free elementary, secondary and university education; child allowances; and old-age pensions (Millar and Wolchik, 1994) – although this view has come under pressure from the new neo-liberal ideologies. This tendency has often been put forward as one of the main reasons for the electoral successes of the former communist parties in elections in Lithuania, Poland, Hungary, Bulgaria and Romania. It is suggested that the electorates, disenchanted with the societal convulsions and the social costs of change (Eberstadt, 1993; European Bank for Reconstruction and Development, 1995), believed that these parties could at least stem the flood of change and slow down the pace of 'streamlining' and 'downsizing' in their workplaces.

The legislation on human rights is for the most part in place. The international covenants have been, or are in the process of being, integrated into domestic legislation. The 'paper guarantees' can, however, unfortunately coexist with more or less extensive discrimination or inequality on grounds of, for example, gender (Scheppele, 1995), or minority status. The new Romanian penal code makes homosexuality a criminal offence (see Chapter 10).

It has been stressed that an awareness of the 'right to have rights' (Arendt, 1973, pp. 296–7) is the first step in developing both an individual and a collective awareness. This should be followed by a learning process whereby it becomes clear to the people concerned that rights actually serve collective interests, by making it possible to have and maintain a certain kind of society with a certain sort of culture. Part of the reason for a system of free speech is that it not only serves to protect the individual speaker, but allows processes of public deliberation and discussion that serve public goals, by, for example, constraining governmental power and making just and effective outcomes more likely (Sunstein, 1995).

Political parties

After 1989 three basic kinds of political parties emerged: the communists recast themselves under different names and with a more centre-left slant; some parties attempted to continue the tradition of the pre-1940s parties; and wholly new parties emerged, most often founded by former dissidents or other individuals who were not linked to communist power-holders in a direct sense. Only the former communist parties have sizeable memberships and significant local organizations. They have inherited the party networks and put them to use in the new environment of competitive politics. This may well be the main explanation for their electoral success in all the CEECs except the Czech Republic and Slovakia, where they were discredited, and Estonia and Latvia, where they are fragmented. Since 1989 very few of the reformed pre-1940s parties have survived, except for peasant parties, which are rather small outside Poland.[6]

Some of the wholly new parties – such as the Union of Freedom (UW) in Poland, the Union of Democratic Forces (UDF) in Bulgaria, and the Democratic Convention of Romania (DCR) – have suffered from childhood illnesses. They have been created from the top down and their memberships are small. Their representatives have, in many cases, no prior experience in practical politics. In societies that seek stability after major transformations it is not a simple task for these new potential politicians to win the trust of the electorates. Also, it is difficult for these parties to build up an extended network of grass-roots party organizations within a rather limited time span. This requires human and financial resources which are not always forthcoming. The result is that party political life gravitates around the capitals and the major cities of these countries.

The transition from a one-party to a multi-party system went through an initial phase of mushrooming political parties, followed by a tightening of electoral laws defining thresholds, usually 3–5 per cent, which in time reduced this great number of parties to five or six important ones in practically all the CEECs.[7] Except in the former Czechoslovakia, a pattern seems to be emerging in which former communist parties are the largest and often predominant parties.[8] Until recently, in Hungary and Slovenia, where these post-communist parties had begun to change during the 1980s, they ruled in coalitions with liberal parties, and a form of consensual politics started to develop.[9] Politics was becoming 'boring', even 'normal'. In other countries, a sharp polarization separates the post-communist parties from the anti-communist opposition. Such is the case in Bulgaria, where former communists are in power, and Lithuania, Poland and Romania, where former communists were recently defeated. Lithuania was the first country in which, in the October 1992 elections, the former communists of the Lithuanian Democratic Labour Party (LDLP) regained power; more recently, in the October 1996 elections, the former communists also became the first such group to be displaced from power. In the case of the Czech Republic and Slovakia, where the communists had been totally discredited, the predominant parties seem to have organized themselves around the personalities of their leaders: Klaus and Mečiar respectively.

Both the former communist and the new parties tend to be highly centralized and to have markedly hierarchical structures. It can be argued that they see themselves, as their communist predecessors did, as instruments for the capture or preservation of power rather than 'transmission belts' for political ideas and debates. The old tendencies to extend party control over various spheres of social life – the media, universities, the newly privatized enterprises – are reducing political space to what Italians call *partitocrazia* (Sartori, 1962), rule by parties dividing up spheres of influence in society.

It is very difficult to distinguish CEEC parties on the basis of philosophy or ideology except for those, mostly peripheral, parties with xenophobic or extreme chauvinistic tendencies, which are to be found in all these countries, some of them attaining 10 per cent of the vote. Most parties express a commitment to the market, to social justice, and to joining the EU, irrespective of whether they are former communist parties – such as the former communists of Romania's National Salvation Front of President Iliescu, the Bulgarian Socialist Party of Prime Minister Zhan Videnov, the Polish Alliance of the Democratic Left of Alexander Kwaśniewski – or right-wing, such as the Czech Republic's Civic Democratic Party of Václav Klaus. These tend to be catch-all parties. There are some differences between those parties which express a more civic orientation, such as the Free Democrats in Hungary, the Union of Freedom in Poland, and Public against Violence (VAN) in Slovakia, and those which accentuate attachment to national and/or religious values: for example, Sajudis in Lithuania; the ruling Movement for a Democratic Slovakia (HZDS); the Hungarian Democratic Forum, in opposition since 1994. By and large political debates have had little programmatic substance. The sharpest debates are either about the past, pitching communism against anti-communism (in the Baltic states, Bulgaria and Poland) or about personalities (Mečiar and Kovač in Slovakia, Klaus and Havel in the Czech Republic, Wałęsa and Kwaśniewski in Poland, and Brazauskas and Landsbergis in Lithuania).

Attempts are being made by the new parties to broaden their membership, but they are coming up against a wall of anti-political sentiments. This reluctance of people to engage in politics has its roots in the negative political legacy of prolonged life in an over-politicized communist polity, but also in a sense of powerlessness, of the inability to influence political or economic events, in a situation in which the perception of parts of the electorate is that agencies such as the International Monetary Fund (IMF) or the World Bank have much greater leverage on their future than internal actors. The absence of a public sphere, a space for true discussion in a sharply polarized situation, often leads to political cynicism and apathy (Vejvoda, 1996).

In most of the CEECs there are extreme nationalist parties, but their support does not exceed the 10 per cent mark in polls or elections. In some cases nationalist strands and factions organize within the larger parties (for example, in the ruling Bulgarian Socialist Party and the ruling Slovak HZDS); in others, larger parties enter coalitions with the smaller extremist ones (Romania's National Salvation Front was until very recently in a coalition government with the small extreme nationalist party, and Slovakia's HZDS is coalesced with 'non-standard groupings . . . characterized by increased degrees of national and social populism, authoritarianism and radicalism' (see Chapter 7)).

Media

The modern media of communication were part and parcel of the former communist regimes, servicing the political monopoly of the ruling party. A parallel public sphere was created through the establishment of *samizdat* journals and informal private lines of communication. Since 1989 the media have been pluralized to differing degrees in all the CEECs. There have been 'media wars' (in Hungary and Bulgaria) and conflicts and often irreconcilable tensions over the control and legal definition of the media. Some countries, such as Hungary, passed their media legislation recently. Others, such as Bulgaria, contrary to constitutional provisions, have still not enacted legislation. The absence of such legislation enables the ruling majority to control the national media directly (see Chapter 11). The plurality of the media and their differing reach and influence have to be considered when assessing the degree of pluralization and the level of independence that have been attained.

The broadcast media, especially television, clearly exert the most powerful influence on public opinion. In each of these countries the state has retained a notable degree of control over the television channels previously operated by the party–state. These have been reformed and liberalized, although the extent of liberalization varies; it is greater in Lithuania (a very successful example), Hungary and Poland than in Slovakia and Romania (the last of these is beginning to open up following the opposition's electoral victory in November 1996). The incumbent governments, which finance these TV channels out of the state budget, tend, with varying degrees of subtlety, to try to influence the way their ideas and policies are presented, while journalists sometimes exhibit too much loyalty to those in power.[10]

There is evidence in opinion polls, in Slovakia for example, that moves to exercise greater control over state-owned broadcast media are arousing growing disapproval and dissatisfaction. People are turning instead to private, commercial channels or to channels from neighbouring countries. People in Slovakia, for example, tuned in to the Czech channel Nova until September 1996, when Slovakia launched its first commercial station, TV Markiza (see Chapter 7).

Numerous independent TV and radio channels have appeared alongside the state-financed channels. For the most part, these are privately owned by domestic or foreign (often expatriate) owners. In many cases they are entertainment, advertisement-driven channels with little political information content, although more balanced private TV channels are beginning to emerge. Journalists have tended to seek a greater degree of professionalization and were among the first to organize independent unions (for example, in Slovenia). It is the lack of financial means and the efforts of politicians to influence the independent boards of media stations that limit the independence of the media.

The basic problem is the difficulty of establishing a public media service which is not dependent on the changing political colour of governments and where, for the benefit of the public good, different political positions can be expressed side by side. In the broadcast media there seems to be a polarization now between government-influenced, state-run channels and independent, commercial or opposition channels. In the print media the situation is more varied, but similar patterns occur. Newspapers resembling *The Independent* or *Le Monde*, which try to cover a wide variety of positions, are rare. In this part of the world, 'independent' media usually means opposition media. Perhaps the best opportunities for the provision of a genuine public service media are to be found at a local level, where both local radio stations and local print media have more space to address local issues, although they reach small audiences.

It is interesting to note that today there seems to be a broader and more intense public discussion in both national and local media in those countries, such as Poland and Hungary, where public debate had already begun during the late 1970s and 1980s, often in very difficult circumstances, and was flourishing by 1989. This debate is probably just as intense in countries such as Slovakia and Romania, but the reach of the print and electronic media in which the debate takes place is less.

Administration

In the aftermath of 1989, the main challenge of transition was the introduction of democratic control over, and the establishment of a public sphere independent of, the state. In this whole process much less attention was paid to the problem of reforming the state itself. Moreover, unlike in East Germany, in none of the CEECs, except the Czech Republic, has there been an extensive programme of decommunization. Lustration laws were introduced in Czechoslovakia before the split; subsequently, the law was abandoned in Slovakia but extended in the Czech Republic. Even in the Czech Republic, however, lustration laws seem to have been used mainly to discredit political opponents rather than to reform the administration (see Chapter 6). An important area for any assessment of the process of democratization is the fate of the extensive former communist *apparat* and its *apparatchiks*.

Not only has there been no extensive programme of decommunization, but the new ruling parties have often inherited the clientelistic assumptions of the previous period. Thus, in almost all of the CEECs the ruling parties have tended to control appointments to the upper level of the civil service. This tendency is especially marked in the Baltic states and in Bulgaria. In Bulgaria, for example, there have been three waves of partisan replacement of the various echelons of the administration: in 1992, 1993–4 and 1995. Moreover, the 'Kapualiev amendment' to the labour code allows medium- and high-level managers in administration and state enterprises to be dismissed without reason (see Chapter 11).

The administrations in the newly democratized CEECs also lack a public service ethos. In particular, there has been a tendency on the part of the younger, more pragmatically minded members of the outgoing communist administrations to transform their political losses into economic gains through the transfer of state property to private ownership, making use of their privileged positions and knowledge of the inside functioning of the state. There is, therefore, an important, complex and often opaque relationship between the administration and the economy.

There have been more or less widespread and more or less regulated and accountable examples of people moving from public administration to private enterprise and corresponding transfers of property in all the CEECs, to varying degrees. In most CEECs the technocrats of the former communist parties are perceived as the winners from the 'transition', having successfully transformed public assets into private property with the help of those in the administration. So-called 'spontaneous privatization' in several CEECs, including Hungary in 1988–9 and the Baltic states, has enabled former managers of state enterprises, members of the *nomenklatura*, to become the new private owners. Various scandals involving members of government, ministers and political figures have been revealed during the privatization process. In Bulgaria the assassination of former prime minister Andrei Lukanov is reported to have been linked to his threat to uncover a scandal involving the coterie around the then prime minister Zhan Videnov and its control over the Orion group of enterprises (Borger, 1996). Romania is a particularly acute example of this tendency, owing to the pervasiveness of the secret police during the communist period.[11] A variety of terms including 'directocracy', 'kleptocracy' and 'new bourgeoisie' are used to describe the power of former directors of currently or formerly state-owned enterprises who are closely linked through former communist and secret police networks and are able to circumvent the existing legal framework and achieve their goals 'invisibly'. A particularly infamous aspect of the Romanian situation is the way in which the Prosecutor's Office has blocked investigations of scandals, such as a Financial Guard report accusing several high-level officials of trafficking influence and the Puma helicopter scandal. In the latter case, revealed by the press, a government party official with a position in the Defence Committee of the National Assembly allegedly received a commission of $2 million for a deal with South Africa (see Chapter 10).

This state of affairs contributes to problems with the civil service in general and the law enforcement agencies in particular. Undoubtedly corruption is a social, economic and cultural phenomenon present under all political regimes around the globe, and liberal democratic countries are not immune from it. What is specific to the post-communist condition is the lack of resources in state budgets to finance adequately their civil services and in particular their law enforcement agencies. This shortage of resources is in turn related to the inadequacy of tax collection, which is due to weak law enforcement, which in turn is paralleled by the growth of a shadow economy and the emergence of various mafia-type networks, often with links to the administration. This situation is most extreme in Romania, Bulgaria and the Baltic states. In Estonia it is estimated that 45 per cent of businesses make payments to the mafia (see Chapter 2). Thus bribery and corruption become a 'normal' way of doing even the most menial administrative business.

Instead of progressively becoming a true 'service', these public institutions are still experienced by people in the CEECs as clientelistic, dependent on ruling party allegiance, and not as neutral institutions working in the

interest of the public. It is still with much unease that citizens enter public
service institutions, where the experience of an over-bureaucratized past has
not changed as rapidly as in other aspects of daily life.

Local government

The need to establish and direct from the top down effective political,
economic and legal institutions, practically from scratch, has engendered a
centralization that stifles local government. The inheritance of the pre-
communist past and, in particular, of the communist centralization of power
has been entrenched by the perceived need for 'expert' governance and
control.

Within each of the CEECs are important regional differences. In local
elections both local parties and local democratically oriented imaginative
leaders have emerged whose attempts to develop a decentralized democratic
arena have been thwarted by a lack of redistribution of resources from the
central state budget and by the impossibility of retaining at least part of the
taxes gathered at the local level, as well as by direct interference from the
centre. In some cases, for example in Lithuania, local government has no
independent tax collection authority. In other cases, financial autonomy is
very limited. In Hungary, Slovakia and Slovenia, for example, a struggle for
power has developed between the regional tier of central government and
democratically elected local government. Romania represents an extreme
example: the Department of Local Administration was actually able to sack
a large number of opposition mayors (see Chapter 10).

Administrative and fiscal impotence has sometimes undermined the legitimacy of locally elected administrators. This is exacerbated by the tendency of
local media to focus on national politics, so that information about local
affairs is not readily available. As a consequence, the local electorate might
try to align its votes with the party in power at the centre to create a lifeline
from the centre to the periphery; that is, to gain access to power and
resources. Depending on the party in power, the regions have benefited or
been excluded from funding in different social and economic sectors. This
phenomenon appears in countries as different from one another as Slovakia
and Romania.

It should be stressed that, despite this situation, local government has
been able in certain circumstances, either through ownership of local
property or because of prolonged involvement in and knowledge of
local needs and interests, to push forward policies concerning cultural or
environmental issues or to acquire resources in ways that have benefited the
local population.

Civil society

The term 'civil society' is associated with the 1989 revolutions. During the 1980s it came to have a very specific meaning, referring to the existence of self-organized groups or institutions capable of preserving an autonomous public sphere which could guarantee individual liberty and check abuses of the state. Essentially, the term was linked with associationalism. In some parts of central and eastern Europe, associationalism has a respectable history. It was very strong in Hungary, which at the time included Slovakia, between 1867 and 1914, as well as in Czechoslovakia and the Baltic states during the inter-war period. It was largely concentrated in towns; hence the term 'civic' also tends to be associated with multiculturalism and contrasted with 'ethnic'. For this reason the term 'civil society' is also used in a normative sense to denote a set of values having to do with democracy and freedom. During the communist period civil society was totally crushed except for brief episodes, such as the mid- to late 1960s in Czechoslovakia. Only in Hungary and Poland after 1956 and in the former Yugoslavia was a limited amount of pluralism permitted within, for example, academia and the arts.

The reappearance of 'civil society' in Central and Eastern Europe during the 1980s paved the way for the 1989 revolutions. The term first came to prominence with the emergence of Solidarity in Poland. Elsewhere in Central and Eastern Europe small-scale clubs and associations developed during this period. Elémer Hankiss (1990) used the term 'second society' to describe the various social, economic and semi-political activities that flourished in Hungary alongside the formal 'first society' of the Party, the Peace Committee, the official trade unions, etc. Slovenia became known as 'NGO country'. Independent peace and environmental groups emerged in Czechoslovakia, and many of the pre-war organizations reappeared in the Baltic states in 1988–91.

After 1989 many of those who had been active in civic groups were absorbed into the new political elites and, as a consequence, some opportunities for creating a firm basis for civil society were lost. This is why, for example, the Hungarian independent trade union movement, FSZDL, failed to replace the official communist trade union in representing employees on a large scale (see Chapter 8). In general, self-organized activities are still very weak in Romania, Bulgaria and the Baltic states, where they are for the most part confined to closed groups of intellectuals. Disillusionment with 'democracy', exhaustion after the frenetic activity of 1989–91, a tradition of apathy and the sheer struggle for survival in the new competitive market era are among the explanations for the decline of civil society.

Nevertheless, new NGOs have developed in all the CEECs. Most are engaged in education, culture, leisure, community development and welfare for such groups as the disabled, although there are also more clearly political groups concerned with racism, human rights and environmental issues. The most active civil society groups are to be found in Hungary, Poland, Slovakia and Slovenia. In Slovenia the new groups have for the most part developed in response to the wars in the region and are primarily concerned with humanitarian activities, especially the welfare of refugees. The most remarkable reported growth of NGOs has occurred in Hungary, Slovakia and Poland. In Hungary, by the end of 1993, there were 11,884 associations and foundations (see Chapter 8). In Slovakia in 1994 the number of registered NGOs rose to 9,800. In 1996 these Slovak independent initiatives were reported to employ 3,500 paid workers and 381,000 volunteers (see Chapter 7). Even more remarkably, in 1996 Poland was reported to have 80,000 NGOs, and some 4 million people are reported to be active in them (see Chapter 5). One puzzle is why Slovakia, which is generally deemed to be one of the least democratic of the CEECs, should enjoy such an active civil society, especially in comparison with the Czech Republic. A possible explanation is disillusionment with party politics. Another is the co-operative, localist tradition in contrast to the more atomistic, individualistic Czech society.

Because 'civil society' has become the fashionable concept of the 1990s it is reasonable to ask how far the growth of these activities is genuinely independent and how far it represents an artificially created demand in response to the various programmes established to support NGOs by Western governments, European institutions and private foundations.[12] Unquestionably there is a clientelistic aspect to many NGOs. But given the legal, financial and bureaucratic obstacles that many of these organizations have had to overcome, it has to be concluded that most of them stem from genuine local impulses. The fact that in Slovakia the state has tried to control foundations has to be explained as a reaction to the independence of these organizations. In many cases civic groups are trying to monitor and control the activities of the state: examples include the Martin Luther King Foundation in Hungary (which campaigns against racism), the Alba Circle (which monitors the Hungarian military), the Slovak Helsinki Citizens' Assembly (which has campaigned against the Language Law and the Law on Foundations) and the Slovak branch of Greenpeace (which campaigns against polluting power-stations).

From a long-term perspective of the creation of a democratic political culture it is clear that the signs of increased individualism and participative energy are very positive, even though apathy, weariness and social fatigue caused by the deep-seated transformations are prolonging an already lengthy maturing process. Many of the above-mentioned civic activities attest to the vigour of both political and social imagination.

A sui generis *post-communist political model?*

The CEECs have all made a definitive break with the communist past. The formal rules and procedures for democracy are more or less in place. In all the CEECs there have been peaceful alternations of power. No one is punished for his or her political views, although arbitrariness and insecurity persist, especially for minorities. Access to alternative sources of information is beginning to spread beyond urban centres (Schöpflin, 1994).

In substantive terms a process of democratization is under way. It is not a linear process, and it is not possible to measure progress or specify overall benchmarks of success. Although there is a tendency to separate CEECs into what appear to be more or less successful models of democracy, these distinctions can be misleading. Thus Slovakia is often contrasted with the Czech Republic as being relatively backward in democratic terms; yet although it is undoubtedly true that Slovakia has one of the worst records among the CEECs in terms of treatment of minorities, authoritarian behaviour by the ruling party and unaccountable police forces, it is also the case that it has an extremely lively civil society and unusually active public participation in political debates. The Czech Republic, on the other hand, which is widely held to be a model of successful transition, only recently, and under considerable pressure, rescinded citizenship conditions that effectively denied citizenship to a substantial minority of its residents, the Roma, and its human rights policy has been rather weak (see Chapter 6).

Table 1.2 summarizes what we have defined as key features of the substantive process of democratization, attempting to indicate a more differentiated approach towards notions of success or failure. There are certain common features in the process of democratization in the CEECs which perhaps make it possible to talk about a *sui generis* post-communist political model. The communitarian character of constitutions, despite the inclusion of individual rights, is linked to the persistent tendency to discriminate against minorities and, in many cases, the absence of an active human rights policy.

The monopoly of power that used to be held by the communist parties has been replaced by the dominance of single parties, in most cases the reformed post-communist party, often associated with a single personality, or a grand coalition. Both post-communist and new political parties have a tendency to extend control over various spheres of social life. While the media are in principle free, the broadcast media tend to be dominated by the government. Government tends to be top down and centralizing. The notion of a public service tradition in the media, administration or police forces is underdeveloped; many former *apparatchiks* have transformed themselves into the owners of newly privatized enterprises; there remains in some countries a

Table 1.2 Substantive democracy: a snapshot of the main features

	Bulgaria	Czech Rep.	Estonia	Hungary	Latvia
Constitutional issues and legality	Constitutional Court strong, acting as a quasi-second chamber	Constitutional stability. Lack of will on part of govt to implement all provisions	Supreme Court is also Constitutional Court. Lack of effective law enforcement	Constitutional Court strong	Concentration of power in the legislative branch. Lack of effective law enforcement
Human rights and minority rights	Roma and Turkish minorities encountering some difficulties	Roma encounter difficulties in acquiring citizenship. Lack of active human rights policy	Limited access to citizenship for ethnic minorities	Record is on the whole positive. Problems with guarantees for Roma	Limited access to citizenship for ethnic minorities
Political parties	Former communists in power. Consolidation of opposition	Centre-right coalition in power. Opposition social democrats are balancing factor	Centre-right coalition. Polarization along ethnic vs Western-oriented lines	Grand coalition post-communist and liberal. Weak opposition	Grand coalition of right- and left-wing parties
Media	Media law contested by opposition. Plurality of media	Independent media	State-owned and private media. Right-oriented print and broadcast media prevail	Independent media. State TV at times 'too loyal' to govt. Media law 1995 not yet implemented	Independent media along with state-run. Media law 1993
Administration	Politicized civil service insufficiently financed. Clientelism	Certain level of politicization and party allegiance persists	Ethnic exclusiveness in higher ranks of civil service	Politicization of civil service	Politicization of civil service. Legacy of past strong
Local government	Democratically functioning local govt, but lacking financial autonomy	Regional tier of govt to be set up. Opposition balancing role at local level	Non-citizens can vote in local elections	Developed local government	Scarce financial means at local govt level
Civil society	Numerous NGOs in a variety of areas	Active NGOs. Low membership. Govt unhelpful	Few civic initiatives and NGOs	Numerous and active NGOs	Civic initiatives are slowly developing, mainly in human rights

Source: Country chapters

Table 1.2 *continued*

Lithuania	Poland	Romania	Slovakia	Slovenia
Negative image of Parliament. Weak judiciary	Presidential interference has occurred under previous mandate	Dispute over constitutional interpretation of presidential mandate	Concentration of powers in the executive branch. Important role of the Constitutional Court	Pending constitutional debate on foreign ownership. Forthcoming referendum on electoral law
Citizenship law is liberal	Record is positive over past period. Periodic appearance of 'anti-Semitism without Jews'	Problems with guarantees of minority rights for Hungarians and Roma. Homosexuality is a criminal offence	Disputes over Hungarian minority rights. Tensions between Roma and non-Roma population	Attempts by right wing to reform citizenship of non-Slovenes. Positive human rights policy
Former communists in power. Polarization of political life; confrontational politics	Former communists in coalition government. Polarization of political life	No alteration in power as yet	Coalition of right/left authoritarian populism. Vibrant but fragmented left-centre-right non-authoritarian opposition	Grand coalition: Christian Democrats and Liberals
Independent media strong but much partiality and prejudice in editorial reporting	Independent media (electronic and printed)	Govt-dominated public TV with a number of private independent networks	Govt-dominated public TV. First commercial TV went on air Sept, 1996. Most private radio and print media independent	Independent media with attempts by parties to gain control over national TV network
Professionalization of civil servants hindered by clientelism, but improving	Attempts at professionalization. Burden of past legacy	High degree of politicization and clientelism	High degree of politicization	Civil service with a certain tradition of expertise
Regional governors appointed by Prime Minister. Little devolution of power to municipalities	Decentralization of power largely fictitious. Local power has formal authority but no financial means	Drastic under-funding. Dependence on government	Pluralist elected local govt restricted by centralizing tendencies of govt	Centralization. Little devolution of power to local govt
Rare civic initiatives (lack of tradition and pervasive apathy)	NGOs very active and numerous	NGOs largely confined to closed circle of intellectuals	Numerous and active NGOs in a variety of areas	Growth of humanitarian NGOs

Source: Country chapters

widespread sense of insecurity and lack of trust in institutions. There is very little substantive public debate about such issues as education, economic policy and foreign policy. In several countries there is sharp political polarization, but this is focused on the past, not the future. The post-communist parties aside, membership of political parties is low, as is participation in public debates.

Many of these tendencies can be explained in terms of the communist legacy: the pervasiveness of the state, the totalitarian tradition of passivity, distrust of the public sphere. In this sense, they are similar to tendencies which can be observed in other post-authoritarian states. Some of the specificity of the post-communist experience arises from the far-reaching nature of the transitions these countries are undergoing. This is not just a transition to democracy. It is a transition to the market, a transition from Cold War to peace, a transition from Fordist mass production to the information age, and for several countries – the Baltic states, Slovenia, the Czech Republic and Slovakia – a transition to renewed or new forms of statehood. The strains of transition – individual insecurity and uncertainty, growing unemployment and social inequality in societies where full employment and social provision had been taken for granted, the egoistic enterprise culture, which affects administration as well as everyday life – have all contributed to a rapid disenchantment with politics, expressed in low voter turnout and a tendency to vote against whoever is in power.

Equally important, however, is the fact that the process of democratization is taking place at this particular moment in history. Several of the characteristics of the post-communist model can also be found in Western countries, albeit in a weaker form. These include the relative paucity of substantive debate, growing public apathy and cynicism about politics, the reliance on media images instead of reasoned persuasion, and increasingly top-down approaches to politics. It is possible to speculate about the reasons: the limited space for manoeuvre for national governments in an increasingly globalized and interdependent world; the difficulty of departing from the pervasive neo-liberal ideologies promulgated by international institutions such as the IMF and World Bank; and the growing power of the broadcast media. One important explanation could perhaps be the absence of a forward-looking project after the discrediting of earlier utopias; hence the preoccupation with the past. Given the constraints on the autonomy of individual nation-states, there seems no progressive alternative to the predominant political consensus. As one of the authors in this book has put it, the tragedy for Central and Eastern Europe lies in the fact that its pre-democratic crisis coincides with Western Europe's post-democratic crisis (see Chapter 5).

There are, however, certain positive tendencies, shafts of light which illuminate this somewhat gloomy depiction of democratization in the CEECs. One is the explosion of energy, at least in some countries, at a local level. It is expressed in the dramatic growth of both voluntary organizations – NGOs, civic groups, etc. – and small and medium-sized enterprises. It sometimes occurs in partnership with local and regional levels of government and is often linked to international networks as a result of the growing ease of travel and communication. This is a phenomenon to be found in both East and West, and it opens up the possibility of a new kind of democracy-building from below, provided political and financial limitation on local and regional autonomy can be overcome.

The differentiated methodology for assessing the process of democratization that we have tried to elaborate suggests the possibility of a differentiated strategy that could be adopted by governments and international institutions concerned to ensure the continuation of democratization. Such a strategy would have to deal with both formal and substantive aspects of democracy. Evidently, international insistence on compliance with formal criteria is essential. In particular, the formal criteria must constitute a condition for membership in European institutions such as the EU. However, it is equally important to focus on the substantive aspects of democracy.

The argument that the weakness of political culture in the CEECs is attributable to contemporary factors as well as to the communist heritage implies that a possible strategy is to promote an alternative forward-looking political project at the European level. Such a strategy might draw on the positive tendencies of democratization and might be associated with support for political decentralization, community development, and 'bottom-up' political and economic strategies generally. The idea could be to overcome the limitations on local and regional autonomy through international efforts. A project of promoting democracy through this type of approach – involving a public–private–voluntary partnership, which would aim to offer a new political model – could contribute more generally to political cohesion in Western as well as Eastern Europe. In the Conclusion to this book, we elaborate this proposal and try to spell out some theoretical and policy implications.

Notes

1. The first criterion, as defined by Lijphart, was the existence of political rights and civil liberties.
2. Juan J. Linz (1978, p. 8), for example, wrote, 'Unfortunately, there is no meaningful, accepted typology of competitive democracies, nor any accepted measure of the degree of democracy. Only the distinction between democracies based on majority rule and those that Lijphart calls consociational has gained wide acceptance.' George Orwell (1957, p. 149), noted, 'In the case of a word like

democracy not only is there no agreed definition but the attempt to make one is resisted from all sides ... The defenders of any kind of regime claim that it is a democracy, and fear that they might have to stop using the word if it were tied down to any one meaning.'

3. In a different vein, in his early writings Marx (1843 [1975], pp. 146–7) expressed a scathing criticism of early-nineteenth-century democracy, considering that formal, bourgeois democracy was insufficient, indeed a veil cast over relations of exploitation, and that a more socially equitable and just society (socialism) in the future would deliver real, substantial 'rule of the people'.

4. The debate between a proceduralist, formal approach to democracy and a substantive and/or normative approach has long been a mainstay of political theory. A variety of authors address these issues. Most recently, for example, Jürgen Habermas (1996) has taken the proceduralist side while Ronald Dworkin (1996) takes the substantive side.

5. See the section on administration and in particular Chapters 7, 10 and 11 on Slovakia, Romania and Bulgaria, respectively; as well as Chapters 2 and 3 on Estonia and Latvia.

6. The Polish Peasants' Party (PSL), the largest such party in the CEECs, won 19 per cent of the vote in the September 1995 parliamentary elections and is part of the governing coalition. Other peasant parties are the Smallholders' Party in Hungary and the Agrarian Party in Bulgaria.

7. This process is almost identical to the one which occurred in Spain in the immediate post-Franco period.

8. In the Czech Republic the ruling Civic Democratic Party (ODS) of Prime Minister Václav Klaus got 29.6 per cent of the vote in the May–June 1996 parliamentary elections and is in a coalition with the Civic Democratic Alliance (ODA) and the Christian Democratic Union/Czech People's Party (KDU/CSL). In Slovakia the ruling Movement for a Democratic Slovakia (HZDS) of Prime Minister Vladimir Mečiar, which won 34.9 per cent of the votes in the 1994 elections, is in a coalition with the Association of Workers of Slovakia (ZRS) and the Slovak National Party (SNS).

9. In Hungary the former communist Hungarian Socialist Party (MSZP), which won 33 per cent of the vote in the 1994 elections but gained 54 per cent of the seats in Parliament, decided to create a grand coalition with the post-1989, liberal Alliance of Free Democrats (SZDSZ), which won 20 per cent of the vote. In Slovenia, in the three years up to March 1996, the Associated List of Social Democrats (the former communists) were in a grand coalition with the Liberal Democrat Party and the Christian Democrat Party (see Chapter 9).

10. See Chapter 8. However, this relative loyalty is due not to censorship but to economic influence.

11. Governmental agencies such as the Financial Guard occasionally have bursts of authority and good intentions, but these remain unsupported by the Parliament and the government itself, so they cannot face up to the problem of generalized corruption, traffic of influence, administrative abuses and lack of effectiveness (see Chapter 10).

12. The Soros or Open Society Foundation has occupied a unique place among the CEECs in fostering independent self-organized activities.

2

Democratization in Estonia

JÜRI RUUS

Introduction

After fifty years of forced integration into the Soviet Union (USSR), Estonia reasserted its independence in August 1991. A non-communist government had emerged in early 1990 after parliamentary elections. The Popular Front of Estonia (PFE) won 43 of the 105 seats and more radical nationalist parties won 30 seats, providing proponents of independence with a majority. Pride of place in the drive for independence must be given to the PFE, originally an umbrella movement encompassing various pro-independence groups. The movement helped ordinary people to participate in pluralist politics and to overcome the alienation towards state structures that they had felt under Soviet rule.

In terms of political institutionalization, the period of transition to democracy ended with the elections to fill the transitional State Council in September 1992. The results verified Estonia's swing to the right. The election coalition Isamaa (Fatherland), composed of five free-market-oriented parties, gained 29 of the 101 seats in the Parliament and formed the core of the new government. On 5 October the Parliament chose the writer Lennart Meri as Estonia's first post-war President.

Independence is not a new phenomenon to Estonia. During the inter-war period Estonia was an independent country and a member of various international organizations. Although the 1920 constitution was democratic and a multi-party system flourished, democracy ultimately gave way to authoritarian rule in the 1930s. The challenges to Estonia's fledgling democracy today are greater than those to which it succumbed during the inter-war period. Ethnic tension is more of a problem and the stresses generated by the transition from state socialism are at least as severe as those unleashed by the Great Depression. Should post-Soviet Estonian democracy survive these pressures when inter-war Estonian democracy could not, it would tell us much about the factors that sustain and undermine democratic government.

Constitutional problems and political parties

During the 1988–91 struggle for liberty and the restoration of independence, popularly acclaimed as the Singing Revolution, the Estonian people and their leaders shared a common foreign policy orientation and were united in legal and political arguments. Victory came without bloodshed, proving the power of discipline and reason. As links with the USSR were gradually severed, the foundations of a sovereign state and a democratic political system were re-created. The legal continuity of the pre-war republic served as the basis for re-establishing state institutions, laws and political parties. In August–September 1991 most of the world's countries recognized Estonia's resumption of sovereignty, and the former member of the League of Nations was admitted to the United Nations.

A republican constitution, granting the Parliament the central role, was approved by referendum on 28 June 1992 and came into effect on 3 July. The constitution was drafted by a Constituent Assembly, jointly appointed in the autumn of 1991 by the Supreme Council and the Estonian Congress (a representative body elected by citizens of the 1918–40 Republic of Estonia). The constitution contains such universally recognized principles of democracy and the rule of law as the separation and balance of powers, the division of authority between central government and local administration, guarantees of human rights and citizens' rights.

Local government

Estonia has a single-tier local government system, adopted in October 1993. Local affairs are managed by elected provincial and town councils. There are 255 municipalities, of which 42 are towns and 213 rural districts. Fifteen county (provincial) administrations implement central government policy within their regions. District and town councils are elected for three-year terms. The first post-war local elections under the new law took place on 17 October 1993.

Political parties

Political parties are an inseparable element of a democratic system. Despite having been on the political scene for more than six years, Estonia's parties are still weak and fragmented, and membership figures are low. This is in part due to still unstructured ownership relations in the society. Reluctance to become involved in party politics, a legacy from the period of one-party dictatorship, is also a factor. The present political landscape – currently 20 political parties are active – is likely to change in the near future through regroupings and mergers. Several of the more traditional parties have become members of corresponding international associations and are likely to survive.

The mass media

A major breakthrough occurred in the late 1980s, when the press regained its independence and once again became a reflection of public opinion and a consistent advocate of democratic ideas. Criticism of the authorities, which could have resulted in imprisonment during the Soviet period, is currently a fashionable activity. The political self-censorship of the past has been replaced by a wide range of political expression. In recent years Estonia's media have again assumed a multi-tiered and multilingual character, where everybody seems to take a stab at publishing. In addition to magazines purely intended for entertainment, there are newspapers and magazines emanating from local government bodies, organizations, cultural societies, political parties and special interest groups. The number of different papers and journals has increased rapidly, although not everyone can afford a daily newspaper. The main battle during the past six years has concerned whether the mass media should be subject to some government control or be left completely free. Two positions have been advocated: (1) all media should be privatized and completely free of government interference; and (2) state-controlled entities should supplement the commercial press. Currently state-owned and private media exist side by side. A right-of-centre political perspective predominates in the mass media.

Challenges to democratization in Estonia

The twentieth century has seen the growth of great industrial societies with their twin problems: the enlargement of government responsibility and the emergence of social conflict as the main motor of political life. Social conflict originates from two sources. The first is the conflict of interests between various forces in society. The more developed the society, the more conscious and active are the groups that contribute to the functioning and viability of that society. The second source is the conflict of values (beliefs, faiths, ideas and customs) among members of society. The two forms of conflict exist in all societies but are particularly acute in transitional ones.

Crime

During the transition period the difficulty of constructing and revising the foundations of the nation-state creates uncertainty and fear. Shortcomings in the institutionalization of the rule of law, particularly the increasing crime

rate, contributed to growing alienation. Almost half of respondents to a
recent survey said that crime is the most serious problem in Estonia (*Estonian
Human Development Report*, 1995). Low wages (32 per cent) and unemployment (20 per cent) were the next most frequently identified problems. Noting
that crime was much worse than expected, Prime Minister Tiit Vahi stressed
in June 1995 that 'Neither our economic success nor the political recognition we have received can make up for the lack of sense of security, and even
fear, experienced today by the people of Estonia as well as by many visitors to
our country.' In the first three months of 1995, 9,000 crimes were reported.
Only 14.7 per cent of cases have been solved, a rate much lower than in
Latvia and Lithuania.

President Meri has linked rising crime with national security, noting that
'When Estonia becomes a corridor for illegal arms trafficking, organised
crime and narcotics trade, there will be no trust in our country. If there is no
trust in our country, what are the prospects of joining the European Union?'
(*The Baltic Independent*, 9 June 1995).

There are several reasons for this high crime rate in the Baltics: gaps in
legislation; socio-economic factors (acute social inequality and no firm social
security net); and the absence of an efficient police system (the Baltic police
forces, created six years ago, are underpaid). The fear of crime has increased
sharply (*Estonian Human Development Report*, 1995). One-third of those
polled are afraid they or their family members will be physically assaulted.

Studies undertaken in the Baltic states show that most Estonians trust
other people but with some reservations (*Pre-election Studies in Estonia,
Latvia, and Lithuania 1992, 1993*). Distrust and suspicion are part of the
legacy of the Soviet past, but a certain degree of trust is necessary for the
consolidation of transitional society and the establishment of a stable regime.
Only after citizens have learned to tolerate compromises can political democracy create conditions for a less suspicious attitude towards other people's
purposes and ideals.

The shadow economy

According to a study by the EMOR market and public opinion research
company, gaps in current legislation, the weakness of the law enforcement
mechanisms, and structural changes in the economy are the main factors
contributing to the spread of the illegal or shadow economy.

Estonian business executives who responded to a poll in autumn 1994 put
the shadow economy at the top of the country's economic problems. Corruption among public servants came second, illegal alcohol and tobacco trading
third. The Estonian Statistics Department estimated that in 1994 the illegal

economy accounted for 13 per cent of the gross domestic product (GDP) (*The Baltic Independent*, 14 April 1995).

Multiple transitions

It was originally believed that the main components of the post-socialist transformation – democratization, property reform and the restoration of the nation-state – would support and reinforce one another. In practice, however, a complex situation has emerged in which these processes may interfere with rather than support one other. For instance, inadequate public control and deficient legal regulation have enabled some influential groups to 'spontaneously privatize' state property.

Social inequality

Instead of enjoying security and stability, which many Estonians consider to have been the most positive aspects of the previous system, many people – particularly families with many children, the elderly, and the young – express feelings of hopelessness. It is regrettable that the generation that suffered Stalinist repression in the 1940s and 1950s is now suffering from the reforms. Privatization and the formation of a market economy are polarizing society. At the very beginning of the transition process, people were predominantly poor, but equally so. As the transition process matured, society became more differentiated with a sharp division between the rich and the poor. The cleavage line lies between the new rich (the country is thought to have 31 super-rich families) and the socially most vulnerable (*Postimees*, 1 July 1996). The development of the middle class, a major source of social stability, has proceeded more slowly.

Sharp social and economic inequalities are widely believed to increase social discontent. Given that the standard of living of many is at or below the poverty line, it is not surprising that trust in the political system is limited, although trust is greater among ethnic Estonians than among minorities (*Pre-election Studies in Estonia, Latvia, and Lithuania 1992, 1993*).

Unrealistic expectations and a disposition towards passivity have also contributed to a growing disillusionment with democracy. Under the Soviet regime many Estonians regarded democracy as a panacea for all political, social, cultural and economic problems. They believed that because almost all the developed countries are democracies and have market economies, democracy would usher in a market economy and make everybody better off. These beliefs led to the conclusion that democracy would automatically entail a better life for everybody. Instead, standards of living have dropped, especially during the first years of transition, and social inequality has increased, leading to alienation, distrust and in some sections of the population a feeling of betrayal (*Estonian Human Development Report*, 1995).

Pervasive passivity

The regimented Soviet state regulated almost every aspect of daily life. Its paternalism fostered passivity. Individuals were inert and waited for the authorities to take the initiative. This passivity has far-reaching consequences. Not only is entrepreneurship, so necessary in a market economy, underdeveloped, but many individuals have had great difficulty in adjusting to changes in the organization of family support, health care, old-age pensions and social services. Elderly, poor and less well educated people have had great difficulty in adapting to these changes because they cannot afford legal counsel and lack the tools to challenge the bureaucracy. These feelings are particularly acute because during Soviet times unemployment was unknown.

In addition, it should be noted that unemployment is disproportionately high among Russian-speakers. Of the 16,109 people officially registered as unemployed in the fourth quarter of 1993, 56 per cent indicated that Russian was their the principal language of communication. This is much higher than the proportion of Russian-speakers in the population generally, approximately 35 per cent. This finding is not necessarily surprising, as Russian-speakers made up the bulk of the workers in the all-Union factories, which were closely integrated into the Soviet military industrial complex (Noorköiv and Annus, 1994) and thus have been hardest hit by the collapse of the USSR and by economic transformation. That these people should fear for their future in an independent Estonia is understandable, because the closing or downsizing of these factories has meant the loss of the preferential treatment (higher wages, social benefits, free housing) previously accorded to them. Moreover, these industrial workers were more fully integrated into the Soviet ideological system than other occupational groups (Kirch and Kirch, 1995).

Nationalism and ethnic minorities

Political polarization is the major source of internal conflict, and the strongest polarizing forces in modern times are ethnic identity, language and religion (Dahl, 1968). Nationalism was one of the two strong ideological movements that gained force in the Baltics after the collapse of the USSR. Western liberalism was the other. The nationalist current steered the new ethnic majorities in an exclusivist direction, while liberalism pointed towards inclusion. Politics in Estonia, as in Latvia, has to a great extent been carried out along ethnic lines. Historical arguments about the injustices of fifty years of Soviet/Russian occupation have prevailed thus far, overshadowing efforts to be more generous in extending political rights to members of national minorities.

The treatment of ethnic minorities in Estonia and Latvia remains a controversial topic. Two models of development have been offered, both as descriptions of actual practices and as prescriptions for future action. According to the first model, Estonia and Latvia display characteristics of social apartheid. Minorities are said to be excluded on the basis of ethnicity or race from integrating fully into the body politic. Used as a means of securing the hegemony of the core nation, citizenship rights (political, civil and social) are limited to individuals on the basis of ethnicity. Consequently, democracy is enjoyed only by members of the core nation. Some Western observers (Smith *et al.*, 1994) have argued that the denial of political rights, notably the right to vote and stand for national elections, to ethnic minorities raises the spectre of apartheid emerging in Estonia and Latvia. This view is shared by the Russian government. In 1993 the Russian president, Boris Yeltsin, argued that Estonia has imposed a form of apartheid on Baltic Russians and resorted to ethnic cleansing in an attempt to secure more ethnically homogeneous polities (*Pravda*, 24 June 1993).

Certain developments give currency to this model. In Estonia, non-citizens, who are mainly Russians, were excluded from voting in the presidential and parliamentary elections in September 1992. Thus the great majority of Russian residents in Latvia and Estonia did not have a say in the first elections of these newly independent states, nor do they hold political office at the national level.

Control of high positions in the state bureaucracy is also overwhelmingly in the hands of ethnic Estonians. The same pattern characterizes the judicial system. In Estonia and Lithuania, only a very few non-indigenous people are members of the judiciary. Thus the core institutions of the state – the executive, the legislature and the judiciary – are insulated from minority influence (Steen, 1994).

Nevertheless, there are serious grounds for doubting that this model accurately reflects reality. Citizenship is based not on ethnic or racial criteria, but on descent from citizens of the inter-war republics *or* length of residency. Thus Russians with historical roots in Estonia automatically qualify for full citizenship while those without roots do not. There are more than 100,000 Russian-speaking Estonian citizens (mainly descendants of pre-war Russian-speaking Estonian citizens), who managed to win six seats in the March 1995 parliamentary elections. The converse is also true. Ethnic Estonians who did not live in Estonia between the wars do not automatically acquire citizenship. They must apply for it.

According to the new (1995) Law on Citizenship, applicants for citizenship must fulfil three basic conditions:

- pass a basic proficiency test in Estonian;
- have at least five years' residency; and
- swear an oath of loyalty to Estonia.

These conditions are defensible. Knowledge of basic rights and obligations as defined in Estonian law is in the interest of everyone taking Estonian citizenship so that they can defend those rights and fulfil their obligations. An understanding of the citizenship process will also ensure that people know that they have the right to challenge, in court, decisions not to grant citizenship (Article 36). The Estonian government, with financial support from foreign governments and international organizations, provides Estonian-language classes for individuals seeking citizenship. However, this has not been enough. Non-Estonians are dissatisfied with the quality and scope of language instruction. They would support any innovations (teaching of Estonian in kindergartens, teaching selected subjects in Estonian) that would facilitate the teaching of the state language. The need is real, for the younger generation of Russians born in Estonia (1950–70) know even less Estonian than their parents (Kirch and Kirch, 1995). The language law stipulating compulsory usage of Estonian in state institutions applies only in theory in parts of Tallinn and parts of north-eastern Estonia, where Russian-speakers form the bulk of the population. Non-Estonians living in monolingual Russian communities in industrial cities such as Tallinn, Kohtla-Järve, Sillamäe and Narva are at a clear disadvantage.[1]

While controversy rages concerning the causes for the slow pace of nationalization, it is evident that most non-ethnic Estonians have not received citizenship. From January 1992 to January 1995, 48,491 aliens were naturalized, 43 per cent of whom were ethnic Estonians. It is quite clear that a large part of the population is disenfranchised and has limited political rights. The bulk of non-ethnic Estonians – primarily Russians, Jews, Swedes, Latvians and Finns – who have gained citizenship have done so because a parent or grandparent was an Estonian citizen in 1940, or because they have married an Estonian citizen, not through nationalization. Approximately 100,000 non-Estonians have obtained citizenship in this manner, bringing to 125,000 the number of Estonian citizens who are not ethnic Estonians (*Estonian Human Development Report*, 1995).

Residents of Estonia can be classified as follows:

1. citizens: 930,000 or 63 per cent of all residents are citizens; 125,000 are not ethnic Estonians;
2. citizens of Russia: on 29 June 1996 the Russian embassy stated that it

had given citizenship to 65,000 people, but most observers believe that 120,000 residents are Russian citizens;

3. residents without citizenship: the estimate varies from 200,000 or 13 per cent to 300,000 or about 20 per cent. Such individuals can be granted foreign passports if they have permanent residence.

The second model for the development of ethnic relations in Estonia, that of ethnic democracy, is composed of three central features. First, an ethnic democracy accords to the core nation an institutional status superior to its proportion of the population. Second, civil and, to a certain degree, political rights are enjoyed universally. Third, certain collective rights are extended to ethnic minorities. By combining elements of civil and political democracy with explicit ethnic dominance, an ethnic democracy attempts to preserve ethno-political stability despite the contradictions and tensions inherent in such a system. As Smootha and Hanf note (cited in Smith *et al.*, 1994, p. 190),

> Since nationalism in Eastern Europe tends to be integral and exclusionary as opposed to western nationalism which tends to be open, inclusive and coterminous with citizenship, there is a strong possibility for some of the democratizing states there to become ethnic democracies.

While the rights and interests of each ethnic community must be respected and balanced, there is also a great need to consider the question of the Russian minority in the broader context of national security. Basically this is the question concerning its political loyalty or lack thereof. Russian-speakers in Estonia can be grouped as follows:

1. those who would prefer that Estonia were part of Russia for reasons having to do with national culture;
2. those who would prefer an autonomous region (in a 1993 referendum on autonomy roughly 60 per cent of the people in the Russian-speaking city of Sillamäe voted in favour of autonomy (*The Baltic Observer*, 23 July 1993)); and
3. those who favour Estonian independence and have linked their fortunes to those of the republic.

Empirical evidence suggests that this last group is the largest. According to data from the Estonian Ministry of Foreign Affairs, 64 per cent of ethnic Russians living in Estonia believe that Estonia offers them better prospects for raising their standards of living than does Russia, compared to 14 per cent who think the opposite. These findings are supported by other surveys which indicate that the bulk of members of ethnic minorities in Estonia would not consider emigrating (*Pre-election Studies in Estonia, Latvia and Lithuania 1992, 1993*).

None the less, there has been a slight outflow of minorities from the Baltic states. Forty-four thousand Russian-speakers have left Estonia during the past five years, mainly for Russia. This relatively modest emigration might be explained by the lower cost of living in Russia.

Several international missions have not uncovered any serious violation of human rights in Estonia. In August 1993 Helsinki Watch found no systematic, serious abuses of human rights in the area of citizenship. Non-citizens in Estonia are guaranteed basic rights under the Estonian constitution, including the right to unemployment benefits and social services. The Law on Local Elections allows resident non-Estonian citizens to vote in local elections. In a letter to the Estonian minister of foreign affairs in April 1993, the Conference on Security and Co-operation in Europe (CSCE) High Commissioner for National Minorities, Max van de Stoel, wrote:

> I am fully aware of the fact that there is no convincing evidence of systematic persecution of the non-Estonian population since the re-establishment of Estonian independence and moreover that there have been virtually no incidents pointing to inter-ethnic violence.

What is more, the majority of Russian-speakers, at least according to some surveys, do not feel discriminated against (Foreign Ministry of Estonia).

The rights of ethnic minorities are protected by the 1993 Law on the Cultural Autonomy of Ethnic Minorities. Based on a 1925 law, it entitles persons of German, Russian, Swedish or Jewish nationality – and any other ethnic minority with more than 3,000 members – to form cultural autonomous groups according to the principle of legal inheritance.

Professor Richard Rose has carried out extensive research on ethnic relations in the Baltics. In one survey he found that 69 per cent of Russian-speakers felt they had a fair amount in common with the Baltic peoples. Moreover, Russian-speakers in Estonia and Latvia tend to be more positive in their views than those in Lithuania, where they comprise only 9 per cent of the total population. Russians in Estonia and Latvia are also divided about what justifies a claim to citizenship: one-third think it should be sufficient to have been living in the Baltic countries at the time of independence; another third think residence of more than 10 years should be required; and more than a fifth think citizenship should be given only to Russian-speakers who were born in the Baltic countries.

Since 1990 there has been a visible shift in the national identities of Estonians, Latvians, Lithuanians and Russians in the Baltics. Indigenous Balts have been slightly quicker to define themselves as Europeans, politically independent of Russia and joined culturally to the West. Many Russians face an identity vacuum and the need to redefine their personal and collective identities. The emerging new identities of Russian-speakers tend to be more Baltic-centred, and this process could be accelerated by a judicious policy of interaction and integration rather than confrontation. It is clearly in the interest of the Estonian government that its residents be loyal, politically aware and active, and this is possible only if the people feel that the political system is responsive to their demands and that its actions are relevant to their lives. It is therefore in the state's interest to incorporate national minorities into Estonian society and encourage their sense of loyalty.

External aspects of democratization

The clear-cut political geography of the Cold War has been superseded by a more nuanced landscape. On one side there is Russia as a nuclear power, together with an unstable constellation called the Commonwealth of Independent States (CIS), and on the other is the North Atlantic Treaty Organization (NATO). Between the NATO member countries in the West and the CIS in the East are the former members of the Warsaw Pact and the Baltic states. None of these countries belongs to a collective defence organization and none has firm security guarantees. The Baltic states are seeking membership of NATO, the European Union (EU) and the Western European Union (WEU) primarily to gain such guarantees for their recently restored independence.

In 1991–5 the Baltic states made significant progress in integrating themselves into Western organizations. They gained membership in the United Nations and CSCE practically automatically as sovereign states. Each applied to and was admitted by the Council of Europe during 1993–6. They now aspire to join organizations – such as the EU, WEU and NATO – that have until now been reserved for advanced Western nations. All three Baltic states have signed association agreements with the EU.

Integration with NATO has proceeded at a moderate pace. In December 1991 a political declaration on joint activities between NATO and the Baltic states within the North Atlantic Cooperation Council (NACC) was signed in Brussels. In January 1994 Baltic leaders endorsed the NATO Partnership for Peace plan, which has already conferred some multilateral security benefits on the participants.

The Baltic states have been quite candid in expressing the conviction that Russia constitutes their main security threat and that NATO membership is the best counter to it. This has placed NATO in an awkward position as it has been insistent that NATO expansion is not considered a means of neutralizing potential Russian aggression. US Defense Secretary William Perry was careful to note on 22 November 1995 that 'We believe that there is no significant threat to the Baltics' freedom' (*The Baltic Independent*, 24 November 1995). While no explicit security guarantees are in the offing, many

Western experts believe that security links will develop through practical co-operation, particularly within the framework of the Partnership for Peace.

Ensuring the development and well-being of its people requires that Estonia co-operate with other states in economic, ecological, security, and other areas. Accession to the EU would offer Estonia the following advantages:

- better access to EU markets for Estonian goods;
- increased security through economic ties with Western European countries;
- reinforcement of Estonians' European cultural identity, which has long been repressed;
- paradigms for legislation, social policy, environmental protection, etc.;
- increasing the attractiveness of Estonia for investors from developed non-EU states interested in EU markets;
- greater stability in economic relations with Russia;
- more foreign investment and accompanying technological development;
- economic assistance during the difficult period of economic reorganization; and
- participation in EU joint programmes.

The EU would benefit from closer co-operation with Estonia (and the other Baltic states) through:

- integrating a region with a high growth potential and which requires minimal financial aid to get back on its feet;
- securing a foothold for developing ties with the large markets to the east; and
- allowing the EU to expand co-operation in transport, communication and environmental protection within the context of development of the whole Northern European region.

The general principles of EU law are already valid in Estonia. However, although the basic laws regulating the fundamentals of economic and social life are in place, more detailed regulations need to be adopted. Discussions are under way to determine which areas should be granted priority in ensuring the compliance of local legislation with that of the EU. It is clear that EU insistence on conformity with its legislation will require a higher level of institutional development (*Estonia and the European Union*, 1995). Further, before becoming an EU member, Estonia must resolve certain problems inherited from the Soviet past, including the status of the citizens of the former Soviet Union and the delimitation of its eastern border with Russia.

Conclusion

Clearly, the state of development of Western Europe and that of the Baltic states differ greatly. However, the Baltic states have made significant advances in developing political democracy as well as market economies. The establishment of a fully consolidated democracy is not an easy task and takes time. In former communist countries democracy has been idealized and imagined to be a miraculous tool immediately available for implementing radical changes rather than as something to be created over generations. Genuine dilemmas and paradoxes must be overcome during the transition. Liberal democracy is not the result of prior unity and consensus but the fruit of successful efforts to transcend stalemate and conflict. It emerges from the interdependence of conflicting interests and diversity of discordant ideals, in a context which encourages strategic interaction among actors. Estonia and the other Baltic states will face major obstacles in ethnic relations, national identity and crime on the road to consolidated democracy.

Democracy in the Baltics must be constructed from a combination of elements that address these challenges and dangers. The most important elements are national integration, an international commitment to Baltic membership in the European family of nations, and the development of a viable economy with Western trade and investments.

Note

1. *The Attitude of Town Residents of Northeastern Estonia towards Estonian Reforms and Social Policy. A Comparative Study of 1993, 1994, 1995,* Tallinn, 1996.

3

Democratization in Latvia

ANDRIS RUNCIS

Introduction

The Baltic states, including Latvia, regained their national independence in 1991 and embarked on the complicated path of creating democratic societies. After independence was restored, Latvia had to solve several difficult tasks that were the legacy of its particular historical development and loss of sovereignty.

The transition process in Latvia, and its Baltic neighbours, has four components: (1) political transformation; (2) transition to a market economy; (3) creation of an independent state; and (4) preservation of independence. The crucial issue of security should not be understood in a narrow military or political sense, but must also focus on demographic matters, including the viability, if not the survival, of the Latvian nation. Since 1940 Latvia has suffered immense losses. Thousands died fighting on both sides during World War II, tens of thousands were deported to and died in Siberia, and almost 250,000 emigrated to the West to escape communist repression. At the same time, hundreds of thousands of Russians were resettled in Latvia. The influx was so great that Latvians almost became a minority in their own land.

The transition process presents policy-makers with both difficult choices and a singular opportunity, for the decisions of today will have a lasting influence on the welfare and development of the people of Latvia.

Historical background

Independence is not a new phenomenon to Latvia. From 1918 to 1940 it was a sovereign country and a member of the League of Nations. Many Latvians remember the period of independence as a time of significant economic and cultural achievement. Political participation, as measured by voter turnout, was high; approximately 80 per cent of the population used to vote in the elections to the Parliament (Saeíma) (Adolfs, 1990).

The 1922 constitution, based on the same principles as those of the Swiss and Weimar republics, gave more power to the legislature than to the executive branch of government. The Parliament elected the president, whose powers were limited; he or she could enact emergency decrees only when Parliament was not in session. Although democratic in character, the constitution had certain drawbacks. The interaction between the weak executive and strong legislature paralysed decision-making. The problem was compounded by the proliferation of minute political parties, most of which, none the less, managed to win seats in Parliament; 28 parties were represented in the last Parliament. The resulting political stalemate meant that the government was usually too weak to carry out necessary reforms. This paralysis set the stage for the imposition of authoritarian rule.

International factors also contributed to the breakdown of democracy in the Baltic states. The growth of extremist political organizations and the emergence of fascist movements in Europe exerted considerable pressure on political life in Latvia. The economic depression of the 1930s also struck hard in the Baltic area. The increased tensions in European politics further undermined faith in democracy.

In 1934 Premier Karlis Ulmanis proclaimed a state of emergency, claiming that there was the danger of a communist *coup d'état* in Latvia. Ulmanis suspended the Parliament and banned party activities. Latvians reacted calmly to his imposition of authoritarian rule. His apologists claim that he would have been elected president anyway if elections had been held; that extremist groups were trying to destabilize the situation; and that matters could have turned out worse if he had not intervened. While this may be true, it is still the case that Ulmanis usurped power. The President did manage to turn the economy around, but he failed to appreciate the changes in the international climate that were endangering Latvian independence. Thus Latvia was unprepared for the Soviet ultimatum in June 1940 that brought the short period of independence to an end.

Nearly fifty years later the transition to democracy began during the period that is now known as the 'national awakening', when political dissidents, environmentalists and intellectuals mobilized in an attempt to influence Soviet policy. The summer of 1988 saw the establishment of the Latvian National Independence Movement (LNNK), which called for immediate independence from the USSR. That same summer, members of various organizations joined together to found the Latvian Popular Front (LPF), which sought the dismantling of the Communist Party's monopoly on power, greater autonomy from Moscow, and protection of Latvian cultural values.

The constitution and government

The instruments of totalitarian rule atrophied during the late 1980s. Several centres of power emerged in Latvia: the Parliament, the government and the Popular Front of Latvia. The Communist Party splintered into two wings: one, headed by Alfred Rubiks, remained loyal to Moscow; the other opted for a more patriotic and reformist course, eventually reconstituting itself as the Latvian Democratic Labour Party.

The LPF was the dominant force during the national awakening. It managed to win widespread support for its programme of greater cultural and political autonomy. In the last elections under Soviet rule, held on 18 March 1990, about 70 per cent of the seats in the Latvian Supreme Soviet were won by individuals who either were members of the LPF or had its endorsement. Shortly thereafter the Supreme Soviet voted for Latvian independence. The LPF, its historical mission accomplished, fragmented and lost its political influence; it did not win a single seat in the 1993 parliamentary elections.

The Supreme Council of the Republic of Latvia restored the 1922 constitution (*Satversme*), which confirmed the legal continuity and identity of the Latvian state established in 1918. Consequently, the government is committed to restoring the legal, economic and civil rights that existed in Latvia prior to the Soviet invasion.

The separation of powers is enshrined in the Latvian constitution, but it has taken considerable time to ensure the functioning of all the elements of the system of checks and balances. Political disagreements delayed the establishment of the Constitutional Court until 1996. It convened for the first time on 11 December but did not hear any cases because not all the judges had been sworn in. The Constitutional Court will have seven judges, each serving a ten-year term. It will review the constitutionality of laws and has the authority to declare null and void legislation that it deems to be unconstitutional.

Other judicial reforms have been implemented more expeditiously. On 15 October 1995 a new three-tier court system was established: (1) regional city court; (2) regional district court; (3) Supreme Court. This reform facilitates the process of appealing against court decisions. Enactment of this law and the establishment of the Constitutional Court meant that the Soviet court system has finally been abolished.

The highest elected body in Latvia is the single-chamber Saeíma (Parliament), which is composed of 100 deputies who are elected to three-year terms on the basis of proportional representation by citizens 18 years of age and over.

The first free elections after the restoration of independence (to select the fifth Saeíma; the first four sat during the inter-war period) took place in 1993. The turnout was high: almost 90 per cent of eligible voters participated. The right to vote had been granted to inhabitants who were citizens in June 1940 and their descendants, about 75 per cent of the population. The change of government that ensued was peaceful. Elections to the sixth Saeíma took place in October 1995. The results were indecisive: nine parties entered Parliament, but none gained more than eighteen seats. After two months of discussion a broad-based governing coalition of six parties was formed.

Both Saeímas have faced the formidable task of reworking the nation's laws so that they protect fundamental human rights and freedoms, facilitate the transition to the market economy and are compatible with European Union (EU) legislation. While no one doubts the diligence of the legislature – several thousand laws have been passed since 1990 – criticism has been voiced about the quality and coherence of the legislation and the procedures by which it is drafted. Critics have lamented the fact that there is no trained body to advise Parliament on whether draft laws will achieve their intended objectives or bring about unintended consequences, and how they will interact with existing legislation.

The Saeíma also elects the president. The constitution grants the president few prerogatives. The prime minister or another minister has to countersign all but two types of presidential decisions: nominating a prime minister and dissolving the Parliament. The latter decision, however, has to be approved by a referendum. If dissolution is rejected, the president is considered deposed and the Parliament elects a new one.

Guntis Ulmanis was elected president in 1993 and re-elected in 1995. A clever politician with a popular bent, he has succeeded in transforming the presidency from an institution whose functions are primarily symbolic into one with genuine political influence.

Human rights

The restoration of *de jure* independence on 4 May 1990 was followed immediately by the Supreme Council's decision to ratify a number of well-known international human rights instruments. This decision states that the Supreme Council recognizes the fundamental principle that Latvia's laws must 'conform to the norms of international law relating to human rights'. Among the 52 basic international agreements recognized to be commitments binding on the Latvian state are the Universal Declaration on Human Rights, two international covenants and other basic human rights instruments. None the less, the separate chapter of the constitution that will deal explicitly with human rights has not yet been approved by Parliament.

Efforts are being made to ensure respect for human rights. The State Human Rights Bureau was established by the Cabinet and granted a firmer base by Parliament on 5 December 1996. The Bureau is subordinated directly to the Parliament, and no other government, political or public organizations can interfere with its activity. It has broad powers to require information from state and municipal institutions concerning cases of possible infringements of human rights. It can also submit legislative proposals on human rights issues to the Parliament. The Bureau's director, appointed by the Parliament, is supposed to be politically neutral.

Human rights have been respected in Latvia. But this does not mean that certain sections of the population have not faced great difficulties during the period of transition. The economic dislocation caused by the shift to the market economy has led to a general decline in the standard of living and a weakening of the social security net. Orphans and abandoned children, handicapped people, mentally ill and mentally retarded persons, old people, former prisoners and other unprotected groups have suffered. Because of limited resources the government has been unable to provide all these groups with the social services that they need. Orphans and abandoned children, many of whom are mentally retarded, have been particularly vulnerable. A special Court of Orphans has been established to address their plight.

The rights of minorities

The most debated issue in Latvia is the ethnic question. Latvians accounted for 77 per cent of the population in 1935, but only 52 per cent in 1989. Ethnic Latvians now make up 55 per cent of the population, owing to the emigration of non-Latvians and a slightly higher birth rate among Latvians.[1] Latvians fear that they will become a minority in their own land. Russians believe that they are denied political rights and are subject to various forms of discrimination.

The most sensitive issues are citizenship and status of resident non-citizens (aliens). The Law on Citizenship, adopted on 22 July 1994, was very controversial. Since 25 per cent of Latvian residents were not citizens in 1940 or descendants of citizens in 1940, they had to apply for naturalization. The original version included an annual naturalization quota of 0.1 per cent of all Latvian citizens, or about 2,000 per year. The Council of Europe, the High Commissioner on National Minorities of the Organization for Security and Co-operation in Europe (OSCE), Max van der Stoel, and human rights organizations protested that the law would have disenfranchised about a third of Latvia's inhabitants. After President Guntis Ulmanis vetoed the bill it was amended to take into account the comments of the Council of Europe and the OSCE. The quota system was eliminated.

None the less, the law is still quite restrictive. Applicants must pass a Latvian language test, demonstrate knowledge of the country's history and constitution, and pay a registration fee of about $60, half the average monthly salary. Moreover, the law provides for the incremental naturalization of non-citizens born in Latvia over a six-year period. Those born outside Latvia can apply for citizenship from the year 2000. Most permanent residents should be naturalized by 2003. According to the provisions of the law, youths between the ages of 16 and 20, spouses of Latvian citizens who have been married for at least ten years, ethnic Lithuanians and ethnic Estonians are eligible for naturalization in 1996. In 1997 naturalization will be offered to persons aged 20 to 25.

The naturalization process is proceeding very slowly. Only about 4,000 residents will have been naturalized by the end of 1996. Of the 33,000 non-citizens eligible for naturalization in 1996, only 450 have acquired it. A poll by the Naturalization Board revealed that two-thirds of 16- to 20-year-olds wish to gain citizenship, but that half believe their knowledge of the Latvian language and history is insufficient. It is estimated that about a third of Latvia's 750,000 non-citizens might not apply for Latvian citizenship. The reasons for their apparent disinterest in Latvian citizenship are contested. Some ethnic Russians believe that the language test is too strict and the registration fee too high. Others note various disincentives: non-citizens do not need to serve in the armed forces, and holders of Latvian passports must pay for visas to enter Russia to visit relatives. Still others may be secretly hoping that Latvia will be reintegrated into Russia or the Commonwealth of Independent States (CIS).

The denial of some political rights, such as the right to vote in elections or run for office, is not the only drawback of non-citizenship. Various prerogatives and privileges are dependent on citizenship. The pension paid to non-citizens was initially only 90 per cent of that of citizens, and non-citizens received fewer privatization vouchers and faced more restrictions when purchasing apartments. In 1996 Latvia's Parliament had to amend the wording of the Law on Civil Service, which would have barred non-citizens from holding government posts. More importantly, non-citizens are excluded from many aspects of the political process, and legislators are usually less responsive to their concerns than to those of citizens, as only the latter can vote them out of office.

Progress has been made in providing the minorities with education in their mother tongues (SDIP, 1994). During the inter-war years the rights of minorities were protected more firmly in Latvia and Estonia than in other European states. But the schools of all minorities, except Russians, were closed soon after the Soviet occupation. Upon regaining independence the Latvian government moved quickly to restore the schools of minorities. The first to open its doors was the Jewish secondary school in Riga, the first school of its kind in the territory of the former USSR. Subsequently Polish, Estonian, Ukrainian, Lithuanian, Roma and Belorussian schools or classes were founded.[2] Maintaining these schools is very expensive. This is particularly true of Russian schools, many of which are situated in small towns where the average number of pupils per class might not exceed five.

The government is aware that knowledge of Latvian is a necessary condition for promoting the integration of the ethnic minorities into the country's political, social and economic life. A Latvian language programme is needed in order to overcome the effects of the Soviets' Russification policy, to abolish linguistic segregation and to ease the anxieties of Latvians about the survival of their language and culture. The government has embarked on a programme to encourage the greater use of Latvian in schools of general education. This will require the revamping of the school system, because there are some school districts in which not a single school has Latvian as the language of instruction. And it is still not possible to study for many professions in Latvian.

During the 1995–96 academic year about 40 per cent of all pupils attended schools in which the language of a minority is the language of instruction. (Most of them attend Russian schools (Mezs, 1996)). However, that number is declining. In 1996 18 per cent fewer pupils studied in Russian than had in 1990. At the same time the number of pupils in Latvian and non-Russian minority schools has increased by 10 per cent. Two-thirds of first-year pupils began their studies with Latvian as the language of instruction. This is a result of the higher Latvian birth rate and a change in orientation among ethnically mixed families, who are now more likely to send their children to Latvian schools.

The government had originally approved a ten-year programme for gradually increasing the number of subjects taught in Latvian at Russian-language schools, but in 1995 the Parliament passed a law requiring that at least two subjects be taught in Latvian in elementary schools and three subjects in secondary schools. A draft bill has been submitted to the Parliament that calls for all secondary education to be conducted exclusively in Latvian by 2005. Ethnic Russians would surely consider such legislation discriminatory.

The Act on Free Development and the Right to Cultural Autonomy of Nationalities and Ethnic Groups, adopted by the Parliament on 19 March 1991, guarantees all residents in Latvia, whatever their nationality, equal human rights, in accordance with international rules. As a result of this legislation, a large number of minority and multicultural groups have been formed. Today there are more than 30 cultural societies in Latvia.

Surveys taken in 1993 and 1995 to evaluate how ethnic Latvians and minority members rated the political systems existing in the Soviet Union and Latvia found that the rating of Latvia's political system had risen significantly (*New Baltic Barometer*, 1993, 1995; Baltic Data House, *Diera*, 11 March 1996). In 1993 only 9 per cent of minority respondents evaluated the political system positively, while in 1995 40 per cent did so. This suggests that the minorities are gradually adapting themselves to their new circumstances. Attitudes towards the Soviet political system appear to be hardening in every national group. In 1993 36 per cent of Latvians and 66 per cent of non-Latvians expressed positive attitudes towards the Soviet political system. In 1995 35 per cent of Latvians and 51 per cent of non-Latvians supported it. Further, although in 1995 Latvians were somewhat less optimistic about the future development of the political system (74 per cent versus 81 per cent in 1993), non-Latvians were slightly more optimistic (74 per cent versus 71 per cent).

The role of religion

On 11 September 1990 the Parliament adopted the Act on Religious Organizations, which was drawn up in consultation with religious groups. The law grants every resident of Latvia the right to freedom of conscience, conviction and religion; to profess individually or together with others any religion or none; to take part in religious rituals; to freely change religious or other convictions; as well as to voice and to propagate his or her convictions and views in accordance with the constitution and national laws.

The most influential of Latvia's many religions are the Evangelical Lutheran Church, the Catholic Church and the Orthodox Church.

The Act on Religious Organizations has been supplemented by the Law on the Restitution of Property to Religious Organizations, passed on 12 May 1992. As a result, the state has begun to return to religious communities properties that were nationalized during the Soviet occupation.

During the occupation the Soviet government made great efforts to root out religion, resorting to various forms of pressure and, if necessary, persecution. The campaign of intimidation was quite effective. In 1985, for example, only 18.9 per cent of newborns were baptized, and just 4.4 per cent of weddings were performed by a minister. The Evangelical Church was the most persecuted. Evangelicals accounted for only 13.4 per cent of the baptisms and 9.5 per cent of the weddings performed in 1985, compared to 61.7 per cent and 83.3 per cent, respectively, for Catholics.

A show of civil courage, however, helped to revive the Church. In 1987 20

Lutheran ministers established a Christian social movement called 'Rebirth and Renewal', which began the struggle for a free Church and free society. Some of these ministers became politically active in the LPF and in the LNNK. The process of change led to the convocation of the Synod of the Evangelical Lutheran Church of Latvia in 1989. It chose a new archbishop, Karlis Gailitis, and a new governing body for the Church. The new administration of the Lutheran Church moved immediately to deal with the urgent problems that pervaded all aspects of Church life. In 1990 the Theology Faculty of the University of Latvia, which had been closed in 1940, was reopened. The fruits of the revival were clear by 1992: the number of children baptized in the Lutheran faith was more than ten times greater than in 1985, while the number of weddings had increased fifteen-fold.

The Catholic Church is the second largest denomination in Latvia with about 500,000 members, the overwhelming majority of whom live in the eastern region of Latgalia. Catholics have tended to be more devout than the Lutherans.

The Orthodox religion has existed in Latvia for more than eight centuries. During the years of Soviet rule the Orthodox Church in Latvia was subject to the same pressures as the other religions and had to overcome similar difficulties, if not even greater ones.

There is considerably less toleration of denominations which lack historical roots in Latvia and which are scornfully described as 'sects'. In December 1996 the government refused to register either the Jehovah's Witnesses or the Unification Church. Registration was withheld from the Jehovah's Witnesses on the grounds that it was a danger to the safety and health of other persons and provoked discord between different religious convictions. The Unification Church was charged with requiring its members to show unconditional submission to its spiritual leader. But there is no legislation that would allow the religious affairs department to apply any sanctions on unregistered religious organizations.

Mass media

In the autumn of 1990 the Latvian Parliament adopted a law on the rights of the media, which called for freedom of expression, the abolition of censorship and the right to establish and publish periodicals freely. The general public is quite satisfied with the way the media are doing their job. A 1995 survey conducted by the Open Media Research Institute indicated that 76 per cent of the respondents in Latvia said that they had 'a great deal of confidence' or 'some confidence' in the media, a rating higher than that for government institutions.

Publications are numerous and diverse, and all the leading newspapers are privately owned. Competition is intense: each year ten to fifteen new newspapers are founded, while the same number go bankrupt. The current economic crisis has limited the number of people who can afford to buy every newspaper, and most people can barely afford one. Most newspapers have specific readerships, so, while the press presents a wide variety of different views, the average reader is not exposed to this variety. This problem is compounded by the division of readers along ethnic lines. Latvians read Latvian newspapers, Russians read the Russian press, but because their content is completely different, neither group is able to learn the opinions and views of the other.

Although state radio and television remain dominant, independent private broadcasters are increasing their influence. By early 1993 more than ten companies had received broadcasting licences. But because of limited financial resources and transmitter capacity their broadcasts are limited to an area within 100 km of Riga. The law on radio and television, passed on 23 August 1995, requires that programming in foreign languages does not exceed 30 per cent of total airtime. This requirement has been waived for foreign television, cable and satellite broadcasters. There are more than ten private radio stations, primarily serving the Riga area (Girnius, 1995).

Political parties

Latvia's political movements and parties, in fact the whole multi-party system, are still being formed. From a formal and constitutional point of view the multi-party system is alive and well in Latvia: there are dozens of parties and nine are represented in the Parliament. But one should differentiate between the multi-party system as a constitutional institution and as a socio-political phenomenon. Many parties lack both a clear political orientation and a sociological base. They barely reflect Latvia's social, religious or ideological conflicts. Many are weak and have very few members. Some are sarcastically called 'sofa' parties, implying that all their members could sit on one sofa. Even the largest party, the Farmers' Union, has only 4,000 members. There are no grass-roots movements.

It would be incorrect to emphasize only the negative aspects of the proliferation of political parties in Latvia. Their sheer number is encouraging evidence of political vitality and of the desire to participate in politics. The profusion of parties recalls the inter-war period, which was also characterized by a plethora of parties. Nevertheless, the new proportional electoral system has had some success in reducing the number of parties represented in the legislature. Twenty-three parties or coalitions contested the 1993 elections, when only 4 per cent of the vote was required to win representation in the Parliament. Only

19 parties participated in the 1994 elections after the threshold had been raised to 5 per cent.

The origins and political success of Latvia's many parties vary greatly. Several – including the right-of-centre Latvian Farmers' Union and the leftist Latvian Social Democratic Party – consider themselves to be the successors of parties that were active in the inter-war period. These so-called 'historical' parties have enjoyed limited electoral success: the Social Democrats do not have a single representative in the current Parliament. Several new parties or movements have mobilized substantial followings and done very well in one parliamentary election only to slide into insignificance because of internal squabbles, the inability to develop a strong organizational structure or the failure to establish the firm social and ideological base necessary for continued political success. The Latvian Popular Front, for example, won the 1990 elections but suffered a crushing defeat in 1993. That year's victor, Latvia's Way, has lost most of its influence. Saimnieks, which garnered the most votes in 1995, is already fragmenting. This pattern of a quick rise and fall indicates both the volatility of the electorate and the instability of the current constellation of political parties. The fact that only a quarter of voters identify themselves with a party suggests that the current pattern will persist for some time. New parties will continue to be formed on an *ad hoc* basis, 'because the prospect of elections brings parties to centre stage in the political drama' (O'Donnell and Schmitter, 1989, p. 57).

The unsettled nature of party politics, however, is not unique to Latvia. In general, during the first, founding election, party identification is likely to be weak, surveys of public attitudes unreliable and public opinion highly volatile. Writing about the democratization of Central and Eastern Europe, Bogdanor (1990, p. 288) states that 'it is probably not until there have been at least two further free elections held under normal conditions that one will be in a position to make meaningful generalisations about the electoral process'.

Latvia's political parties cover a broad political spectrum. The Farmers' Union, To Fatherland and Freedom, the Latvian National Independent Movement and Latvia's Way represent the right. They have called for the deepening of economic reforms and for economic integration into Europe, convinced that the free market and individual initiative are the best means of stimulating economic development and ensuring increased welfare. Leftist political forces, such as the Unity Party and the Socialist Party, seek to preserve and strengthen the state's role in regulating the economy as well as ensuring the welfare of individuals.

The programmes of the individual parties differ from one another in analytical sophistication and comprehensiveness. Some are quite detailed, but six do not even mention such issues as the economy or social politics, prompting the quip that 'the majority of political parties in Latvia behave as ignorant people at the Swedish table – putting pineapple, herring, milk and flakes, cake and mustard on their plate' (Inkens, 1996).

The current ruling coalition is an improbable mixture of rightist and leftist parties that includes almost 70 per cent of all deputies. The Prime Minister is a successful businessman and is not a member of any party. Although there has been a fair amount of internal squabbling, and no precise coalition agreement was drawn up, the government has proved more stable than many observers expected. The political diversity of the coalition serves as another reminder of the fluidity of the political system, which, while it offers the voter a wide choice of parties, gives the voter little knowledge of or control over how the party and deputy of his or her choice will behave subsequently. Thus accountability to the voters, a cornerstone of democracy, is still embryonic.

The debate on European integration

Much remains uncertain about the potential development of the Baltic region. Although it has rarely played a key role in European politics, it has often been the battleground of the Great Powers fighting for spheres of influence. At present the Baltic states find themselves in a security vacuum without the resources needed to protect themselves from external aggression. They do not know who will guarantee their security or how this will be done, but look with hope to the Western countries, convinced that the enlargement of the EU and North Atlantic Treaty Organization (NATO) will guarantee not only their security, but also the stability of the Baltic region as whole. Security must, of course, be understood in broader terms that include the demographic and ethnic situation, ideology and religion, protection of the environment, social and cultural conditions, health and education issues, and public order.

Because of Latvia's historical experience, its difficult demographic situation and its proximity to Russia, Latvians tend to frame the debate concerning membership of the EU in terms of security rather than on an assessment of the functions of the EU. Thus in a sense the discussions about entry are not really debates about the EU at all. This is an unfortunate development. Because the consequences of EU membership are so massive and permanent, all the relevant decisions should be made with great deliberation and with full realization of their import. The experience of other European states has shown that governments that have failed to engage the public in an open dialogue concerning the ramifications of EU membership have at times inadvertently encouraged Euroscepticism. Moreover, the exaggerated emphasis on the need to join European economic and security structures distracts the attention of the government and provides justification for the failure to deal with urgent domestic concerns, such as the need to reform education and revamp the health system.

Further, a psychological barrier must be overcome if membership of the EU is to be considered of great value. Because of the circumstances in which the Latvian state was born, Latvians tend to equate the concepts of national sovereignty and national identity. The idea of a sovereign Latvian state, which emerged together with the formation of a distinct national self-consciousness, is considered a necessary foundation for the preservation and development of the national identity. The two concepts need to be disentangled before Latvians can realize that members of the EU delegate part of their sovereignty, though not their identity, to the EU. The united Europe of the future must be seen as compatible with the preservation of numerous national identities. No European nation is willing to lose its identity, just as the Latvians seek to retain theirs.

Notes

1. Although the rate of emigration has decreased – from 46,900 in 1992 to 18,800 in 1994 – the population continues to fall: from 2,661,000 in January 1990 to 2,485,000 in October 1996.
2. The belief that Russians are the only ethnic minority in Latvia is a common misapprehension. In 1995, Latvians comprised 55 per cent of the population; Russians, 33 per cent; Belorussians, 4 per cent; Ukrainians, 3 per cent; and Poles, 2 per cent.

4

Democracy in Lithuania

KĘSTUTIS K. GIRNIUS

Introduction

Procedural democracy is firmly established in Lithuania. Free and fair elections are taken for granted, and no political figures of distinction harbour anti-democratic designs. But democracy has generated little enthusiasm, for the government's flaws are more evident than its virtues. Even allowing for the immense difficulties of the transition, the performance of politicians has been below par. Nor does moral achievement compensate for its intellectual failings. Many government officials are paternalistic and arrogant, corruption and greed are rampant, studied indifference is the usual response to the genuine suffering of many citizens. Opinion polls have consistently shown deep scepticism towards government institutions. According to a March 1996 poll, only 20 per cent of those questioned expressed trust in the government, while 68 per cent voiced distrust. The figures for the Parliament were 18 per cent and 72 per cent; for the presidency 23 and 52 per cent respectively.

To say that citizens get the politicians they deserve would be an unnecessarily harsh judgement on Lithuania. Because it was incorporated into the Soviet Union, the deformations of Soviet rule were entrenched more deeply in Lithuania than in other East European countries that retained elements of sovereignty. The fractious nature of public life, the bitter quarrels that have rent most private organizations, the disappointing failure of efforts to reconstruct civil institutions are but part of the heritage of totalitarian life. A decade, if not a generation, must pass before Soviet modes of thought and action, often beyond the conscious grasp of those most afflicted, are uprooted. The effects of this bitter legacy are aggravated by the deep polarization of society, a fissure that runs all the way down from the commanding heights of government to informal groupings of private citizens.

These developments are all the more tragic because they have been accompanied by the squandering of the great goodwill and enthusiasm that flowered in 1988–90. No longer is the nation animated by a sense of common purpose and naïve faith in its ability to forge its own future. The onerous task of rejuvenating civil society and implanting a democratic culture will have to take place in an atmosphere of cynicism and fatalistic resignation.

Recent opinion polls have registered the growth of disenchantment. Results of the 1995 Eurobarometer poll make depressing reading: 66 per cent of those polled expressed dissatisfaction with the development of democracy, while 26 per cent viewed it positively. In 1991 democracy had a rating of +28 per cent; four years later it had slumped to −40 per cent. Only Hungarians and Ukrainians were more pessimistic about their nation's course of development (report of the polling organization Baltic Surveys, published in *Respublika*, 20 March 1996).

Formal democracy

Lithuania's experience of democracy is limited. The country was a democratic parliamentary republic from independence in 1918 until 16 December 1926, when a putsch by the army and nationalist elements installed a mildly authoritarian regime which ruled until the Soviet occupation in June 1940. Democracy was re-instituted after parliamentary elections in February 1990 and the re-establishment of independence on 11 March 1990.

The basic elements of a democratic state have been established in Lithuania. Free and fair elections are the norm; the rule of law, human rights and the constitution are generally respected;[1] minorities are not subject to discrimination; the mass media are independent.

Elections

There have been five national elections in Lithuania since 1990: parliamentary elections in 1990, 1992 and 1996; presidential elections in 1993; and municipal elections in 1994. All were free of major distortions and each resulted in a transfer of power. The 1992 parliamentary elections, however, had significant potential to destabilize Lithuania's fledgling democracy. The election campaign was extremely bitter, and speculation was rife about a possible putsch or the government refusing to relinquish power. The neo-communist Lithuanian Democratic Labour Party (LDLP) won a totally unexpected 42.6 per cent of the vote in the first round of the elections, compared to 34.7 per cent garnered by the Sajudis coalition. The second round took place as scheduled three weeks later, and the LDLP took over the reins of power unchallenged.

In 1996 the results were reversed. The Sajudis coalition, reorganized as the Conservative Party, won 70 of 137 seats, while the LDLP won only 12. The campaign was sedate, even boring.

Human rights

Human rights are generally respected in Lithuania. Individuals are not persecuted for political beliefs or religious convictions. Great tolerance is shown to political protesters. In April 1995 the Parliament ratified the European Convention on Human Rights and Basic Freedoms, although it has not abolished the death penalty. Concern has been voiced about the lack of changes to the criminal code, inherited from Soviet times, which limits the rights of suspects. The police can keep a suspect in custody for ten days without filing charges. Individuals have been held in pre-trial detention for more than eighteen months. Particularly odious is the Law on Preventive Detention, in force since 1993, which allows the police to detain suspected violent criminals for a year without making formal charges. This law has been rightly criticized as a violation of human rights and as an ineffective measure, liable to administrative abuse. Critics have also charged that the civil rights of soldiers are curtailed and that the government has turned a blind eye to police brutality. Conditions in the overcrowded jails are extremely harsh.

National minority rights

Lithuania has two substantial national minorities: Russians, who make up 8.4 per cent of the population, and Poles, who constitute 7 per cent. A very liberal law, passed in November 1989, granted citizenship rights to all permanent residents of the republic, regardless of nationality. More than 90 per cent of non-ethnic Lithuanians chose citizenship. The new citizenship law is more restrictive, requiring a rudimentary knowledge of Lithuanian. The language law also requires that public-sector employees have a functional command of Lithuanian. The test is not very rigorous, however, as more than 80 per cent of those taking it pass.

In order to better integrate national minorities into political life, the 4 per cent barrier for proportional representation in Parliament has been waived for national minority slates; they need to win only 1.4 per cent of the vote. This exemption enabled the Polish minority to win two extra seats in the 1992 elections. On 27 June 1996, however, the election law was altered to raise the threshold for representation in the Parliament to 5 per cent and to eliminate the exemption granted to ethnic parties. None of the three national minority parties cleared the threshold in the autumn 1996 elections.

Although concentrated in several large cities, the Russian minority is a collection of disparate individuals rather than a community. It has neither organizations nor spokespeople who could credibly claim to speak for their compatriots. The Russians have not complained of discrimination. The Poles, on the other hand, are primarily rural inhabitants, well organized, and vocal about being mistreated. Their accusations, albeit sincere, are questionable and concern minor matters. Some Polish activists have castigated plans to expand the borders of the city of Vilnius as an attempt to dilute the voting power of adjacent Polish regions, although others insist that such expansion will not harm Polish interests. Some Lithuanians accuse the government of failing to assert its legitimate prerogatives and defend the rights of ethnic Lithuanians in predominantly Polish regions.

Although violations of national minority rights are few, real tensions between the communities do exist. Their roots lie in past enmities and unrealistic expectations. Some Poles would like the regions they inhabit to be treated as if they were part of Poland, while the Lithuanians would like the Poles quietly to assimilate. Memories of past injuries will not fade quickly, and government action will not fulfil expectations.

The rule of law

If widespread voluntary compliance to legal norms is the measure of successful implementation of the rule of law, then Lithuania has not fared very well. There are three major problem areas: violations; 'secondary corruption'; and problems with interpretation and implementation.

A substantial number of Lithuanian citizens and public officials routinely violate the law. Lithuania has a high crime rate, the shadow economy is flourishing, and a majority of citizens working in the private sector fail to report a substantial share of their income. Corruption is endemic. According to a June 1995 survey by the World Bank, 54 per cent of the 200 Lithuanian businesses questioned stated that they had paid bribes to government officials, and 80 per cent of 200 foreign investors claimed that they had been asked for bribes, while 90 per cent asserted that corruption was an obstacle to expanding their business and increasing their investments (*Verslo žinios*, 28 September 1995). Public awareness of corruption and tax evasion has had a demoralizing effect, leading many citizens to believe that in present circumstances honesty is equivalent to foolishness.

Equally pervasive and pernicious is the growth of what could be called 'secondary corruption'; that is, the granting of various bonuses, rewards and perquisites to government officials to increase their salaries. Bonuses paid to leading members of the Foreign Ministry in 1995, for example, were 335 per cent of their regular salaries. Staff of the Bank of Lithuania were allowed to purchase apartments for a fifth of their market value. The University of

Vilnius granted the Prosecutor General's office the right to recruit a special contingent of students for admission to the Faculty of Law, thus allowing staff children to avoid the stringent competition for normal admission.

Further problems occur regarding the interpretation and implementation of laws. Much legislation is poorly drafted, inconsistent with previous laws, and imprecise in formulation, leaving government agencies wide discretion in interpretation and application. The frequent amendment of laws leads to further confusion. The legislature lacks means to determine whether the executive branch has faithfully implemented legislation or to compel compliance in the event that it has not. Committees have no subpoena power or other means to force officials to testify or hand over records and information. During the latter half of his premiership, particularly in 1995, Adolfas Šleževičius's authority was so ascendant that he felt free to ignore the Parliament. Many judges are poorly trained, susceptible to bribery, and lack the expertise needed to be able to interpret and apply legislation concerning economic matters.

Independent media

The mass media are independent, diverse and free from censorship. The government's ability to control the media is practically non-existent. There is no government newspaper, and the government does not regulate the sale of newsprint. The influence of state-owned radio and television has declined as independent stations have constructed their own transmitters and aggressively expanded audience shares. Moreover, state radio and television have stopped following the 'suggestions' of government officials. State television, for example, broke the story of Prime Minister Šleževičius's withdrawal of his deposits from a bank about to be declared bankrupt, an action that led to the fall of his government in February 1996. That the position of director of state radio and television was allowed to remain vacant for two years is another indication that it is no longer a compliant tool of government. The media have played a significant role in uncovering corruption and incompetence, and have been rewarded by public trust. Surveys have consistently indicated that about 70 per cent of respondents trust the mass media.

The mass media have their shortcomings, but obsequiousness is not one. Editorial criticism of the authorities is excessively strident, unmeasured, and blind to the government's point of view. Partiality and prejudice, masquerading as wit, have helped poison the atmosphere of public debate.

Tension between the government and media persists. On 18 October 1995 the directors of major mass media concerns established the Free Speech Foundation to combat perceived threats to free speech and free enterprise. The organization announced that Lithuania was 'only a single step away from the watershed dividing democracy from dictatorship'. The catalyst for the charge was the Parliament's expressed intention to limit alcohol and tobacco advertising. The government rejected the criticism as exaggerated. A more serious cause for concern is the regulation that allows government officials to sue the media for injury to their 'honour and dignity'. In a notorious case the court ordered the daily *Lietuvos aidas* to pay compensation to President Brazauskas for quoting the assertion of an assistant prosecutor that the president had lied; this despite the fact that the prosecutor assured the court that he had been quoted accurately. A new law on public information, passed in July 1996, eliminated the last vestiges of censorship and ensures access to all unclassified government documents.

Informal democracy

If free elections, rough equality under the law, and respect for basic rights were the only defining criteria of democracy, Lithuania would easily pass muster. Matters become more complicated if democracy is considered to be more than a procedure for electing rulers, and genuine democracy is thought to be impossible without a political culture that emphasizes mutual respect and open dialogue.

Such respect and dignified debate are in short supply in Lithuania. In an age in which a consensual approach to politics is considered the norm, Lithuanian politicians are non-conformists. Opponents are often viewed as representatives of criminal or anti-state elements rather than as proponents of the legitimate interests of a section of the population. The dominance of confrontation and undisguised enmity is but one indicator of flaws in Lithuanian political culture. Others include an underdeveloped civil society and a top-down, paternalistic mode of government. But the longest shadow is cast by the polarization of Lithuanian society.

The polarization of Lithuanian society

Lithuanian society is deeply divided, and the level of strife has been increasing rather than decreasing. The main division is not ethnic or religious but political: between former communists and anti-communists. Unlike in the other Baltic republics, neo-communists are a major political force in Lithuania. This is a result of several factors. First, in 1988–9 the Lithuanian Communist Party (LCP) did not discredit itself by blind obedience to Moscow. Second, its leader, Algirdas Brazauskas, retained his personal popularity among a broad cross-section of the population. When popular sentiment turned against Sajudis, he and his party were considered the natural alternative. Third, ethnic Lithuanians made up the overwhelming majority of the LCP and held most responsible positions. Not pressured to leave their posts for ethnic or linguistic reasons, they remained in their positions.

Initially, Sajudis considered Moscow loyalists rather than communists in general to be its opponents. It could hardly be otherwise, as many of its leaders were Party members. But once the need to choose between Sajudis and Party membership arose during the 1990 parliamentary elections, the seeds of antagonism ripened quickly. Within six months the rupture was complete. The quarrels within the elite etched themselves into the political landscape, where they found an easy resonance among the general population.

Although many benefited from communist rule, more suffered from Soviet repressions. The victims of Soviet terror and their children had little sympathy for their compatriots who had luxuriated in the perquisites of privilege but now dressed their actions in the cloak of patriotism. Particularly unpalatable was the glib identification of self-interest with national ideals captured by President Brazauskas's frequently repeated assertion that 97 per cent of LCP members were patriots and 3 per cent communists.

The depth of the cleavage has been captured by surveys assessing public opinions of the Soviet past and the post-Soviet present in the three Baltic republics (Gaidys, 1996). The surveys, performed in 1993 and 1995, revealed *inter alia* that (a) Lithuanians had the most favourable view of the past; (b) their evaluation of the past was correlated with their political preferences (supporters of Sajudis having a very negative opinion, the supporters of the LDLP an extremely positive one); and (c) the gap between the opposing Lithuanian perceptions of the Soviet era has increased.

The more upbeat evaluation of the past among ethnic Lithuanians is probably a consequence of their major role in administering the republic under Soviet rule and the low level of Russification. The correlation between political affiliation and perception of the past reflects contrasting life patterns. But the most important and most ominous result is the increased polarization of perceptions. The growing proclivity to portray the past through a Manichean prism of undifferentiated good and evil is a projection into the past of current political discord. Rather than the past becoming enshrouded in myth, as Gaidys (1996) suggests, the past is now the mirror of a troubled present. The statistical findings are not surprising; they confirm what is intuitively evident.

The divide is also broad. Between one-sixth and one-eighth of the population stand on each side of the barricade. Well organized, politically committed and vocal, they wield influence disproportionate to their numbers and for the worse. Lithuania's dialogue of the deaf has imposed its logic even on moderates who would prefer to discontinue it, but who have found themselves sucked into the endless circle of recrimination and counter-accusation.

The dispute between anti- and post-communists, originally about power and interpretations of the past, embraces other issues, such as relations with Moscow, social justice and inequality. While the heart of the LDLP may be on the left, its wallet and numerous supporters are firmly on the right. In contrast, elderly Sajudis adherents, who find collectivism ideologically abhorrent, lambaste the LDLP for disregarding the disadvantaged and favouring the wealthy. This sensitive social issue makes the dispute even more acerbic.

There are no major countervailing forces to offset the trend towards division. Neither the President nor the Catholic Church seems capable of serving as a focus for national unity. Although Brazauskas suspended his membership of the LDLP upon assuming office, as required by the Constitution, he remains a partisan figure. Open in his sympathy and support for the LDLP, he has been aloof from, and distrustful of, the opposition. Even had he adopted a more balanced stance, his past as a Communist functionary made him unacceptable to many. Opinion polls regularly show that the Catholic Church is the institution most trusted by Lithuanians, but this popularity is neither as widespread nor as deep as conventional wisdom would have it. Expressing faith in the Church is more a matter of convention than of commitment. Moreover, the Church has angered some with its stance on various moral questions and its attitude towards sects, and anti-clerical sentiments are gaining ground. The idea of statehood cannot serve as a neutral rallying ground, for its very meaning and the problem of its continuity are among the major issues that fuel political division.

In these circumstances the demise of 'ritual politics', as opponents of Sajudis christened it, only exacerbated the situation. In 1988–91 meetings attended by hundreds of thousands were common. Appealing to emotion rather than reason, preferring rhetoric to analysis, prescribing clear answers to complicated problems, the gatherings created a sense of unity, purpose and mission. And although they gradually became more partisan and exclusive, they remained a powerful forum for reconciliation.

Confrontational politics

Consensus politics prevailed in the Lithuanian Parliament for about six months in 1990. Initially friction arose in the Sajudis coalition, where deputies who had expressed doubts concerning the decisions of the majority were castigated by their colleagues amid suggestions that they were agents or dupes of Soviet State Security (KGB). Materials from the KGB archives, some of them of questionable value, were publicized in an effort to compromise opponents. As the number of disenchanted deputies increased, ever stronger proofs of loyalty were required, leading to the disintegration of the Sajudis bloc in a paroxysm of Donatist fervour. In the summer of 1992 supporters of Vytautus Landsbergis, now in the minority, boycotted parliamentary sessions and assembled instead in a conference room in the Parliament building. Upon ascent to power the LDLP promised to eschew confrontation and heal old wounds. Although it spoke in more measured tones, it adopted measures that enraged its opponents and undermined conciliation. In line with its general policy of portraying the past in rosy tones, the LDLP sought to rehabilitate odious individuals and institutions, as if the very act of rehabilitation would lay to rest doubts about their integrity. Important posts were given to activists of the Communist Party of the Soviet Union (CPSU) who continued to serve the Kremlin even after Lithuania's declaration of independence and the killing of Lithuanians by Soviet forces in January 1991. The Parliament passed a law that granted degrees from the former Communist Party higher schools the status of university diplomas despite universal protests by the academic community. In January 1995 LDLP deputies adopted legislation that would have severely restricted the Church's ability to regain ownership of property nationalized by the communists, although the LDLP government was negotiating a concordat with the Vatican that addressed this issue. President Brazauskas defused the issue by returning the law to Parliament for further consideration.

Opponents of the LDLP have been quick to denounce such measures as part of a concerted plan of 're-Sovietization'. Such talk is exaggerated, but the failure of LDLP moderates to foresee the response to such provocative decisions indicates a breakdown in comprehension and communication.

The habits of confrontation will remain in the ascendant as long as deputies do not know how to act when in the majority and cannot accept being in the minority. The LDLP majority, aware that it had sufficient votes to impose its will, rarely tried to reach a consensus or win over the opposition. It justified its reluctance to seek an accord by asserting that the voters had empowered it to rule. In turn, the opposition accused government deputies of being parts of a 'mechanical voting machine', impervious to rational argument and thus not worth arguing with. The opposition was reluctant to admit that the majority may have been justified in voting along strict party lines and ignoring vigorous opposition arguments. When one side feels it has a popular mandate to rule and the other feels marginalized, debate becomes ritualized and voting does become 'mechanical'.

Organizational defects contribute to the malfunctioning of the Parliament. Individual deputies and standing and special committees have minuscule staffs; a deputy usually has only one or two advisers, a committee not many more. Because committees are so understaffed, they have little input in draft legislation, rarely serve as focal points of debate, and are generally ignored by parliamentarians. Instead of trying to forge compromises in committee, opposing factions draft their own proposals with little outside consultation and present them to the full Parliament, where matters are usually decided by up-and-down votes along party lines.

Most legislators are poorly trained for law-making. Few are lawyers or businessmen; rather, many are either faithful party workers (in the case of the LDLP) or fiery orators with a literary background (in the case of the right). Such deputies – a large proportion of the total – have little understanding of economic and business matters, which are the subject of the bulk of legislation, and little inclination to master the necessary detail, preferring to question the motives and probity of their opponents. In these circumstances widespread absenteeism has become the mark of the Lithuanian Parliament.[2]

The Parliament is Lithuania's most salient political institution. The disappointment and anger engendered by its flawed performance have been prime contributors to negative attitudes towards politics and democracy as a whole. This perception will remain unaltered until political passions in parliament subside.

Governmental attitudes

The LDLP had a top-down style of government, which was captured by the expression 'pyramid of government' so beloved of its leaders. The 'pyramid' concept of government is one in which power flows from the apex into everbroadening layers, but retains clear and unchallenged lines of authority. Just as a pyramid is a single structure without wings or outlying growths, so all government institutions must form a unitary structure without any parallel lines of command. To former members of the Soviet elite the pyramid model of government is a self-evident part of the natural order. Its ancestry in 'democratic centralism' is obvious.

This model and its associated mind-set have their lighter moments. For example, the chairman of the Parliament, Česlovas Juršėnas, explained that the establishment of the office of the ombudsman completed the creation of the pyramid of state authority, blithely unaware that the ombudsman is one official who should remain a sceptical observer of the pyramid rather than be a constituent part of it. But the mind-set can also distort efforts to modernize government. A case in point is administrative reform. Aware that a redistribution of authority was needed to make local governing bodies more effective and responsive to the public, the government sought to devolve power from the central ministries. The country was divided into 56 municipalities on the lowest level together with an intermediary level of ten regions. The regional governments were to be the linchpin of administrative reform, charged with implementing government policy at the local level and serving as intermediaries between the municipalities and Vilnius. The central ministries were to transfer some of their functions to the regional authorities, while supplemental powers were to be granted to the local authorities. The opposite has happened. Central ministries have jealously retained their authority, while the power of the regional governors, appointed by the prime minister, has grown at the expense of the municipalities. Instead of responsibilities flowing from the centre to the regions, the regional governments have appropriated functions that had been the prerogative of local governments. While it is doubtful whether efficiency has increased, the reform has clearly diluted democracy, as a government appointee, the regional governor, has more power than elected municipal officials. The lack of local accountability is aggravated by the difficulty of dismissing regional governors, even after a change of government, because they are considered regular civil servants.

The concentration of power in the hands of regional governors has been incremental but steady. The Law on Regional Administration, adopted on 15 December 1994, granted them wide-ranging powers to administer policy in the areas of social security, health, culture, education, regional planning and land administration. The local police are now subordinate to the Ministry of the Interior rather than the municipalities. The regional governor has been granted the right to administer all state-owned land in the regions, stripping the municipalities of a crucial function and a potential source of revenue.[3] Finally, the municipalities have no control over tax collection. Without independent sources of revenue, they have limited capacity to launch local initiatives and are reduced to serving as conduits for orders from above.

Politics and finance have further complicated the situation. The Conservative Party and its allies were victorious in the March 1995 municipal elections. Each side now blames the other for the shortcomings of local government, although the central cause of strife – shortage of funds – will not be resolved until there is an improvement in the economy.

As a result of substantial budget deficits, payments to the municipalities are frequently delayed or reduced. More disconcerting is the central government's policy of increasing the salaries of local government officials without supplementing the municipalities' budgets, forcing them to cut back expenditures on other matters. It is unclear whether the situation will improve now that the Conservatives have regained control of the Parliament.

The governmental pyramid remains a goal rather than reality. Its structure is flawed in part because of the lack of professionalism in the Parliament. The quantity of legislation adopted is imposing but, as mentioned above, its quality is dubious.

The professionalization of civil servants and their protection from political pressure was another commendable goal perverted by Soviet thinking. The law on government employees divided officials into two categories: political appointees, subject to summary dismissal; and protected civil servants. But, seeking to secure jobs for party loyalists, the Parliament extended civil service protection to individuals, such as deputy ministers and regional governors, who formulate policy and perform clearly political functions. Because no government can permit its ministers to be deprived of the right to choose their most important aides, the law will be repealed eventually. This is one of many cases in which legislation was adopted with the aim of advancing one's friends. Such patronage has also sullied the privatization process.

The tendency of government officials to distrust and look down on ordinary citizens, endemic in the Soviet system, remains pervasive. Many bureaucrats believe that politics is the province of experts and that the involvement of the people should be kept to a minimum. Justas Paleckis, President Brazauskas's foreign adviser, epitomized this imperious attitude by stating that the role of the 'man in the street' is to perform his civic duty by voting every five years; he should not concern himself with the president's foreign policy decisions.[4] In other words, he is to empower government mandarins, who are entrusted with the affairs of state until the next election. This conception of passive citizenship leaves little, if any, room for dialogue and debate, for participation by an informed citizenry in public affairs, for feedback between governors and the governed.

Civil society

Lithuanian society is more atomized than it was ten years ago. The conditions for reinvigorating civil society have deteriorated. The economic crisis and the demands it makes on an individual's spiritual and material resources have fostered not only cynicism and apathy, but also an almost exclusive concern with personal matters to the detriment of wider civic and cultural commitments. The weight of the past belies any hope for rapid improvement in the near future.

Civil society does not have deep roots in Lithuania. Before 1918 Lithuania was a predominantly agricultural society of small producers. Ethnic Lithuanians were strangers in cities and semi-urban communities that have traditionally been the spawning grounds of civic society. During the interwar years, however, substantial progress was made in developing the relatively thick network of interlocking horizontal organizations that constitutes civil society. Boy Scouts and other youth groups, religious and mutual aid societies, patriotic and paramilitary organizations, farmers' and producers' co-operatives found fertile ground in a society engaged in conscious nation-building and endeavouring to buttress its identity and sense of difference.

The communists, however, not only persecuted the religious, nationalist and youth organizations that were the strongest pillars of this network but also uprooted the very basis of civil society. The most socially conscious farmers were repressed, the rest suffered under forced collectivization. In the 1960s the younger generation fled the ravaged countryside, leaving behind the sick, the elderly and the broken in spirit. The cities had fared no better. Their Jewish, Polish and German inhabitants either emigrated or were killed, while ethnic Lithuanian intellectuals fled to the West. The old structures disappeared along with their human capital. The new inhabitants inherited a civic vacuum, in which only communist-controlled organizations were permitted.

Because of the ferocity of Lithuanian resistance to Soviet rule, officials in both Moscow and Vilnius were extremely sensitive to manifestations of 'bourgeois' nationalism and quick to ban organizations suspected of fostering national aspirations. Consequently, many ethnic associations were kept under surveillance and disbanded.

The leading role of the Catholic Church in the dissident movement during the 1970s and 1980s bears witness to the poverty of Lithuanian civil society under Soviet rule. The Church became a haven for dissidents by default because it was the only organization free from government control. Defenders of human and national minority rights, even those of an anti-clerical bent, eventually gravitated to the Church because they could find comfort and support nowhere else.

After the collapse of most Soviet organizations – sports clubs and folk ensembles being notable exceptions – in 1988–90 frantic attempts were made to resurrect the civic order of the inter-war years. Lithuania once again became home to Scouts, traditional political parties, a National Guard (Šauliai), sodalities.[5]

In most cases these rebirths were as short-lived as they were artificial. The new organizations succumbed to internal strife amid savage recriminations, particularly between neo-communists and anti-communists. The Scouts split into two groups. The main Catholic youth organization, Ateitininkai, retained its unity, but only by expelling many potential leaders. Journalists split into two competing associations, whose members barely speak to each other. The Union of Artists is on the verge of a breakup.

Political parties fared no better. The Liberal Party and the Democratic Party have undergone several purges, and only a very small number of their founders are still members. The most poignant symbol of the retreat from civility was the transformation of Sajudis from the symbol of unity into a faction.

Many factors combine to undermine efforts to reinvigorate civil society: naïve and unrealistic plans, personal ambitions, inexperience with co-operative ventures. The result has been a further tearing of the social fabric. The withdrawal of the disappointed from public life was accelerated by the economic dislocations of economic transformation.

Lithuania has been particularly hard hit. Alcoholism, suicides, divorces, unemployment and infectious diseases have increased, while the average life span, standard of living, birth rate and public confidence have fallen. The fraying of the social security net and the loss of job security have been accompanied by what some estimate to be the greatest income and social inequality in the former socialist bloc (Milanovic, 1994). Economic hardship has forced many to concentrate their energies on finding second and third jobs, leaving neither time nor energy for civic activity.

Although sheer exhaustion accounts for much of Lithuania's political apathy, the absence of examples of successful democratic policy should not be underestimated. The citizens of Lithuania, unlike those of the Western democracies, have almost no experience of challenging the government on important social and economic issues and forcing it to relent. Moreover, the government's callous indifference to massive corruption and failure to prosecute suspected grafters reinforce feelings of hopelessness. One could even say that under current circumstances avoiding civic commitments is rational; the likelihood of success is small and the energy could be expended better on providing for one's family.

It is not just embittered social activists who have turned from civic life. Young Lithuanians are perhaps even worse afflicted. While they have not seen their best hopes dashed, they have grown up in an environment free not only of the heavy hand of communist organizations but of all organized after-school activities. A 1994 sociological poll by the Ministry of Culture of 14- to 19-year-olds found that only 14.9 per cent of respondents had ties with a youth organization and only 6.7 per cent considered themselves to be active participants.[6] Their social indifference mirrors their political apathy.

Lithuania and Western Europe

The exuberance of the Sajudis years has been replaced by a deep-seated pessimism and cynicism that will not easily be dispelled. This is part of a mind-set that colours the perceptions and actions of a very large number of individuals. The fissures in Lithuanian society further strengthen the general feelings of malaise. These attitudes are all the stronger for being the result of shattered expectations.

For most Lithuanians, Europe and its institutions are a distant presence, despite nightly television coverage and Lithuania's slow but steady integration into West European political and economic structures. Contacts between ordinary Lithuanian citizens and those of European Union (EU) countries are limited, while knowledge of the nature of European institutions is very sketchy. Even members of the elite frequently fail to differentiate between the Council of Europe and the EU.

It is difficult to gauge the effects of Lithuanian integration into European institutions. Concrete signs are few and far between. The free trade agreement with the EU came into effect on 1 January 1995 and Lithuania's association agreement (Europe Agreement) was signed the following June. Although the agreements required changes in trade and customs policy, ordinary citizens can be forgiven for being unaware of the connection between the agreements and the policy changes.

The most visible sign of integration into Europe has been an amendment to the Lithuanian constitution that allows foreigners to own land in Lithuania. Supporters of the measure made a tactical mistake by emphasizing that passage of the amendment was a necessary condition for membership in the EU, rather than arguing the economic merits of such legislation. This played into the hands of Eurosceptics, who emphasize the burdens rather than the benefits of integration. Although the amendment was finally adopted on 20 June 1996, surveys indicate that a majority of the population did not approve of the measure.

The impact of membership of the Council of Europe is also unclear. The government recognizes the need to respect the various human rights conventions, but cautions that implementation may have to wait for an improvement in Lithuania's financial situation. Thus officials agree that prisoners and illegal migrants should be better housed, but add that there are no funds to make the necessary improvements. There are, however, some exceptions. For example, in 1996 President Brazauskas suggested that it might be time to abolish the death penalty.

The idea of integration into Europe profoundly affects attitudes, but is difficult to measure. An aura of respectability is attached to the idea of Europe. Pride in being European is one of the few threads that unites the overwhelming majority of Lithuanians. Even for Eurosceptics, to label an attitude or stance as anti- or non-European is to condemn it. This positive emotive association is firmly entrenched, although it might be jeopardized if officials continue to justify unpopular actions in terms of the need to comply with European demands. The dearth of visible benefits from integration has contributed to a decline in support for European institutions, although the pessimism generated by internal developments is the primary cause. Similarly, clear and concrete indicators of the benefits and grounded expectations of more to come could serve as a stimulus for halting the decline in expectations.

Notes

1. The claim about respect for the constitution needs some qualification. It has been openly violated several times, although on minor matters. The Election Commission allowed the émigré Kazys Bobelis to run for Parliament even though it was clear that he was not telling the truth about renouncing his US citizenship. Generals have been appointed as ministers of the interior, although this is not permitted by the constitution.
2. Very rarely are more than 75 per cent of deputies present at a session of Parliament. Roughly 50 per cent seems to be the norm.
3. Although the amended Land Law does not explicitly state that municipalities no longer retain the right to administer any state-owned land, and several government decrees explicitly mention the right of municipalities to administer state land, there seems to be no category of land that remains in the control of local government.
4. The remark was made during an interview for Radio Free Europe on 4 October 1994.
5. The tendency to resurrect old groups rather than found new ones was in part due to the belief that this was the best way to tap the purported wealth of émigrés.
6. The findings are contained in an unpublished report by Algirdas Augustaitis, a government adviser on youth affairs.

5

Democracy in Poland

MARCIN KRÓL

Introduction

I should like to make my assessment of the state of democracy in Poland in two parts. The first addresses the structure of the democratic institutions, the second cultural or mental and social aspects of democracy. This decision is justified by the fact that it was relatively easy, at least in Poland, to introduce institutional democracy, but it seems to be much more difficult to introduce democratic customs and patterns of social behaviour. In the final section I shall make some personal reflections on the Polish situation.

Before describing Polish democracy, I shall mention some characteristic features of the tradition of democracy in Poland and of the Polish mentality (if such a thing exists). Poles boast about Poland's having been the first modern country to have a quasi-democratic system of government, which is true if one limits democracy to the nobles, who introduced the division of powers and parliamentary system as early as the sixteenth century. The legacy is a very strong individualistic tendency of the typical Pole, which has, in the twentieth century, made introducing democracy more rather than less difficult. I can, without doubt, say that liberal attitudes are easier to accept in Poland than are democratic rights and obligations. One also has to remember that Poles have a very strong tradition of organizing themselves without the help of the state, which did not exist during the nineteenth century or World War II, and was undemocratic in the recent past. The state, therefore, is treated with more suspicion than anywhere else, which complicates the business of introducing democracy from above. Further, it is unclear whether the relatively developed 'civil society' of the underground opposition in the 1970s and 1980s has helped or hindered the installation of 'normal' democracy. This morally sensitive civil society created characters who do not readily accept the everyday rotten compromises that are required by democracy.

Democratic institutions

Practically all the formal features of a democratic system exist in Poland. One should mention the separation of powers, including an independent judiciary with a very strong Constitutional Court, the judgments of which can be overturned only by a two-thirds majority of the members of Parliament; strong and independent media; and a decentralized political system. The constitution dates from 1952, although it has been amended many times. Work on a new constitution has started several times, but in each case a political crisis stopped it. There is a fair chance that a new constitution will be ready soon, but there is no great need for hurry as the current one with all its amendments seems to work quite well. There are certain problems, however, which, although not major, are symptomatic of the weakness of the cultural substructure of democracy.

First, the decentralization of political (executive) power is largely fictitious because local government exists at only the lowest administrative level; local government has strong authority but no local money; citizens are rarely interested in the working of the local government; and turnout in local elections is very low, less than 30 per cent.

The decentralization of the executive (and to an extent legislative) powers since 1989 has been perceived by nearly all governments as an important, but not much loved, decision. I can only speculate why, but some reasons seem pretty obvious: radical change was thought to require strong central government; so-called society was not considered ready to take matters in its hands; successive governments were afraid of losing their influence over the privatization of the local economy; and the strength of local mafia-type structures justified centralized authority. Although some of these explanations are quite reasonable, the slow process of introducing local government has created a considerable obstacle to the development of local democracy.

Second, the independence of the media is limited by two factors: insufficient resources to create a strong newspaper or private TV station; and repeated efforts by politicians to influence the boards of the public TV and radio stations. There are two very strong national daily newspapers in Poland and quite a lot of local ones (although local newspapers are not generally very sophisticated). Several major efforts to create new major national daily newspapers have failed owing to the insufficient financing. Although both *Gazeta Wyborcza* and *Rzeczpospolita* are free from any political influence, there is no solid, centre-oriented daily, such as *The Independent*. What seems even more odd is the fact that politicians, of all political tendencies, do not as yet understand the importance of good relations with the press and therefore tend to struggle against it and accuse it of being biased.

The independence of the public TV board is not totally secure in legal terms, because board members are nominated by the two houses of the Parliament and by the president. This means that if one party monopolizes all these institutions, the board can become politically dependent. We have seen efforts in that direction, although as yet none has been successful, because of the strength of public opinion.

Third, although the existence of the voluntary sector is legally guaranteed, there has been very little government effort to make the life of foundations, associations and other non-governmental organizations (NGOs) easier or to connect them to other functions of society. The development of the voluntary sector has been relatively slow, although stable. This is due to the complicated legal framework, which has been changed several times since 1989 in response to abuse by non-profit institutions; the complicated and questionable tax deduction system; and the bureaucratic and formal regulations (both domestic and foreign) that have limited the influence of foreign institutions and made external funding difficult to obtain.

There is of course also a problem with social attitudes, which, in a period of mass interest in money-making and economic survival, do not tend towards altruism or even promotion of the idea of civil society. That is only to be expected. All the same, whenever people see that there is a really worthy cause they are ready to help and get involved. Social attitudes therefore are not as strong an obstacle as the lack of tradition on the one hand and administrative nuisance on the other.

Democratic culture

The less formal aspects of the development of democracy in Poland should also be described. I shall now proceed from institutional problems to more cultural and spiritual ones, although it is not always easy to discern the difference between the two.

Political parties

The political parties in Poland can be divided according to different criteria. The most important is whether or not they existed in some form before 1989. Those that existed before 1989 are not necessarily post-communist (although that is the case with the Alliance of the Democratic Left (SLD)), but they do have at their disposal much better local structures, surprisingly good managerial skills and closer connections to business structures. For these reasons they have recently succeeded in both parliamentary and presidential elections.

A second criterion is the traditional difference between right and left. The liberal right was very popular in the first three years after independence, but for obvious reasons (economic hardship and very slow practical and tangible effects of the major free-market reforms), leftist or, let us say, social-security-minded parties now have better standing. This includes both socialist parties and the totally unreformed communist Union of Labour. The interest of the so-called left in social security and related matters may well be limited to words, but words seem to be at the moment the major political issue.

Third is the total collapse of Solidarity, which is due to both political rivalry (despite the fact that the old enemy, namely the post-communists, are still quite strong) and a lack of experience in democratic politics. I shall come later to some very important psychological factors. The weakness of the new political parties may well lead to political domination by the post-communists in the next five or six years.

One should also note that political parties in Poland – with the exception of the post-communist social democrats, the Peasant Party and the Union of Freedom (which was originally *the* main opposition party, but now seems to have influence only among the intelligentsia) – have very short and eventful lives. Names change; alliances are created and destroyed in a matter of weeks. These problems are most severe for the right-of-centre parties. Changes are common, and thus they lack firm programmes. Even though these parties think of themselves as rightist, their social and economic programmes are often more leftist than those of the present government. In anticipation of the next parliamentary elections there are many attempts to create a common camp of the right, but so far this has produced only more chaos than before. It is therefore practically impossible to describe the party system on the right of the political scene. Perhaps it is worth mentioning that the leadership of the right is now in the hands of the trade union Solidarity.

The police and military

The democratic framework of civilian control over the military in Poland is quite strong, stable and durable, although there are occasional political games in which politicians try to become more powerful by gaining the approval of generals. The same is true of the police force, which can be praised for its apolitical stance, and there are only a few points of concern. First, a lack of money and of experience with modern free-market society makes the work of the police very difficult. Also, the police are not yet well adapted to the new, mafia-style of crime which is flourishing in Poland. Second, the biggest security problem is created by the inability of the customs services to cope with the enormous black-market transportation of goods through Poland to the east. Third, some accusations have recently been formulated against the former secret services after former Prime Minister Józef Oleksy was accused of spying. It is not yet known whether he really was a spy or was just an incautious politician, but it seems that the secret services behaved correctly. In a country that did not go through the process of total decommunization there is always a danger of blackmail, but it seems quite improbable that such a danger will come from present intelligence circles.

The poverty of public debate

One of the peculiar aspects of Polish politics is the lack of public debate about major political issues and the abundance of arguments about the past. The following issues are raised only occasionally, although they seem to be of the utmost importance:

- accession to the European Union (EU) and the North Atlantic Treaty Organization (NATO);
- relations with neighbouring former Soviet republics, particularly Russia and Ukraine;
- reform of the social security and retirement systems;
- reform of the entire education system;
- radical changes in the structure of agriculture and rural life;
- decisions concerning obsolete state-owned industrial complexes.

There are many such issues that are mentioned neither by the ruling coalition nor by the opposition. Instead of debating these issues, Poles seem to be totally immersed in the discussion of the past and its influence on the present. This outdated type of debate fascinates politicians but bores the people, who have to take decisions in election after election – decisions that, because of the poverty of public debate, cannot be based on hard facts but rather are based on emotions, stereotypes and symbols. Politicians from all parties conspire to avoid major controversial issues. This may be the consequence of insecurity or of politics that centre around personalities and not problems. The lack of public debate, however, creates a formidable obstacle to the development of democracy, as major issues are not discussed or well understood. A clear example of this is presented by the issue of accession to the EU. Everybody agrees that it is very important, but practically nobody understands why or what the potential costs and benefits are.

Another explanation for the lack of debate, which is even more telling concerning the state of democracy in Poland, is that the politicians are probably convinced that the people do not need to be informed about major decisions, because they are not yet prepared to understand them or the reasons for taking them. The mistrust of society has been apparent on several occasions when politicians from all political parties have declared that Polish society is not adult, experienced or honest enough. In fact, the opposite is probably true. Sociological research and practical observation show that Polish society is probably more reasonable and liberal-democratic than its political leadership.

Tolerance and civic sentiments

Poland is probably the only country in Central and Eastern Europe that has minimal national minorities. Consequently, nationalist tendencies are relatively weak and the parties invoking nationalist arguments have not achieved any significant success. This tolerance, however, is negative rather than positive; very secondary disputes between Poles and Ukrainians, Poles and Jews, Catholics and Orthodox Christians could easily become major issues. Nationalism is closely related to some Catholic Church officials, although one cannot make a general statement about the nationalistic tendencies of Polish Catholicism.

There is a strong tendency towards privatization not only in the economy, but also in civic and social life. Poland was traditionally a country which, for many reasons, had a very solid idea of the Fatherland. This idea has disappeared astonishingly quickly and no new vision or project has taken its place. What therefore really endangers democracy is not weak nationalism but the lack of a common project. Individualism and utilitarian attitudes – which are not dangerous when accompanied by a solid moral vision of society – seem to be overwhelming. This rather astonishing development has several causes, the most important of which is the rapid construction of a new middle class which has no idea of civic virtue and misinterprets liberal ideology by more or less reducing the concept of liberalism to the survival of the fittest. The liberal idea of negative freedom has become the only way of understanding freedom, which limits any feeling for public life.

These social and psychological factors produce a very limited interest in politics and practically no interest in political strategies. Thus a stupid technical decision concerning taxation can create a social uproar, but the general strategy and long-term consequences of high taxation provoke little interest. There is a vicious circle of rapidly growing lack of interest in politics. The more politics focuses on the short term and lacks vision, the less people feel involved. One has to remember that Poles went through the experience of Solidarity, which means that common action and common decision-taking was a very valuable part of their life. The present political scene may be described as having exactly the opposite social and psychological features as compared with those pertaining to the Solidarity years, which understandably creates further frustration and tendencies to depoliticization.

Decommunization

Because of the specific character of the events in 1989 – the fact that independence was regained as a result of round-table talks – any type of massive decommunization in Poland was out of the question. Even in politics you do not shoot the partner of a major agreement. This fact, which cannot yet be fully evaluated, has created numerous problems which are largely responsible for the present political situation. These include the weak authority of the ruling post-communist group: they are elected but not trusted. This weakness prevents the post-communists from introducing proposed reforms that are, at least in theory, quite reasonable. Without successful reforms, they have to offer something else to the people before the parliamentary elections of autumn 1996, and it can only be money (salaries, pensions), which may lead to a new wave of inflation. The opposition, instead of promoting positive and concrete political programmes, has to seek votes on the basis of anti-communist and historic arguments.

The Church

The Catholic Church in Poland is often said to have a very strong and sometimes negative influence on the development of democracy. This is, however, open to doubt. The influence of the Church, as shown by all types of elections, on politics is relatively small, and its impact on morality astonishingly low. The Catholic Church without any doubt creates obstacles to modernization, but it is at the same time immersed in its own problems.

Some reflections on specific Polish problems

When Poland regained independence and the Berlin Wall fell in 1989 we thought not only that it was the end of one world and the beginning of another, but also that we should be very proud of our achievements. True, there was some joy, and for a moment people felt very happy, but only for a moment. Then came the practical implementation of democracy and of free-market economics, and virtually overnight everything changed. On the surface this seems easy to explain: life is more difficult than we had thought; we have to work harder; we do not have enough democratic culture; and communism destroyed civil society, which will take decades to rebuild. All this is probably true, but I do not feel satisfied by these explanations.

For a short time I was involved in Tadeusz Mazowiecki's presidential campaign (in 1990). Mazowiecki ran against Lech Wałęsa, who during the campaign often used the keyword 'acceleration', hoping to indicate that things were not happening quickly enough and that under his leadership problems would be solved immediately. That was, of course, not true. Here I would like to describe our efforts to refute Wałęsa's claim and explain why they were fruitless.

Responding to the idea of 'acceleration', we decided to contrast on TV the situation under communism and in 1990: then there were queues for food, now there was abundance of everything; then there was censorship, now there was none; then there were problems with passports and visas, now there were open frontiers; and so on. This approach proved totally counter-productive. First, people did not want to be reminded about how things had been under communism. Second, food was abundant but expensive, and only a few people are interested in freedom of speech. Third, we tried to be reasonable, sensible, practical and therefore we offered nothing that would really capture people's imagination and will to act.

After the elections I tried to find out why Wałęsa was so successful. Polish society proved to be well informed, relatively well educated and, after years of underground activities, quite aware of politics. So how was it possible that this society elected a man who (I do not speak about his enormous past achievements, but about his electoral campaign) promised impossible and stupid things, such as that everyone would get 100 million złotys, who always thought about short cuts and not about real solutions, who was obviously good in specific circumstances but was not good for everyday leadership?

The answer is simple, and it came to my mind only after seeing the recent political turmoil in Poland and in other post-communist countries. Perhaps those of us who were engaged in the struggle for independence and freedom were mistaken about the values for which people were yearning. We thought they wanted freedom, and to an extent we imposed it on them, but it seems now that people do not know what to do with the freedom they have regained. This is not a criticism of society, it is merely a statement of fact. Perhaps the value of freedom is not self-evident, at least to those who do not know what to do with it.

If I am right, it is not only a problem for the post-communist societies, but a problem concerning the whole of Western culture, even though demo-cratic countries during the past two centuries have introduced many ways of keeping people active and suggesting different uses of freedom. If I am right, the hope that civil society and associations will become the core of democ-racy is an illusory one, because civil society was introduced from above and not from below.

Here we come to another problem, which makes things even more complicated. In all post-communist societies we observe a tendency, of whatever strength, towards populism and against rule by intellectuals. This reaction is quite understandable. Intellectuals were involved in the struggle against the totalitarian system, some even went to prison, but the enormous majority of people do not want to be constantly reminded that they behaved in an opportunistic way. Therefore societies have rebelled against intellectual rule, but they have done so at a moment when the traditional functions of intellectuals – criticism and experimentation in patterns of social behaviour – are particularly important.

On the other hand, intellectuals have betrayed their mission, because they so readily accepted active participation in politics, which excludes criticism. Similarly, the Catholic Church did not set an example of moral behaviour, because it became involved – unsuccessfully – in political struggles. All social authorities became obsolete because they betrayed the functions that they fulfil in so-called 'normal' democracies.

People need some guidance as to how they are supposed to use their freedom. Without such guidance they tend to behave in primitive ways which are deplored by intellectuals and churches, creating a vicious circle. If someone makes some money and, instead of thinking about the future of his family or the good of society, buys a new Mercedes, we think that he has wasted his money, that he does not know what to do with his profits. And that is exactly true. He does not know. He does not even know how to look for what gives him pleasure. Why do we expect him to know? Where is he supposed to have acquired such knowledge?

Three, perhaps four, years ago the most popular word in Poland was 'liberalism'. Everybody wanted to be liberal. Everybody was for the free market and for all kinds of individual freedoms. Now the same word has a pejorative connotation. What has happened?

The liberal tradition – which was familiar to some, but rarely discussed – grew as a result of social and economic changes and not as their cause. One can be liberal in a free and affluent society, but it is a very strange task to be a liberal in a poor society in which individual freedoms exist but signify almost nothing because the means to implement them are lacking. Liberalism is very vague, and that is precisely what gives it power. Liberals say, 'Do what you want, on the condition that you do not harm your neighbours.' Therefore, liberal ideology presupposes that people know what they want to do, but lack the opportunity to do it. Liberal ideology is appropriate for grown-up societies, but even in those societies it creates a lot of problems. But liberal ideology is not sufficient for societies that have just started their journey towards democracy.

We are not sure what we really need, but we can say quite firmly that we need solid proposals. We do need concrete patterns of behaviour, and although it is important to know that everything in human life is relative, we would prefer to be informed that some things are better than others and that some ways of life, such as participation in voluntary associations, really do help. We do not want to be left alone, although we may understand that this eventually is the fate of all human beings.

And here comes Europe. Hope for membership of the EU and NATO is currently the most important factor in Polish politics. Without this hope we would already have had a lightly authoritarian political system. There is no doubt that everybody in Poland wants to be in Europe, therefore people and political parties have to behave properly. In this sense Europe has a very positive impact. Fear of membership of the EU is practically non-existent. On the other hand, Europe has provided neither moral and intellectual standards of social behaviour nor a political philosophy that could serve as the foundation for new societies. I have a strong feeling that Europe has not provided such a philosophy because it has problems itself in this regard. The post-communists have made good use of this ambiguous situation.

International opinion and the pressure, both real and supposed, of the West worked marvellously in all the post-communist countries of Central and Eastern Europe, with the obvious exception of the former Yugoslavia, which is perhaps not that exceptional. It is not obvious that all practical and short-term problems are best resolved on democratic and free-market bases. However, any undemocratic measure was immediately and strongly criticized by both the internal opposition and international opinion (governments, non-governmental institutions, such as the Helsinki Committee, and the mass media).

We did not have a violent revolution only because of our restraint. We also knew that hanging people is not 'politically correct' in a democracy. We strongly favoured the free-market economy not only because we thought that it was a right way, but also because we had read Hayek and Friedman and we had the World Bank and International Monetary Fund on our backs. We thought that democracy and freedom are a marvellous thing, because we read and reread de Tocqueville and because thousands of foreigners arrived in our countries to teach us how to be democratic, how to create and use self-government. We did not treat the older generation harshly, not only because to do so would have been dangerous internally, but also because Western standards of social justice would not permit such treatment. I may add that we have not been adequately reimbursed for our good behaviour. The West also made many mistakes, the most important being the lack of any practical proposition for integrating our countries into the Western community.

I have to conclude by saying that, if we take all the arguments above into account, the apparent *accident de parcours* in the last two Polish elections is easily understandable. But is it really only *accident de parcours*, or the beginning of a new time? One Polish prominent post-communist recently wrote that the old regime was a thesis, the Solidarity governments an antithesis, and now we are going to have a synthesis or a new quality. I am not happy with what happened, but I do not believe that this is true. We may have before us several years of paternalistic and leftist governments, but the road to democracy and to a free-market economy is not closed. Basic human freedoms will not be limited and we shall have some time to think and act not only concerning democracy but also concerning the socialization of democracy. There is, however, one condition: if the West uses the results of the last two – parliamentary and presidential – elections in Poland as an excuse for doing even less for Central and Eastern Europe (which is hard to imagine, as it has done so little to date), we and our neighbours might remain forgotten in chaotic, paternalistic, chauvinistic, populist and boring countries. It may happen, and, if so, it could appear to constitute universally valid proof that democracy is, in the last resort, not such a good thing. And that may be the beginning of a new period in modern history – a period that hopefully will not happen.

On 2 April 1997 the National Assembly (Sejm) passed the text of Poland's new constitution, which was subsequently adopted in a nationwide referendum on 25 May 1997, by a margin of 53 per cent in favour and 46 per cent against, with a turnout of 43 per cent of all eligible voters. The constitution, which came into force on 16 October 1997, was attacked throughout the constitution-making process by the right-wing parties, Solidarity Union and the Catholic Church. It was the subject of a political conflict focused more on the legitimacy of its adoption than on its actual wording and substance.

The parliamentary elections held on 21 September 1997 led to another change of power in Poland. The Solidarity Electoral Action (AWS), a broad coalition of rightist, centre-right and Christian-national parties anchored by the Solidarity trade union, won 33.9 per cent of the vote and thus displaced the ruling Democratic Left Alliance (SLD), a successor party to the former Communist party. The new ruling coalition is composed of two parties: the AWS and the centrist Freedom Union (UW).

6

Democracy in the Czech Republic

ZDENĚK KAVAN AND MARTIN PALOUŠ

A *methodological remark*

Our chapter should answer two fundamental questions. The first concerns the political model which is emerging in the process of transition in Central and Eastern Europe. The preliminary presumption is that it is a *sui generis* model which, although it shares something with the liberal democracies in the West, has at least some features peculiar to the region that derive both from the legacy of the past and from the impact of contemporary global developments. To what extent can this model be described as democratic or as authoritarian? What can be said about the underlying mind-set? What varieties can be distinguished within the species called post-communist or post-totalitarian political culture?

The second question touches upon what has been characterized as a set of vicious and virtuous circles. The more successful and 'virtuous' a country is in its transition to democracy and a market economy, the more favourable are relations with the European institutions which in turn enhance democracy and contribute to prosperity. The implication is clear: the countries which are less successful in the post-communist transitions for all sorts of reasons – be it economic hardships, social or political tensions or adverse international developments – find themselves in a very different situation: in a 'vicious' circle, being increasingly marginalized and separated or even excluded from the processes of European integration. The different positions of the Czech Republic and Slovakia in the North Atlantic Treaty Organization (NATO) enlargement debate and the growing gaps between Slovenia and the other Yugoslav successor states are possible examples of such 'virtuous' and 'vicious' circles.

The case of the Czech Republic demonstrates that the characterization of post-communist political models as either democratic or authoritarian is too crude and that greater subtlety in differentiating between them is needed. First we must take into account that we are dealing with complex and dynamic processes that cannot be reduced to claims about either the common heritage of communism or the specific cultural legacies of individual post-communist countries. These models cannot be separated from the external environment into which they emerged and in which they operate. All of them are undergoing complex interactions between the status quo and various transformation strategies. The key problem is, as Dahrendorf (1990) pointed out in his seminal study of the revolutions in Central and Eastern Europe, that of timing: the relation and proper ordering of various agendas in the process of transition. It means, however, more than sequencing 'constitutional' and 'normal' politics in the transformation of the form of government and relating them to the far-reaching economic and social changes being implemented. What must also be taken into account is that the observed process is not just one transition, but the conjunction of transitions in the domestic, regional and international systems. The collapse of state socialism in Central and Eastern Europe was accompanied by the collapse of the Soviet empire, which has sparked further and broader processes occurring on a global scale. It is this set of reactions, the reality of complex interdependence in the post-Cold War world and the problem of concentric multiple transitions, that lies hidden behind the 'virtuousness' and 'viciousness' of Europe's post-communist circles.

A brief historical background

Unlike most of the former communist states, Czechoslovakia had a certain amount of experience with democracy. As a matter of fact, egalitarianism – the lack of hierarchical structures, the building up of a society 'from below' – belongs to the natural, 'genetic' equipment of small central European Slavonic nations, reborn in the period of Enlightenment at the end of the eighteenth century. The first republic, an independent Czechoslovak state which appeared on the map of Europe after the dismemberment of Austria-Hungary at the end of World War I, was essentially democratic, with a well-functioning economy, pluralistic party political system and the rule of law. Its weaknesses included the failure to resolve successfully the problem of national relations within the country, which, in the deteriorating international situation, contributed to the eventual demise of the state.

A more limited form of democracy was established after World War II and functioned between 1945 and 1948. It involved a curtailed form of pluralism – the right and the centre-right were excluded – and the Communist Party assumed a dominant position in the government. The intensification of the Cold War and the increasing radicalism of the Communist Party resulted in the demise of this 'democracy' in February 1948.

Last, but not least, the 1960s saw a gradual thaw of the Stalinist variety of socialism, culminating in the radical reforms of the Prague Spring of 1968.

The termination of this democratic experiment by the Soviet military intervention confirmed the perception that threats to Czechoslovak democracy were largely external.

Although these historical experiences with democracy were limited in time and scope, and represent, for the majority of the population, a distant historical memory rather than any actual experience with democracy, they provide an enduring myth of the democratic national culture.

The dissolution of Czechoslovakia

The key aspect of the Czechoslovak model of transition is the fact that the legal solution to the problem of coexistence between Czechs and Slovaks turned out to be a more important and more powerful issue than anything else. The correction of the asymmetry that characterized all past constitutions of Czechoslovakia became a task of the highest priority, and the solution found in the end was unexpected and was received by the majority of both citizens and politicians with mixed feelings: Czechoslovakia, the only state in Central and Eastern Europe with a real democratic tradition, disintegrated in the name of its democratic revolution after more than 74 years of existence.

The general conviction, however, that both Czechs and Slovaks were democrats did not change. In fact, the peaceful and relatively constructive way in which the divorce between Czechs and Slovaks was organized was generally recognized as further proof of the solidity of Czechoslovak democracy. Both successor states were able to overcome practically all the consequences of the split relatively quickly and to lay solid foundations for peaceful co-operation.

It has to be noted, however, that the dissolution of the country raised some hard questions about the nature of the democratic process. The dissolution occurred without the prior and explicit consent of the people. They did not vote for it in an election – none of the leading parties had advocated it in their campaigns – or in a referendum, and opinion polls taken at the time showed that the majority of the electorate in both parts of the country favoured preserving the common state. It might, perhaps, also be speculated that by creating, for the first time in modern history, a relatively ethnically pure Czech state, the dissolution of Czechoslovakia has brought about a shift towards an ethnic understanding of civil society. This has some implications for the one important and sensitive problem that was created by the sudden termination of the Czechoslovak state: the question of citizenship (see below).

The Czech model as a result of the dominant transformation strategy

The main feature of the Czech transformation strategy has been the combination of elements which may not look quite compatible, at least at first sight. Neo-liberal economic doctrines, rejecting the concept of a paternalistic welfare state and relying uncritically upon the omnipotence of market forces, have been combined with policies aimed at keeping practically untouched a strong and heavily centralized state administration. The spontaneous activities of civil society reborn from below and all forms of politics built upon the concept of civil society were considered more dangerous and potentially more destabilizing even than the forces of the *ancien régime*. The reason for this surprising étatism of post-communist liberals is obvious: they came to believe (the American founding fathers served as a good example) that the biggest threat to democracy during the period of transition is a weak government. Regardless of their anti-étatist ideology, the neo-liberals' highest priority in their transformation strategy is the strengthening of existing state structures and, of course, the gaining of sufficient public support to do so.

The successful Czech transformation strategy – liberalization planned from the top down – was described by one of its main protagonists, Prime Minister Václav Klaus, as an example of the practical application of the 'turnpike theorem', which in micro-economics defines the fastest way of achieving an optimal situation. It implies that one simply cannot know all that lies ahead in the transition process. Therefore instead of making speculative plans for the future, 'instead of using a winding road of half-measures, of ill-motivated concessions, delays and ideological errors and prejudices', one should prepare 'all necessary preconditions for a successful take-off into the "normal" world' of the Western, i.e. free-market, economy. The liberalization of domestic markets – a significant degree of price liberalization accompanied by a restrictive macro-economic policy – together with the opening up of the Czechoslovak economy to world markets and rapid privatization were the main pillars of the economic transformation and, consequently, stood at the top of the political agenda. In order for economic reforms to be successful, however, more is required than the readiness of their proponents to drive along a straight ideological and economic turnpike; a viable political strategy is also necessary for their implementation. Such a strategy required the acceleration of political polarization. The original post-revolutionary political consensus, which had been built round civic values and public virtues and which unified the people round the concept of revitalized civil society, was deemed not compatible with the basic precondition of successful economic transformation, a strong centralized state. As speed is crucial for the success of this strategy, everything that can slow down the initial operation of the 'turnpike', such as the spontaneous activities and institutions of civil society, must be set aside, at least for a while. No doubt the rule of law is the key principle of an open society, but this strategy subordinates it to other priorities. The political bodies which emerged victorious from the revolution have to be transformed into political parties which would be able to start standard Western political processes centred not only on principles but also on defined and balanced interests. The substance of these processes is the struggle for political power, and therefore a strong reform party must be created capable of winning elections and of forming a strong government.

The state of Czech democracy

As mentioned above, the Czech Republic is generally considered to be an example of successful transition. Seven years after the collapse of the communist regime and in the fifth year of its independent existence the country seems to be remarkably stable. The basic democratic institutions have been reconstructed and the principle of the rule of law has been reintroduced.

The achievements of the Klausian model

Elections and political parties
There is little doubt that the electoral system, largely based on proportional representation, is democratic and functions fairly. The Law on Political Parties is fair and just, and there are few formal restrictions on political activities, with the exception of prohibitions on the advocacy of racial hatred and intolerance and on activities designed to destroy democracy and the pluralistic regime. The requirement that a party must win 5 per cent of the vote to be eligible to sit in Parliament has meant that the number of parliamentary parties is limited and that a degree of clear crystallization of political forces is emerging. The coalition government, re-elected in May 1996, consists of three right-of-centre parties. It is led by the neo-liberal Civic Democratic Party (ODS), is dominated by Prime Minister Václav Klaus and is the largest party in the Parliament. It fared less well in the May 1996 elections than had been anticipated and signs are appearing of internal pressure for more dialogue and greater pluralism. The other two coalition parties are the conservative Civic Democratic Alliance (ODA), which has a small, rather elitist, membership, and the centrist, Catholic, Christian Democratic Union/Czech People's Party (KDU/CSL), which puts much greater emphasis on social issues and policies than the ODS and is in some policy areas much closer to the Social Democrats. The coalition is thus not

monolithic and there are some significant differences in policy preferences among its members.

Three other parties are represented in Parliament. The Czech Social Democratic Party (CSSD) – which, unlike in the other Central and East European countries, is not the former Communist Party but a reconstituted social democratic party – is the second largest in the Parliament, having been significantly strengthened in the May 1996 elections. The Communist Party – an unreconstructed former governing party -- and the Republican Party – which is xenophobic, racist and populist, and displays many fascist tendencies – are the other two parliamentary parties. There are also dozens of extra-parliamentary parties and other political entities and groupings active in the public arena.

The May elections suggest several developments. First, a more traditional left–right system seems to be emerging in which the long-term monopoliza-tion of power by the centre-right no longer looks assured. Second, owing to the lack of a parliamentary majority, there should be more informal co-operation between the coalition government and the main opposition party, the Social Democrats. Third, negotiation and compromise between the coalition partners should intensify. Fourth, as almost 20 per cent of voters voted for parties with dubious commitments to democracy, some potential for anti-democratic developments remains.

Economic and social transition
The market-based economy (two-thirds of gross domestic product (GDP) is produced by the private sector) grew strongly in 1995 and 1996, though growth declined in 1997. Macro-economic indicators such as inflation and unemployment are favourable, though there are also some indicators of problems ahead, particularly regarding the increasing balance of payments deficit and the relative decline of exports. The relative lack of structural reform is also a source of potential weakness.

Social tensions, which were expected to accompany economic transforma-tion, have thus far turned out to be much less of a problem than had been predicted, and the so-called tripartite negotiations between the government, employers and trade unions have worked well as a means of constructive and efficient communication. Despite some currently hotly disputed issues, such as the reform of the health service, the cohesion of Czech society does not seem to be immediately threatened.

However, some potential threats to democracy arising out of the economic transformation are already visible. The 'enormous and opaque power of the banks, odd transformations of some investment funds and huge financial frauds' (Bělohradský, 1992) create the risk of public disillusionment with the new system. Some of the recent fraudulent economic and financial activities have raised some doubts concerning the way in which coupon privatization, the central and lauded plank of the Czech economic transformation, was carried out. It is now acknowledged that the emphasis on speeding the process resulted in its not having a clear legal regulatory underpinning, and thus provided the scope and the opportunity for the subsequent misuse of funds and other forms of unfair enrichment. A remark by the father of the privatization scheme, V. Ježek, explaining the lack of legal framework – 'We had to save privatization from the lawyers' – is quite revealing of the tendency to perceive law, and by extension the rule of law, as an obstacle to desired ends.

Formal democracy

The constitutional system

An important problem stems from the fact that the government lacks the will to implement fully the constitution, thus weakening elementary legal awareness and respect for law. The second house of the Parliament, the Senate, came into existence in November 1996, almost four years after the Czech constitution was adopted. Self-governing regional bodies have yet to be established, although the changed configuration of forces produced by the May elections did force the leading governing party (the ODS) to agree to their establishment and Parliament accepted the government's proposal for the establishment of fourteen such bodies in October 1997. Their power and competence are yet to be agreed and the implementation of this arrangement is not envisaged until 1 January 2000. Previously Klaus's party had strongly opposed such moves towards the devolution of power and further conflicts over these bodies' competences can be expected before implementation. The Supreme Administrative Court has likewise not yet been established, nor is it clear when it will be.

The government's opposition to referendums, a result of its emphasis on representative democracy, despite constitutional provisions for their use, means that the necessary procedures have not been adopted.

Some problems also remain with regards to human rights. The Declaration of Basic Rights and Freedoms and the international agreements on human rights and fundamental freedoms referred to in Article 10 of the constitution are often not considered as primary and enforceable law in administrative and legal practice.

The judiciary

Although the independence of the judiciary is firmly established by the constitution, serious problems remain concerning the length of proceedings and the absence of a fully functioning and organizationally complete administrative judiciary. The speed of proceedings particularly affects public trust in the administration of justice.

The military and the police

The military remains firmly under civilian control and poses little threat to democracy. The rising crime rate has pushed crime to the forefront of public concerns and has raised questions about the effectiveness of the police force. The issue of public control over the state security forces, particularly the Parliament's role, remains hotly debated.

The civil service

Two problems have affected the performance of the civil service: brain drain and patronage. The private sector offers much greater opportunities to the more able members of the civil service, and the politicization of the civil service that took place under the communist regime has to some extent been maintained. Appointments to the top positions still tend to be made on the basis of party allegiance.

The media

The media are basically free, operating without any political control by the state, and have become a lively and politically diverse force. Criticism of the government is considered normal and desirable. Expressions of government hostility towards the media have largely been absent. Some problems relating to press law have, however, emerged (see below). There is also disquiet in some quarters about the fact that 80 per cent of the press is German-owned.

Foreign policies and the international standing of the Czech Republic

The 'return to Europe' was one of the central slogans, or aims, of the 1989 revolution and it was linked explicitly to democracy. The identification of democracy with the European West as against the totalitarian East not only has affected external policies but also has exercised great symbolic power. This symbolic identification with the West in part contributed to the dissolution of Czechoslovakia, because a portion of the Czech elite perceived that the path to Europe would be smoother without the more eastern-oriented Slovakia. The symbolic power and usage of Europe have somewhat declined since 1993 but have not entirely disappeared. A great many people from across the political spectrum still link membership of Western institutions, particularly the North Atlantic Treaty Organization (NATO) and the EU, with guaranteeing democratic transformation.

The North Atlantic Treaty Organization

Most of the parliamentary parties (the coalition parties and CSSD) support early membership of NATO. There is some disagreement between the government and the opposition on the use of the referendum (the government opposes it). The decline in public support for accession is linked to the public opposition to the stationing of foreign troops and of nuclear weapons in the country.

The European Union

The issue of EU membership is potentially more divisive. As with NATO, all the leading parties are committed to membership as soon as possible, and the government formally applied for membership in 1996. There are, however, significant cracks in most of the parties between Eurosceptics and Europhiles. Klaus has been publicly identified with the sceptical tendency, having expressed strong support, in truly Thatcherite terms, for the idea of a Europe of nation-states. Some other members of the government, however, have taken a much more pro-integration position. The CSSD takes a strongly pro-EU line, emphasizing the social provisions and going as far as to claim that the EU is basically a social democratic institution. Klaus has also referred on a number of occasions to the danger of having socialist policies foisted upon the country by Brussels. The general public remains relatively ill-informed about the issue and the debate in the media at present is relatively poor.

Civil society, non-governmental organizations (NGOs), and human rights

Non-governmental organizations and social movements

Since the collapse of communism a number of NGOs have appeared, dealing with a variety of concerns including the environment, gender, human rights and ethnic minorities. They operate across the political spectrum. Their combined membership, however, remains relatively small, and the government has tended to view their role negatively. It has been particularly keen to limit their impact on political decision-making by stressing the primacy of formal representation. The government has also obstructed their activities by delaying the law on non-profit-making organizations and by not making charitable donations tax-deductible.

Human and legal rights

THE OMBUDSMAN

The Commission of Ministers of the Council of Europe recommended that an ombudsman be established, and the Czech Parliamentary Committee for Petitions, Human Rights and Ethnicities presented the Parliament with a bill on the Public Protection of Rights in 1996. However, the ODS's opposition to such an institution has meant that there has been insufficient political will to adopt the bill, a situation which is likely to continue during the current Parliament.

THE RIGHT TO LEGAL ASSISTANCE

The main problem in the area of legal assistance concerns the rights of those who cannot afford it. Although the right to legal assistance is guaranteed under Article 10 of the European Convention on Human Rights and by the existing law on advocacy and the professional rules of the Czech Bar Association, the new law on advocacy does not include it. Instead it requires that legal services be provided for a fee.

RIGHT TO AND ACCESS TO INFORMATION

The issues of the right to information and of access to it became topical in 1995, particularly in relation to the preparation of the new press bill. Important developments concerned the deletion of the obligation to respect the confidentiality of the press's sources and the removal of the right of access to information. The latter was justified on the grounds that the Declaration of Basic Rights and Fundamental Freedoms guarantees access to information for all without exception. The legislation implementing this provision, however, has not yet been prepared. Therefore, journalists' right of access to information is limited.

As far as the public administration is concerned, access to information is based on the principle of discretion rather than the principle of publicity. Even when this right is positively formulated in law, legal protection against the unlawful limitation or denial of access to information is lacking. Fundamental rights specified in the Declaration, such as the right to timely and full information concerning the state of the environment and natural resources, are severely circumscribed in practice.

RIGHTS OF ETHNIC MINORITIES

The current situation with respect to the rights of ethnic minorities is characterized by the following tendencies:

- improvement in the internationally guaranteed legal standard for the protection of minorities. The Czech government joined the Council of Europe's Framework Convention for the Protection of National Minorities in 1995. The Czech government pledges, once this convention becomes part of the legal order, not only to protect the rights of minorities but also to enforce a policy leading to the elimination of ethnic inequalities in social, economic, cultural and political life;
- movement towards the emancipation of most ethnic minorities. The Polish and German minorities in particular have received their own institutions

and formulated their own interests and needs, a process undoubtedly influenced by positive relations with their 'mother' countries;

- formation of effective minority organizations and periodicals within the Slovak community in Prague. Immigration from Slovakia has continued, immigrants having included members of the Slovak elite;

- continued poor treatment of the Roma. The segregation of the Roma in Czech society is deepening. It is both a cause and a consequence of their deteriorating chances for employment; their declining participation in the educational, health care and housing systems; their growing poverty; and their relatively high rates of criminality, including participation in serious forms of organized crime;

- increases in intentional, violent and racially motivated attacks by organized neo-Nazi and nationalist groups on members of ethnic minorities, particularly the Roma. Revenge attacks by the Roma have begun to occur and are at least partly due to the Roma's perception that the state offers inadequate protection against racial violence;

- the existence of open non-violent discrimination against the Roma, by stores, restaurants, etc. This can include refusal of service as indicated by notices such as 'We do not serve Gypsies'. Such acts go largely unpunished because the necessary direct legal instruments are inadequate and the will to use indirect instruments is lacking. Similarly, racist and extremist publications have seldom been prosecuted;

- persistent strong latent racism directed against some ethnic/racial minorities, particularly the Roma, Vietnamese and non-white immigrants. Although only one person in ten supports the extremists, the majority do accept maximum spatial, social and cultural segregation as a basis for the solution of ethnic and racial tension. The idea of close neighbourly coexistence with Romanies is unacceptable to seven out of ten Czechs;

- increased sensitivity to the dangers of racism, although this has not yet translated into a public search for and debate on positive policies;

- poor performance by Roma candidates in the local elections. There are almost no Roma representatives in local government. This is in part due to poor Roma participation in elections, which has not been adequately addressed by the government's lax formal approach, which in turn is shaped by the state's and political parties' lack of political will;

- persistent divisions within the Roma community. There has not been significant progress towards a consensus among its elite about the major aims, interests and requirements of the Roma minority. This is at least partly due to the fact that many Roma who integrate successfully into

Czech society abandon their community and do not transfer their experience to it;

- increased NGO activity regarding the Roma minority. NGOs are conducting a number of small projects focusing on regional, short-term or experimental programmes which seek to test the possibilities of integrating the Roma minority. Town and school organizations have also tried several co-operative projects, including experimental schools and programmes, though the positive experience and knowledge coming out of these projects have been ignored by the central authorities;

- little impact of *ad hoc* meetings between the representatives of the Roma minority and state officials on government policy. This lack of results is due in part to the failure of the Roma representatives to clarify their aims and the small amount of influence the responsible partner bodies have with government ministries;

- government hostility to criticism from foreign governments and international governmental and non-governmental organizations. Several times in 1995 the Czech government dismissed such critics as incompetent or insufficiently aware of specific Czech conditions. That international pressure can have some impact, however, was demonstrated in April 1996 when the Parliament finally amended the much criticized citizenship law (see below).

LUSTRATION

The lustration law was passed by the Czechoslovak Federal Assembly in the autumn of 1991 and sought to exclude from elected posts and appointments in the public administration all those persons who had at any time between 25 February 1948 and 17 November 1989 been members of the secret service (StB); were registered in its files as agents or collaborators; had knowingly collaborated with the StB; had held positions as secretaries of an organ of the Communist Party from the level of the district committee upward; or who, as members of either the ruling bodies of the party or its apparatus, had been involved in setting the political direction of the secret service; and those who had held any position of authority in the People's Militia. Subsequently the process was extended to cover other spheres, including the media. The law, which was to be valid for five years, was extended by the Czech Parliament in 1996 for another five years.

The major weaknesses of this law are its reliance on official StB documentation and its quasi-judicial procedure, which is based on the presumption of guilt. Thus the accused has to prove his or her innocence or seek redress in a court of law where the proceedings would take an inordinate amount of time. The lustration process, it soon became clear, acquired a political purpose: to discredit political opponents by associating them with the most disreputable practices of the previous regime. Important rights deriving from natural justice, such as the right to a fair hearing, were trumped by political expediency (Wheaton and Kavan, 1992).

CITIZENSHIP LAW

The citizenship law has been severely criticized both at home and abroad for one of its provisions and for its implementation. The criticized provision set two years' residence and five years with a clean criminal record as conditions for citizenship. It was impossible for a number of people to fulfil these conditions within the period specified for application for citizenship following the dissolution of the Czechoslovak state. Further, the demand for a five-year clean criminal record was perceived to be anti-Roma (given the high numbers of Roma of Slovak origin with criminal records). In April 1996 the Czech government finally responded to international pressure – particularly from the Council of Europe, the US Congress and the US State Department – and the Parliament amended this provision by giving the Ministry of the Interior discretion to waive this condition for Slovak citizens residing permanently in the Czech Republic since the dissolution of Czechoslovakia.

In addition, in implementing the law the government did not always fulfil the obligation to provide applicants, particularly Roma, with assistance and instruction so that they would not be handicapped by their lack of awareness or understanding of the regulations.

The weaknesses of the Czech citizenship law are obvious and its impact on significant sections of the Roma people is negative. However, it should be recognized that new states face greater difficulties in constructing their citizenship laws than established ones. Claims as to the membership of this new polity have to be not only coherent but also legitimate as far as the majority are concerned, and the search for the legitimating principle can lead to provisions which are too restrictive and exclusionary.

The weakness of democratic culture

There is little doubt that the full transformation of Czech society into a democratic one depends on the creation of a democratic culture, and this will be a long-term process involving a generational change. The authoritarian culture fostered by the communist regime is too deeply ingrained in people's outlook and behaviour to alter easily. It is still evident in the public preference for a government with 'strong hands', particularly in the fight against crime. A significant majority, according to opinion polls, would accept a reduction in democracy, human rights and fundamental freedoms in exchange for the successful reduction of crime. Our assessment of democratic changes ought to take into account the long-term nature of this problem.

Conclusion: the human rights alternative to the dominant model

The central question concerning the dominant Czech model of transformation is whether it is sustainable in the long run, its short-term successes notwithstanding.

The crucial weaknesses of Czech democracy are the weakness of 'politics from below'; an underdeveloped legal and political culture; the vacuum that has been created between individuals motivated by self-interest and institutions of public power; the lack of interest in a proper dialogue; and the difficulties of public communication and understanding. The principle of respect for human rights should be revitalized as a remedy to these problems. The question is what kinds of strategies are available under the prevailing conditions for raising public awareness of the importance of human rights and how to empower the structures of civil society, which have been seriously weakened by the Klausian reforms.

The enforcement and fulfilment of human rights would require more than a high-quality legal system and state institutions. Other necessary conditions are public awareness of the law and a high political culture involving citizens' respect for these rights and their willingness to defend them effectively. The principle of human rights requires foremost that there be permanent two-way communication between citizens and public authorities. The legal system and state apparatus of an open society must be, above all, trustworthy and transparent. Information from below, voicing the experience of individuals and expressing their demands for rights, should not get lost in the bureaucratic machinery, but should play a crucial role in the development of the legal system, provide effective feedback and serve as an important corrective.

At the same time, it is clear that the protection of human rights in the Czech Republic does not depend solely on the state of Czech society, on the willingness of citizens and public authorities to engage in a permanent dialogue; it also depends on communication with the outside world. The issue is not only how the international mechanisms for the protection of human rights are integrated into the Czech legal system and how the state fulfils and enforces its international obligations, but also whether and how the discussions in Europe and elsewhere affect debates and decision-making in the Czech Republic. The issue is to what extent the Czechs are able to make use of the experiences of others; to join in the dialogue taking place beyond the country's borders; to understand their own situation in a broader context; and to resist the illusions of transformational ideology, which currently seems so convincing and popular.

There seems relatively little doubt that formal democracy has been reconstructed relatively successfully in the Czech Republic. A number of substantive problems remain, however, which, given the multifaceted and complex nature of the transformation process, is to be expected. Further, in spite of the long-term problem of developing a democratic political culture, significant progress has been made, and that process appears irreversible provided that no catastrophic economic decline occurs.

It is perfectly natural that there are some misunderstandings between individual citizens and those who represent and govern the state. These ensue from the different perspectives from which different groups contemplate social and economic realities. For these different perspectives to coexist peaceably in a democratic society, continuous horizontal and vertical communication is required. In this permanent dialogue political power cannot be primary, and parameters for arbitrating among contending interests have to be continually renewed and reconstructed.

7

The Present State of Democracy in Slovakia[1]

MARTIN BÚTORA

Introduction

Despite some positive macro-economic achievements in recent years, Slovakia has become the most problematic of the Visegrád countries (the other
countries in the group being Poland, Hungary and the Czech Republic). The
increasingly visible exclusion of Slovakia from the first rank of candidates for
membership of the European Union (EU) and North Atlantic Treaty Organization (NATO) is a response to the disturbing domestic policy trends which
followed the 1994 parliamentary elections. These trends reflect the unstable
democratic political culture in the country. The ruling coalition's efforts to
concentrate and monopolize political power in the hands of the executive;
the political confrontation resulting from government's efforts to remove
Michal Kováč from his presidential post; the strengthening of state authority
and paternalism in legislation; changes in the privatization process leading
towards clientelism; the ruling coalition's confrontational attitude towards
ethnic Hungarians; the government's intervention in the media; the exclusion of the opposition from the control of Slovakia's secret services; and the
unsatisfactory development of the investigation into the kidnapping of
Michal Kováč, Jr, are examples of the disturbing trends which sow doubts
about the consolidation of the democratic regime in Slovakia.

Historical legacies

Democratic traditions and party politics

Slovakia is one of the few European countries that has experienced all three
main political systems of the twentieth century: capitalism with parliamentary democracy; a domestic variety of fascism, which oversaw the
deportation of more than 70,000 Slovak Jews, and subsequent strong
domestic resistance; and socialism in all its varieties from Stalinism through
attempts at reform in the 1960s to the petrified post-Stalinist 'real socialism'

of the following two decades. Slovakia not only endured these regimes, but also contributed to shaping them and was itself shaped by them.

As for the party system, two main traditions can be discerned: political pluralism with a broad spectrum of parties, which gradually emerged within Austria-Hungary (1860–1914) and flourished in the first Czechoslovak Republic (1918–38); and one-party rule, first by the Catholic Andrej Hlinka's Slovak People's Party (1938–45), then by the Communist Party (1948–89). The geopolitical environment and external pressures were inauspicious for democracy, but in addition, Lipták (1995) explains the relative success of the authoritarian tradition by the way hegemonic force appealed to certain traditional domestic political currents, tendencies and forces, existing ideas, concepts or, at least, illusions. He sets out a series of economic, social, political and psychological factors – including the disruption of private ownership, the destruction and loss of confidence in the system of parliamentary democracy, the undermining of civil society, the strengthening of the state and enlargement of its sphere of interventions, the discrediting of traditional political groupings, and the principle of collective guilt – 'which facilitated the transition from one form of dictatorship and one form of hegemony to another' (Lipták, 1995).

The post-1989 development reflects both traditions, and, especially since the early elections in the autumn of 1994, the cleavage between the forces of democratic pluralism and the political groupings with authoritarian inclinations has become the most conspicuous characteristic of the political scene in Slovakia. The 'authoritarian amalgam' of the pre-war traditionalist nationalist populism and the post-war socialist collectivism has hampered the formation of an organized and institutionalized democratic consensus.

A mentality of 'unfinished modernization'[2]

The processes under way in Slovakia are those of a country with a delayed and still incomplete modernization. Urbanization and industrialization took place here later than in the Czech Republic and occurred primarily under socialism. Therefore, modernization processes happened without the presence of either a market economy or a political democracy.

These circumstances resulted in the spread of particular configurations of values, beliefs and modes of behaviour. Socialist social engineering did not give birth to individualism. On the contrary, initiative, creativity and personal responsibility were largely absent as the people became used to depending on the state, large enterprises and industrial mono-cultures which, in most cases, colonized their work and social life. Further, as some social rights were achieved while civic and political rights remained limited, people grew to believe that, unlike in the democratic countries of the West, civilization's progress was possible without freedom and democracy. In addition, as socialist modernization did not occur under the rule of law, constitutionalism and respect for law did not develop.

Structuring of the political scene

As in some other post-communist countries, changes in Slovakia's social structure have not kept pace with the development of individual parties. As Mesežnikov (1995) observes, those political entities – such as the Christian Democratic Movement (KDH), the Democratic Union (DU) and two leftist parties, the Party of the Democratic Left (SDL) and the Social Democratic Party (SDSS) – that strive for clearer self-definition and for closer alignment with models along the continuum of conservativism, liberalism and social democracy do not yet have a sufficiently strong social base. In contrast is the Movement for a Democratic Slovakia (HZDS) – the party without manifest international contacts which has repeatedly won the elections, has the strongest social background and has deliberately profiled itself as a 'pragmatic wide centrist movement' (Mesežnikov, 1995).

Szomolanyi (1995) describes the political scene in terms of 'fragmented polarization' rather than 'structured plurality'. In other words, in contrast to what happens in countries such as Hungary, the Czech Republic and Poland, the 'programmatic' parties, which are compatible with existing international party structures, have repeatedly achieved less electoral success than the parties with charismatic leaders. Two 'non-standard groupings' – the Slovak National Party (SNS) and the Association of Workers of Slovakia (ZRS), which are characterized by increased degrees of national and social populism, authoritarianism and radicalism – have won parliamentary representation and have even been invited to join the government (Szomolanyi, 1995).

Many authors repeatedly point to the main cleavage in Slovak society, which is urban–rural rather than between the socio-economic left and right. Using Kitschelt's (1995) classification of the formation of party cleavages in post-communist democracies, Szomolanyi (1996) speaks of the conflict between the advocates of 'left and right authoritarianism' and 'left and right libertarianism'. An analysis provided by Krivý (1996) has proved that 'due to the 1994 elections political power was shifted to parties rooted especially in the rural and less educated environment as well as to the parties with electorates that are authoritarian and state-paternalistic'.

Government and opposition: diverging interpretations of democracy and constitutionalism

The government's commitment to democracy and the rule of law stated in its manifesto of January 1995 and reiterated in the memorandum that accompanied its application for membership of the EU in June 1995 is in sharp contrast with the events which have occurred since the night in November 1994 when the parties of the current coalition government started to implement what the political science literature classically refers to as the 'tyranny of the majority', including concentration of political power, purging of the state apparatus, drastic interference with privatization and the establishment of total control over state television. Unlike during 1990–4, the opposition does not have a parliamentary vice-president; the chair of any parliamentary committee; a representative on the parliamentary body that oversees the Slovak Intelligence Service (SIS); a representative on the National Property Fund (FNM), which has complete control over privatization; or a single representative on the councils for public electronic media.

The results of such political conditions are evident in the progress of privatization during 1995–6, when the managers of state-owned companies and the industrial lobby, who have close ties with the ruling coalition, strengthened their positions. After November 1994 privatization was managed by coalition politicians unhindered by any overseeing power of Parliament, opposition parties or independent institutions. The process was opaque and uncontrolled, and property transfers benefited persons close to the government coalition (Juris *et al.*, 1995). Privatization has thus become one of the hottest issues in Parliament, with the opposition accusing the government of selling firms to members of the HZDS and other ruling parties through direct sales orchestrated by the government-controlled FNM.

It is quite evident that the government coalition and the opposition hold fundamentally opposing views and interpretations of democracy and constitutionalism, and that there is a lack of dialogue between them. One reason for this is the specific political style of Prime Minister Mečiar, chairman of the HZDS. While he can win elections, his confrontational style prevents him from building and maintaining a consensus and sooner or later brings him into conflicts with his allies (Fisher, 1996).

Because of internal disputes, however, the opposition has not been able to produce a viable political alternative to the ruling coalition. But the process of social learning continues. At the end of 1996 opposition parties were close to agreement on a mechanism for mutual co-operation, and the chances of creating a broader democratic coalition increased.

The constitution and the division of power

For the most part, Slovakia's constitution corresponds to the standard of modern democratic states. Despite many political changes since its adoption in September 1992, the country's constitutional system has remained stable, with a strong Constitutional Court. The constitution includes a Bill of Rights, and international covenants on human rights and freedoms take precedence over the legislation of the Slovak Republic. Slovakia, as an associated member of the EU, is expected to respect the standards of political life characteristic of the EU countries. This creates an important reference framework for internal political developments in the country. While there are some contradictions and shortcomings in the constitution regarding management of political crises and clear delineation of the division of competencies between the highest institutions of the state, the constitution has had a crucial role in preserving the division of power in Slovakia.

While the basic division of power has been preserved, the ruling coalition has sought to remove President Michal Kováč from office. Because it did not have the necessary two-thirds parliamentary majority to dismiss the President, it tried to minimize his power. It amended the Slovak Intelligence Service (SIS) Law so as to strip the President of the right to appoint and recall the head of the SIS and similarly that of the chief of the General Staff of the Armed Forces. Institutional confrontation culminated with the Parliament's vote of no confidence in the President in May 1995. The ruling coalition also imposed restrictive financial measures on the office of the President. Staff members of central state authorities and other state institutions were urged to sign petitions against the President; in some cases, the signing of the petitions was tied to the declaration of loyalty to the government.

At the end of August 1995 an event took place that markedly affected domestic political developments in Slovakia. Michal Kováč, Jr, the President's son, was abducted by unknown persons and taken to Austria. The timing and style of the act, as well as the reactions of constitutional representatives and the course of the investigation, indicate that the abduction was politically motivated.

Besides the President, the Constitutional Court has been one of the most important pillars of democracy and constitutionalism. In several of its rulings it has demonstrated its power to limit the 'tyranny of the majority'. In May 1995, for example, it ruled that the post-privatization law passed during the 'nocturnal' November session breached the constitution. In April 1996 the Court declared the 'golden shares' section of the Law on State Strategic Interests in the Privatization of State-Run Companies unconstitutional. This section would have enabled the state to purchase a 'golden share' of a company, thereby enabling it to intervene in the firm's legal status and limit the rights of the owners.

In September 1996 the court ruled that the Ministry of Foreign Affairs had violated the constitutional right of a Slovak citizen (M. Kováč, Jr) between 5 January and 23 February 1996: from the time he asked in writing that the ministry request his extradition to the time when he actually returned to Slovakia. The court ruled that, pursuant to Article 23 of the constitution, a Slovak citizen cannot be made to leave the country through any law, judicial decision or executive order. The opposition press interpreted the court's decision as sending the message that the constitution protects citizens against state power and not the other way around.

Some of the court's decisions are met with disapproval by the representatives of the ruling coalition. The Prime Minister, for example, famously labelled the court a 'sick element on the political scene'. Officially, however, nobody from the government or the Parliament has declared that the court's decisions should not be obeyed. In some controversial cases, though, the government has delayed the implementation of or simply ignored the court's rulings.

The Slovak judiciary, taken as a whole, preserved its independence during 1995–6. This was possible because the judges themselves articulated quite clearly their independent position and resisted attempts to introduce a political dimension into the judicial decision-making.

A more troubling situation has emerged in the police force. This was particularly evident during the investigation of the abduction of Michal Kováč, Jr, when almost undisguised political pressure was put on the police, directly influencing the course of the investigation. These pressures intensified after a link was established between the abduction and the activities of SIS officers. Two police investigators who disclosed this connection (as well as some other members of the Investigation Section) were removed from the case. The state-run television service waged a campaign suggesting that the President's son actually organized his own abduction in order to escape criminal liability for financial fraud – a conclusion which contrasts with the opinion of the Austrian court that dealt with the case.

Recently the executive was granted new competences and extensive personnel changes were carried out in the state administration. Under the new law regulating the state administration, the Office of the Government was given the power to control the fulfilment of state administrative tasks. According to legal experts (Prusák, 1995), these steps violate the principle of separation of powers and herald the advent of a special form of concentrated 'executive-parliamentary' power.

The new territorial-administrative division of Slovakia

In March 1996 a new and controversial law on the administrative division of the country was passed. It was adopted without sufficient effort to reach a broad social consensus on such a crucial issue. There was no meaningful dialogue with the Hungarian minority or important institutions such as the Association of Towns and Villages of Slovakia or the Union of Towns. Not surprisingly, there have been some squabbles between towns in connection with the determination of district seats.[3]

While the government hails the measures associated with the new administrative division as part of a large-scale decentralization,[4] the opposition claims that they will strengthen the power of the local state administration at the expense of local self-government. The 2,500 new officials appointed by the government to the newly created posts were selected on the basis of their loyalty to the government rather than on merit and were seen as the clientelistic base of the ruling coalition. On the whole, the relationship between the central political power and the local self-governing bodies is problematic, at times verging on hostile.

Media[5]

During 1995–6 the government strove to increase its control over the media, especially the electronic ones. While it did not succeed in the case of the printed media, Slovak Television (STV), though a publicly owned institution, was transformed into a government mouthpiece. A 'monochromatic' board guaranteed this metamorphosis of independent journalism into government propaganda.

STV's exaggerated loyalty to the ruling coalition resulted in a decline in public trust in the institution. The less partisan Slovak Radio preserved greater credibility among its listeners. While STV has exerted influence over the majority of Slovakia's population, the diversification of television broadcasting continues. STV's dominant position changed in September 1996 when Slovakia's first commercial television station, TV Markíza, the latest entry from Central European Media Enterprise (CME), went on air with signal reaching 60 per cent of Slovak territory and achieved a rapid and continuing increase in the number of its viewers.

Although the government tries to influence the press both directly and indirectly (e.g. by regulating advertising), the printed media are rather pluralistic. However, about 30 per cent of the population do not read a newspaper.

Coping with the past

The crucial issue in the political discourse about the national identity has not been the communist period, but that of the wartime Slovak state (1939–45). Circles around the Matica Slovenská and the Ministry of Education, which are close to the SNS, openly strive to rehabilitate this state and its president Jozef Tiso, and to reduce his responsibility for the deportation of the Slovak Jews. However, this reinterpretation of history has not achieved sufficient political support and was officially rejected by the government and Prime Minister. The anti-fascist Slovak National Uprising of 1944, by contrast, is commemorated as the national holiday. The general public, according to opinion surveys, also reject the idea that Slovakia should seek value continuity with the wartime Slovak state. The most highly appreciated historical personalities are Alexander Dubček, a reformed Communist, known from the 'Prague Spring' of 1968, and Milan Rastislav Štefánik, the co-founder of Czechoslovakia.

The protagonists of the SNS and Matica Slovenská also emphasize the friction between Slovaks and Hungarians.

Minorities

Approximately 14 per cent of the population of Slovakia claim other than Slovak national or ethnic origin. The most numerous are the Hungarian minority, who, in the most recent census (taken in 1991), accounted for 10.76 per cent of the population. Hungarians are concentrated in southern Slovakia along the Hungarian border. The Roma are the second most numerous minority. In 1991 76,000 persons declared themselves to be of Roma ethnic origin, although the actual number is estimated to be several times higher. In the same census 59,300 persons claimed Czech origins. Other minorities include Ruthenians (17,200) and Ukrainians (13,300), most of whom live in eastern Slovakia. Among the smaller national minorities are ethnic Germans, Poles, Bulgarians and Russians. A relatively small Jewish community also lives in Slovakia.

Most national minorities have their own cultural associations, cultural institutions and periodical press. Only the two most numerous minorities have political representation. The Roma have several political groupings, none of which has significant influence or representation in the Parliament – a situation criticized by younger, educated Roma, who seek more efficient representation. The entities representing the Hungarian minority are of much greater political relevance, having 17 seats in the Parliament.

The rights of national minorities are laid down in articles 33 and 34 of the constitution. Under the constitution members of minorities and ethnic groups are guaranteed the right to develop, with other citizens of the same national minority, their own culture; to receive and disseminate information in their mother tongue; to form associations; to create and maintain educational and cultural institutions; and to participate in decisions affecting national minorities and ethnic groups.

There is a remarkable difference between the problems experienced by the Hungarian minority, the Roma minority and the less numerous minorities respectively. According to O. Dostál (1997),

> small minorities are faced with a problem of preserving their own identities, and their efforts are mainly in the cultural area. The Roma's problems are linked, in particular, to their socioeconomic situation and to the difference in lifestyles between them and the rest of the population. The Hungarian minority's concerns are connected with the place of ethnic Hungarians in the Slovak society and are manifested at the political level.

Developments between 1990 and 1996 have clearly shown that whereas the problems of the Hungarian minority (and of the other and smaller minorities) could be reduced by a more tolerant government policy towards minorities, the problems of the Roma are much deeper.

In 1995–6 the representatives of the Hungarian minority criticized the government for its confrontational policy and considered some laws (such as the Law on Territorial and Administrative Organization and the Law on the State Language) as limiting their rights. In 1995 they campaigned successfully against the Ministry of Education's proposal for 'alternative education', which had been prepared without consulting the Hungarian community.

Although intolerant acts aimed against the minorities (racism, anti-Semitism, extreme forms of nationalism) were no worse in Slovakia in 1995–6 than in other countries, Slovakia's problem is that while similar acts in other countries are confined to marginal political groupings, in Slovakia they are also manifested by some politicians from the ruling coalition. Democratically minded members of the population display a strikingly feeble response to such acts. Racist acts reached a new stage in 1995 when Slovakia recorded its first racially motivated murder.

Non-governmental organizations

During the inter-war period there were more than 16,000 associations in Slovakia, but associational life was suppressed by both authoritarian regimes. In view of the decades of political regimentation, since 1989 the third sector has recorded remarkable development (there were almost 6,000 NGOs registered in Slovakia in 1993 and 9,800 in 1994). In 1996 there were more than 15,000 organizations altogether; 9,976 of them were civil

associations – clubs, societies, movements, trade unions, and their organizational units – and 1,687 were foundations. These two types (civil
associations and foundations) manifest all the core characteristics of third-
sector organizations: they are organized, private, self-governing, non-profit
and voluntary. The remaining organizations are churches or religious
societies, interest associations of legal entities, political parties and professional associations.

Surveys have found 11 to 13 per cent of the population to be involved in
some kind of unpaid activity for an NGO and about a half the population to
be involved in some form of giving. There is a high level of self-organization:
there is the elected Gremium of the Third Sector, there are service-providing
clearing-houses and regular nation-wide conferences (Bútora *et al.*, 1997).

Despite the achievements of the past six years, challenges also face the
non-profit sector in Slovakia. It is not easy to reach a meaningful collabora-
tive partnership between the non-profit sector and the state in Slovakia, a
country with strong traditions of state paternalism. The campaign, in 1996,
against the bill on foundations drafted by the government and designed to
increase its control over the activities, resources, donors and representatives
of foundations was a test of Slovak society's capacity to defend itself against
the government's excessive tendency to control spontaneous public activity.
By joining the campaign many organizations 'came out of the shadows' and
had to redefine their missions and mobilize their resources. The campaign
generated a great deal of literature concerning what the third sector really is
and whom foundations and civic organizations serve (almost 12,000 articles
and/or short reports were written on the topic in 1996). The NGOs' activities
helped to improve the quality of the third sector as well as the quality of at
least one of the more recent laws passed to regulate the third sector (Law on
Non-investing Funds). The campaign has proved that the struggle to establish a civil society in Slovakia will be long and difficult. However, it is playing
a major role in the birth of a modern and democratic Slovakia.

A positive public attitude to NGOs was reflected in opinion surveys which
found that the majority of respondents considered foundations and other
NGOs to be useful and claimed that the state should create favourable
conditions for them. A surprisingly high proportion of the population would
be willing to volunteer in the future if they were asked.

Three new elements were visible during recent protests. First, different
segments of civil society strove to improve mutual networking and collaboration. Second, some of these actions were supported by the trade unions,
which tended to be more sensitive to broader political issues, not only to
economic and/or social agenda. Third, several protest meetings were co-

organized by political parties and civil activists, which could open the door to more efficient co-operation in the future.

Relations with Western Europe and towards the EU

As for foreign policy orientations, most of the population supports Slovakia's pro-European integration and pro-Western foreign policy. However, although not dominant, Slovakia's so-called 'own road of development', or neutrality, was conspicuously supported (one-third in favour) by adherents of the ruling coalition parties. Respondents recognize the discrepancy between the ruling coalition's actual policies and its proclaimed pro-integration stance. At the end of 1995, less than a third of Slovakia's residents believed that their country was actually heading towards the EU.

It has been repeatedly stressed by EU representatives that all countries intending to join the EU must respect human rights and democratic pluralism. Public opinion surveys have found that most people responded favourably to European criticisms of developments in Slovakia. In general Slovakia meets the formal criteria for integration better than those of a substantive nature. President Kováč, however, has expressed concern that the exclusion of Slovakia from integration could aggravate its domestic situation: 'We would find ourselves in even greater isolation from the surrounding world, we would lose the possibility of exerting a certain positive influence and a broader space would open for other than the democratic development in our country.'[6]

This is an issue not only for Slovakia. For a democratic West, it presents a challenge to formulate Europe's political, security and economic strategy anew, with democratic perspectives not only for the next members of the club, who will be adopted soon, but also for the current laggards. The mission is clear: to prevent the laggards from becoming the losers, to strengthen the democratic habits of the third-wave democracies. But after the changes in Bulgaria and Romania, Slovakia's democrats seem to understand better that the task of making the glass full again instead of half empty must, first and foremost, be accomplished at home.

Notes

1. Among other mentioned sources, this chapter draws on the results of several studies in Bútora and Hunčík (1997).
2. Generalizations used in this section are based on the studies by Pavel Machonin, Jiří Musil, Soňa Szomolanyi, Vladimír Krivý, Ján Pašiak *et al.*
3. Some of the arguments advanced in this dispute illustrate the increasing acceptance of clientelism in political culture. For instance, some advocates of a prospective new district noted that the Prime Minister had studied at the local

gymnasium while their rivals asserted that their town deserved to become a new district because it had registered one of the strongest showings for the ruling Movement for a Democratic Slovakia.

4. See the interview with A. M. Húska, vice-chairman of the HZDS and of the Parliament in *SME*, 23 August 1996.
5. This section uses data from Gindl (1997) and Gyárfášová (1996).
6. See an interview with him in *Pravda*, 7 September 1995.

8

Democracy in Hungary, 1990–97

ANDRÁS BOZÓKI

Introduction

In this chapter, I aim to describe the main social and political features of Hungarian democracy from the viewpoints of democratic theory and post-communist practice. My main point is that, in an institutional procedural sense of the term, Hungary is a 'fully democratic' country, and the existing deficits of democratic legitimacy stem not from the institutional arrangements, but from the 'simultaneity problem' (Elster, 1993), which is the need to (re)build a market economy and a democratic society in a parallel process. My focus is on Hungary, although most of my findings can be applied to all the Visegrád countries (the others being Poland, the Czech Republic and Slovakia).

Historical background

Hungary has never had as broad a democracy as it has now. Between 1867 and 1918 it was a part of the dualist system of Austria-Hungary, which was a constitutional regime but did not guarantee universal suffrage. From 1919 to March 1944, Hungary had an old-fashioned, irredentist, authoritarian regime, albeit with some limited democratic features – elements of a *Rechtstaat*; a multi-party system, including the legalization of the Social Democratic Party; and relative freedom of the press (until 1938) – but it was far from being a democracy. Nazi Germany invaded the country in March 1944 and imposed puppet governments until April 1945.

The period 1945–7 can be regarded as a huge step towards democracy. In the free elections of 1945, an absolute majority of voters supported the centrist Smallholders' Party. Nevertheless, the Soviet forces occupying the country firmly backed the Communist Party and forced the Smallholders' Party to form a grand coalition with the Communists, Social Democrats and the pro-communist Peasant Party. The 1947 elections were almost free, but far from fair. The quick turn from limited multi-party democracy to the party–state rule of Bolshevik totalitarianism took place in 1948.

Between 1948 and 1989, communist one-party rule existed in Hungary. From 1948 to 1963 communist rule can be regarded as totalitarian; from 1963 to 1989 it was post-totalitarian, paternalist, liberalizing and authoritarian. The twelve days of the 1956 democratic revolution did not allow enough time for elections, which is why one is justified in saying that the 1990 elections were the first really free and fair elections in Hungarian history.

The communist legacy is mixed but non-democratic. Communism urbanized and industrialized Hungarian society; some welfare policies were introduced, and, in its second phase, there was a reformist process of liberalization in non-political (economic, cultural and leisure) activities, although the political monopoly of the party–state was maintained. From the 1970s onwards, members of the nascent underground opposition lost their jobs or could not study in the main universities, but they were rarely imprisoned. By exercising their human rights in a challenging manner, the opposition contributed to the emergence of public consciousness concerning human rights, minority rights and civil liberties (Csizmadia, 1995). The nature and impact of the communist centrally planned modernization are still the subject of heated debates, but there is no doubt that Hungary was economically closer to 'Europe' in 1938 than in 1990.

Constitutional problems and parliamentary democracy

Hungary's constitutional–legal system was crafted in 1989 during the trilateral negotiations between the ruling Hungarian Socialist Workers' Party (MSZMP), the Opposition Roundtable (nine opposition parties) and the 'Third Side' (the then satellite organizations of the MSZMP). The new constitution kept the structure of the old one, but it was substantially revised, sentence by sentence. It was accepted and declared on 23 October 1989, a few months before the first free elections. From then on, the Republic of Hungary may be regarded, constitutionally, as a *Rechtstaat*, or law-based state. Some remaining political questions were solved by the November 1989 referendum, and the constitution was amended in the summer of 1990, following an agreement between the two biggest parties, the Hungarian Democratic Forum (MDF) and the Alliance of Free Democrats (SZDSZ).

The Hungarian transition process was in many respects very similar to the Spanish transition during the later 1970s. After 1994 the Hungarian Socialist Party (MSZP)–SZDSZ coalition government committed itself to elaborate a new, 'final' constitution in co-operation with the opposition parties. Although the constitutional moment had already gone, they created a special committee in the Parliament to do the preparatory work.

Constitution-making was viewed by the coalition as a legal and policy question which most people were not interested in or did not recognize as important. No wonder that the constitution-making process seems to be deadlocked at the time of writing (the summer of 1996).

Hungary has a parliamentary democracy, not a presidential one. The president possesses primarily symbolic functions.

Major constitutional debates have occurred in three areas: the appointment and discharge of the heads of the media offices; the extent of the president's foreign policy powers; and the interpretation of the president's role as commander-in-chief of the armed forces. These debates are somehow natural in the new democracy, especially since the Hungarian constitution does not clearly delineate the relationship between the head of government and head of state. The Constitutional Court's rulings have attempted to dispel confusion over the interpretation of the law and have tended to cut back the president's powers.

The constitutional debate has centred on institutional questions, rather than on personalities. For the first time in the history of the Hungarian constitution, the head of state completed his five-year tenure of office and participated in the first democratic transfer of power. In the summer of 1995 Árpád Göncz was re-elected president.

Hungary has a parliamentary tradition, which continued after the 1990 elections. The six main parties remained in Parliament after the second elections in 1994. The Hungarian Parliament conducts its work through plenary sessions, standing committees and special committees. One of the standing committees is concerned with European integration affairs, and enjoys high prestige.

The key decision-making figure is the prime minister. Individual ministers are responsible to the Parliament only as members of the Cabinet. The Parliament cannot dismiss a minister even if he or she is unable to answer questions. The prime minister is responsible for the activity of the Cabinet, and only he or she can make changes to it. The constitution introduced the constructive no-confidence motion, which enables a simple majority of the Parliament to dismiss the prime minister, but only if they are able to nominate a replacement at the same time.

This makes the position of the prime minister constitutionally very strong. (Some observers even feared the office would hold too great a concentration of power.) The Parliament has not thus far replaced the prime minister in the way describe above. In this sense the Hungarian prime minister has constitutional powers and entitlements similar to those of the German *Bundeskanzler*. The above-mentioned clashes between Prime Minister József Antall and President Árpád Göncz could be judged as inevitable consequences of some not very clearly formulated paragraphs of the constitution. These conflicts had to be clarified by a new, and important, institution, the Constitutional Court.

The Constitutional Court (following the Austrian–German model) was set up in January 1990 as an outgrowth of the trilateral negotiations. Some judges were selected by the negotiating partners and some (a little later) by the newly elected Parliament. The appointments are for nine years and can be renewed once. The court has exceptionally wide jurisdiction. In fact, it became the functional equivalent of a second legislative chamber. The Constitutional Court has taken the standpoint that Hungary has been governed by the rule of law since 23 October 1989, which means that all regulations concerning the consequences of the communist past must stay within the framework of the rule of law. In some cases, justice and legality contradicted each other, and the court always emphasized the importance of the latter. It resisted all claims that sought to extend retrospectively the rule of law, which resulted from the negotiated transition. Some politicians and legal scholars have blamed the court for its activism (Pokol, 1994). In the final analysis, however, one can claim that the court has significantly contributed to the spread of legal consciousness in Hungarian society and, by so doing, has strengthened the belief in liberal democracy.

Political culture, political cleavages and the party system

The Hungarian transformation was a peaceful, elite-controlled change, a 'negotiated revolution' (Bruszt, 1990). Opposition leaders (writers, historians, philosophers, sociologists and constitutional lawyers) and reform-oriented young technocrats played crucial roles in the process. The claim for a regime change came from the idea of 'radical reform', which was a kind of common denominator for these groups during the 1980s. This idea has had a positive impact on the political culture: it has promoted the acceptance of such principles as non-violence, self-restraint, political pragmatism and readiness for negotiations. All the political leaders – radicals, moderates, reformists or supporters of the status quo – wanted to avoid violent solutions.

On the other hand, the prevalence of humanistic intellectuals in the transition process strengthened the temporary revival of an old cultural division in the Hungarian intellectuals: the populist–urbanist cleavage. This cleavage gave a tribal character to some party elites, especially the MDF and the SZDSZ. Early MDF leaders committed themselves to the idea of a 'third way' between Soviet communism and Western consumerism and wanted to develop a new Hungarian identity which refused both. On the other hand, SZDSZ leaders advocated the pattern of Western liberal democracies and described other directions as provincial. This division infected the elite politics of the first two years of Hungarian democracy. Nevertheless, this was not a real social cleavage, as it was first termed by Lipset and Rokkan (1968), since the overwhelming majority of the voters were not interested in these issues at all. This is one reason why the pragmatic Federation of Young Democrats (FIDESZ) was popular during the years between the two elections, and why the pragmatic, former communist MSZP gained victory in 1994. People became bored by the decade (1985–94) of symbolic politics and turned to those parties that remained untouched by these ideological politics. Hungarian political culture is characterized by its moderation; voters always prefer moderate, centrist politics, opposing all kinds of extremism. Three types of parties can be distinguished in the Hungarian party system according to their ideological stances: the Christian-conservative, the liberal, and the socialist.

The Christian–conservative bloc

The most important party in the Christian-conservative bloc is the Hungarian Democratic Forum (MDF), established in September 1988. Between 1990 and 1994 it was the senior partner – the others being the Christian Democratic People's Party (KDNP) and the Independent Smallholders' Party (FKGP) (till 1992) – in the governing coalition. It started as a 'third way' movement, but party leader József Antall remoulded it in a Christian–conservative–national liberal image. There was always a tension between the more radical grass-roots of the party and the conservative leadership. This led to the secession of the right-radical István Csurka and his group in 1993.[1] After the death of Prime Minister József Antall in December 1993, Péter Boross succeeded him as prime minister and party-president. In the 1994 elections, the MDF received only 12 per cent of the votes and became an opposition party. Internal fights divided the party, and, in February 1996, a clash between the radical and moderate wings led to formal separation. Sándor Lezsák, founder of the MDF, took over the party, while the 'national liberals', led by Iván Szabó, left the MDF and founded the new, less significant, Hungarian Democratic People's Party (MDNP).

Another party in this bloc is the Christian Democratic People's Party (KDNP), which was re-established in March 1989 and became a junior partner in the first post-communist coalition government. It is based on the religious (mostly Catholic) constituency, which has provided a rather small but solid foundation. Its support is strongest among older, rural, uneducated, religious and female voters. This is a major problem for the party leadership since the party's capacity to increase its popularity is thus limited. On the other hand, its support is (and will be) strong enough to push the party over the 5 per cent threshold. The Christian Democrats, led by László Surján

(1990–5) and György Giczy (since 1995), are also members of the European Democratic Union (EDU).

The FKGP has a rather dubious ideological character. It won the 1945 elections with a centre-right, plebeian, moderate and agrarian profile. It was re-established in November 1988, and received 12 per cent of the vote in the 1990 elections, supported mainly by an uneducated, agrarian, older male constituency. The FKGP started in government as the MDF's junior coalition partner. In 1991, however, József Torgyán, a populist leader, took over the party and took it out of the coalition in February 1992. Since then, it has been in the opposition. Torgyán reformulated the FKGP into a truly populist party with a charismatic leader and a rather incoherent political pro-gramme. It is economically on the left but culturally on the right. Voters who feel disappointed about the change of regime find the FKGP attractive, and, with the support of those who have lost out in the transformation, the party has increased its popularity to 25 per cent, according to public opinion surveys. It is unlikely, however, that all these protest voters will remain faithful to the party at the next election.

In summary, the Christian–conservative–national camp has based itself on the non-secular and older voters, but it holds only 23 per cent of the seats in the present Parliament. (It had almost 60 per cent of the seats between 1990 and 1994.) These parties sought an identity for the new Hungarian democracy in the pre-communist past. They created a new, symbolic politics, but were reluctant to compromise with the younger, technocratic intelli-gentsia of the late-communist regime. They tended to over-ideologize political issues. Probably all these factors contributed to their electoral defeat of 1994. Today the division between populist radicalism and moderate centre-right conservatism is sharp, and seems unbridgeable.

The liberal camp

The liberal camp consists of two parties. The larger, the Alliance of Free Democrats (SZDSZ), is the descendant of the underground democratic oppo-sition of the 1980s. Founded in November 1988, it is liberal both economically and socially. It has a solid constituency among the urban, secularized, educated, younger and more cosmopolitan voters, who reject both the pre-communist and the communist pasts and seek to implement a truly Western model. According to the SZDSZ's critics, copying the West in a backward country can lead to an unintended contrary consequence, such as to a society sharply divided between an 'enlightened', Western-oriented, well-to-do *comprador* elite and everyone else living in poor conditions. The harsh economic liberalism of the party has been softened, and the SZDSZ has recently taken a rather social-liberal stance. That change made it possible to reformulate the party's identity, bridging the anti-communist and 'anti-anti-communist' cleavage. The originally heavily anti-communist party membership finally accepted the party elite's decision to enter a coalition government with the former communist socialists (MSZP) in 1994. The constituency of the party has remained stable: the SZDSZ won 21 per cent of the votes in 1990 and 20 per cent in 1994. It spent the first four years in opposition, as the senior opposition party, and since 1994 it has been the MSZP's junior partner in the socialist–liberal coalition government. The SZDSZ's president has been Iván Petö since 1992.

The second liberal party is the Federation of Young Democrats (FIDESZ), which was one of the most curious phenomena of the regime change. Founded in March 1988, the party started as a radical, anti-communist youth organization, but later, as a party, received 9 per cent of the vote in the 1990 elections. This is the only parliamentary party which has been continuously in opposition since 1990. The original age limit (35 years) for membership was lifted in 1993, when the party changed its character from being a radical–liberal– alternative–pragmatist party with a strong commitment to market liberalism to becoming a centre-right moderate– pragmatist party. This change of image hurt FIDESZ. Protest voters had greatly liked the party during the years 1991–3 because it was different from all other parties and represented a fresh spirit. During that period FIDESZ was by far the most popular party in Hungary, receiving support from 35–40 per cent of respondents to opinion polls. Yet it gained only 7 per cent of the vote in the 1994 elections. After the elections the representation of Hungarian liberalism became politically divided, with the SZDSZ entering the government and FIDESZ remaining in opposition, refusing the invitation of the socialists to participate in government. Despite the catastrophic election results, the party, under the leadership of Viktor Orbán, maintained its move to the right. It is now both economically and culturally on the right, although the party has softened its former harsh market liberalism and is still much more secular than religious. In the spring 1995 it changed its name to FIDESZ–Hungarian Civic Party (FIDESZ–MPP) and sought closer co-operation with other centre-right parties under the name Civic Alliance. The alliance did not work out, however, and the party must prepare for the next election alone.

The socialists

The former communist Hungarian Socialist Party (MSZP) is really the only socialist player in town. The party is the legal successor of the ruling Communist Party of the dictatorship (MSZMP). It renamed itself in October

1989 and adopted social democratic values. The MSZMP already had a reformist image in the 1980s, and the party was an arena for the struggle between the old communists and bureaucrats on the one hand, and the emerging younger pragmatic technocrats on the other. During 1988–9 the technocratic soft-liners slowly but surely marginalized the 'old comrades' and became more open to reform. They initiated economic reforms first, but the emerging 'reform circles' of the party pushed forward the idea of political reform as well. The relative openness of the Communist Party helped the negotiated, non-violent transition. Younger party experts soon realized that they could be winners, not losers, in the transition. The phenomenon of spontaneous privatization, during 1988–9, marked the beginning of so-called 'original capital-accumulation' by the *nomenklatura*. Despite the reform steps of the party, voters did not reward them in the first elections, in which the MSZP gained just over 10 per cent of the vote. Between 1990 and 1992 the party lived in a political ghetto, but it remained strong in its local organizations and presence.

When the political mood of the general public moved away from symbolic politics, voters found no better alternative than the MSZP for pragmatic policies expertly carried out. The party won some by-elections in 1992–3, and by early 1994 was the most popular political force. In the 1994 elections it received 33 per cent of the vote, which provided it with an absolute (54 per cent) majority of the seats in the Parliament. Paradoxically both winners (non-ideological technocrats, managers, business-oriented people) and losers (the older, urban, secular, uneducated, former Communist Party members, unemployed and pensioners) voted for the MSZP. The contradictory expectations of these groups have made it hard for the party to please both. Although it could have governed alone, it offered a coalition partnership to the SZDSZ in order to share the responsibility for unpopular policies and to bridge the communist–non-communist gap. After long hesitation, Prime Minister Gyula Horn, who always liked to play the role of man-of-the-people, committed the government to large-scale privatization, and even supported Lajos Bokros's harsh economic stabilization package. The major achievement of the MSZP and Gyula Horn himself is that the party is still one of the most popular parties in Hungary, despite a dramatic 10 per cent decrease in real wages in 1995.

Apart from the reformist MSZP, the old Hungarian Social Democratic Party (MSZDP) was also re-established (in January 1989). Largely because of bitter internal fights, it has failed to pass the threshold for parliamentary representation. Some communists had continued to operate inside the extreme-left MSZMP, which later changed its name to Workers' Party (MP). It too has failed to enter Parliament, although it is still probably the strongest extra-parliamentary party, with roughly 3 per cent of the vote.

To sum up, the characteristic feature of the Hungarian party system is that it has three poles: Christian–conservatives are culturally right-wing, economically closer to the left than to the right; liberals are now culturally divided (although both secular), but economically right-wing; socialists are culturally left-wing and economically ambivalent. During the first four years of the new democracy, cultural divisions played a bigger role than economic ones. In foreign policy, those parties which are closer to the economic right (SZDSZ, FIDESZ–MPP, MDF, MDNP, MSZP) are also much more pro-European and pro-NATO than the others. Extremist extra-parliamentary parties are divided along cultural left–right lines, but are very similar in their support for leftist, autarkic economic policies, their opposition to European integration and their advocacy of neutrality.

Herbert Kitschelt (1995) recently differentiated between three types of parties: programmatic, charismatic and clientelistic. Using his typology for the Hungarian party system, I would say that the SZDSZ, MDF, MP and KDNP are roughly programmatic; the FKGP and MIEP are charismatic; and the MSZP, MDNP and FIDESZ–MPP are clientelistic.

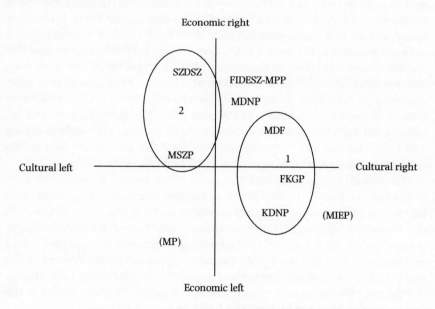

Figure 8.1 A 'map' of Hungarian political parties

Figure 8.1 summarizes the ideological locations of the different parties. It also reveals that ideological (left–right) and political (government–opposition) maps are not necessarily the same. The first group of parties (1) constituted the governing coalition after the free elections of 1990. The core of the MDF around József Antall was culturally and economically on the right, while the KDNP and FKGP were culturally on the right but economically closer to the left. The second group of parties is the MSZP–SZDSZ coalition elected in 1994 (2). It too is not very homogeneous. The MSZP is a coalition in itself: a meeting-place of trade unionists, the business elite, people from the lower classes and from the technocracy. The party is culturally on the left, but economically in between. The SZDSZ is slightly to the left culturally, while clearly on the right economically. The MP on the extreme left and the Hungarian Justice and Life Party (MIEP) on the extreme right are not represented in the Parliament, while the centrist FIDESZ (FIDESZ–MPP) is the only parliamentary party which has not taken part in any governing coalitions.

The role of the media

The degree to which the media were controlled during the 1980s was selective. Sometimes the authorities were tolerant, but the most important media were still under the strict control of the Communist Party. Journalists in the official media remained basically loyal until 1988. The emergence of *samizdat* journals in the early 1980s created a second public sphere, and this duality existed until the regime disintegrated. The rigid borderline separating the two kinds of press began to weaken in the mid-1980s, and a 'grey zone' appeared in low-circulation periodicals (Bozóki, 1995). The 'culture of critical discourse' (Gouldner, 1979) was replacing party jargon, and an alliance between the new 'politocracy' and the 'mediacracy' evolved during 1988–9. The normative model that inspired the journalists and media experts was the practice of openness in Western societies.

The Antall government and the party elites behind it suspected most journalists of loyalty to the previous regime. Some formerly communist journalists realized that their only means of survival was to move closer to the liberals in criticizing the government; while most journalists simply wanted to do their job well. By confusing these two groups, the Antall government alienated itself from the main opinion-forming centres of the mass media. The government wanted to control the media administratively, but did not care about how it appeared in the media. This tension led to the 'media war', which lasted from 1991 to 1994.

The roundtable negotiations had not been able to solve the problem of media control. Media privatization was frozen, the result being a lack of competition in the information market (Bozóki, 1993). No wonder, then, that the main battles of the 'media war' centred around the control of public radio and television. Most journalists working in these media fought for independent, government-free media, and the opposition parties also took this stance. The first presidents of radio and television, who had been nominated and accepted consensually, were forced to resign in January 1993. MDF and KDNP radicals vigorously criticized the state-sponsored mass media. In the last year of the first electoral term a group of rightist journalists (even to the right of the centre-right government) sacked 129 journalists and took over the most important news magazines. This tough course provoked a boomerang effect in the 1994 elections, in which the coalition parties lost out. The sacked journalists returned and now they dominate the public media.

The socialist-liberal government is using softer and more indirect forms of media control: big firms do not advertise in opposition dailies; non-opposition publishers bought some opposition magazines (which still represent the voices of opposition, but in a much softer, less critical way). So the post-1994 government tries to utilize the difficult economic situation of these newspapers to soften their criticism. The present newspaper market is not one-sided, but it is unbalanced. The economic power of the left-liberal papers is much greater than that of the much poorer centre-right magazines. By the end of 1995 the Parliament adopted the Media Act, which abolished this unconstitutional situation (as the Constitutional Court had declared it). Freedom of the press and the freedom of information do exist as civil liberties in Hungary, although the media tend to be too loyal to the present left-liberal government. This relative loyalty was gained not by censorship, but by economic influence.

Civil society, intermediary bodies and the role of NGOs

During the 1980s the notion of civil society had a variety of meanings. First, it was understood to be an arena, independent of the state, in which autonomous civic initiatives could emerge. Second, it was regarded as a liberating force against the oppressive state. Third, it was connected to a sort of political consciousness-raising, critical discourse in which the attitudes and virtues of the *citoyen* could be exercised. Civic courage and civility were the primary focuses of this understanding. Fourth, the emerging second economy was also understood to be a civil society, because it brought some independence from the state for its participants. According to this interpretation, the process of embourgeoisement and bourgeois values in general were emphasized. The second economy, in short, was the 'small capitalism' of 'socialist entrepreneurs' (Szelényi, 1988). To sum up, the term 'civil society' was a 'new evolutionist' political strategy of liberation (invented by the Polish opposition), rather than a well-defined social science concept (Szöcs, 1996).

The flourishing club life, the emerging political networks, the peace and environmental movements, loose coalitions and successful symbolic politics gave the participants the ecstatic feeling that a victorious civil society was going to take over communism. What actually happened was that the movements turned into political parties on the eve of the regime change (Jenkins, 1992). Those intellectuals who had been the major proponents of an independent civil society suddenly found themselves in the new party elites, following and representing particular political interests. Although political pluralization seems necessary and inevitable during the transition to democracy, it became clear that, in a political vacuum, many intellectuals had been sucked into party politics, and without them civil society remained very weak.

One of the victims of this speedy party formation was the Democratic League of Independent Trade Unions (FSZDL), which failed to capitalize on a historic opportunity to replace the ex-communist trade unions as the primary representative of employees' interests. By the time of the 1993 trade union elections the opportunity had passed, and the ex-communist National Federation of Hungarian Trade Unions (MSZOSZ) enjoyed a sweeping victory, thus anticipating the results of the 1994 parliamentary elections.

In the first years of democracy, a new, hyperactive political class could be found in Hungary. And although a lively political society (composed of intellectuals and represented by some daily newspapers and weekly magazines) surrounded it, civil society at the grass-roots level was weak. Disappointed individuals and groups faced a new, self-confident power, enjoying the democratic legitimacy of popular election.

The meaning of civil society has changed in the last few years. It is no longer a rebellion against the oppressive state, but a self-organizing society existing alongside the democratic state. It is wider than just the non-profit sector, because it includes those who aim to make elected politicians accountable (i.e. lobbying groups), but the main thrust of its activity consists of non-governmental organizations (NGOs) helping independent initiatives.

The number of associations grew very fast after the collapse of communism: there were 8,396 associations in 1989 and 22,926 by the end of 1993. Even more spectacular was the development of foundations: 400 in 1989, 11,884 by the end of 1993. Most associations and foundations are active in cultural, educational and leisure activities. Thirty per cent of the non-profit organizations operate in Budapest, even though 72 per cent of income is concentrated in Budapest (Bullain, 1996).

The non-profit sector is still heavily dependent on the state, although the share of non-state income is continuously increasing. Recently, some civic organizations have emerged that aim to control the activity of the state:

offering legal assistance (the National and Ethnic Minorities' Legal Defence Centre; the Hungarian Centre for Defence of Human Rights), monitoring the military and legislation concerning it (Alba Circle); watching the independent public sphere (Fekete Doboz [Black Box], Publicity Club). Nevertheless, the formation of a new democratic political community, which is neither an atomized society enjoying negative freedom, nor the symbolic community of the nationalist right, is just beginning.

Role of the churches

Hungary is a rather secular country. Fewer than 20 per cent of people regularly go to church. About 60 per cent of the population claim to believe, in one way or another, in God. Traditionally, the Roman Catholic Church is the most influential of the churches, embracing two-thirds of believers. Since the time of St Stephen, the founder of the Hungarian state, Roman Catholicism has represented, in a way, Hungary's ties to the West. Catholicism is dominant in central and western Hungary, roughly the area west of the river Tisza. The Catholic Church was westward-looking and loyal to the Habsburgs. It was not a strong supporter of Hungarian nationalism or the idea of an independent Hungary, which is why it played no important political role during the post-Trianon Horthy regime. Under communism the Catholic Church was oppressed and controlled. Its imprisoned conservative leader, Cardinal Mindszenty, became a symbol (mostly for believers) of spiritual resistance to communism. In the immediate post-communist period the Catholic Church did not get involved in everyday politics, although its support for the newly formed Christian Democratic People's Party (KDNP) and the Catholic wing of the Hungarian Democratic Forum (MDF) was clear. The first democratically elected prime minister, József Antall, a Christian–conservative politician, was convinced that 'only a country basing itself on Christian values has a future'. Since the return of 'rebaptized' communists to power, the Catholic Church has played an even less active role in politics.

The second largest church is the Hungarian Protestant Church (Református), which has historically represented a commitment to national independence and resistance to the Habsburgs. The Protestant Church is dominant east of the Tisza and among the ethnic Hungarians in Transylvania. For the latter group, Protestantism is part of their Hungarian identity. Communism treated the Protestant Church as badly as the Catholic one. During the period of regime change the Protestant Church was not politically active, although it supported the MDF. This party, early in its development, had a plebeian, Protestant, reformist orientation with a strong emphasis on national values and democracy, which was attractive to the Protestant

Church. As a young MDF leader of the time put it, 'Let's go to Europe – but with all of us!' Protestants tended to be suspicious of the elite-controlled modernization and democratization, sometimes regarding this modernizing elite as a comprador bourgeoisie or as agents of foreign interests.

Hungary also has an important Jewish minority, concentrated in Budapest. During the Nazi occupation most of the Hungarian Jews in the countryside were sent to extermination camps. Unlike in the other CEECs, however, most of the Jews living in the capital avoided mass arrest and the Holocaust. Part of this community left Hungary for Israel in the late 1940s. Nevertheless, there are still about 100,000 people in Budapest who consider themselves culturally Jewish, although only a minority are religious, belonging to the Israelite Community. In the post-1989 period the religious Jewish community was cautious and did not play any political role, although a rabbi was elected to Parliament on the liberal SZDSZ's list. Outside politics, however, a remarkable cultural and religious revival of this community could be seen.

Eastern past, western future?

Historically, Hungarians have often defined themselves as being between East and West: an island of people with a unique language and identity. But clearly they prefer to see themselves as the last bastion of the West, having defended continental Europe from the Tartars and Ottoman Turks, and as those who sacrificed themselves under Soviet rule for the luckier fate of the West. Under communism, on the other hand, Hungary was often known as the 'happiest barrack of the camp', the most Western-oriented country of the East. Although, under communism, the idea of 'Finlandization' (which meant neutrality and the retention of sovereignty) represented the most optimistic aspiration, in fact most Hungarians do not like this *cordon sanitaire* status. Now they want to push forward 'Finlandization', following Finland into the EU. Their other model is Austria, with its wealth and its softer, well-elaborated conflict resolution process.

As I mentioned before, the parties in Hungary's current ruling coalition government are strongly pro-European; having joined the Organization for Economic Co-operation and Development (OECD) in 1996, they seek membership of the EU and NATO. The opposition sometimes accuses them of being willing to sacrifice the interests of ethnic Hungarians living in neighbouring states in order to achieve that goal. The MDF and KDNP (now both in opposition) are also pro-European, but the issue of the ethnic Hungarians abroad is equally important. They do not use the term 'Europeanization', because to them Europe is not a programme of modernization: rather it is a geographical area where people follow civic and Christian values (Wolek,

1996). The populist FKGP follows an ambivalent policy on Europe: while it prefers the reconstruction of Hungary's national identity, it sometimes supports American, Korean, Japanese and Taiwanese investments in order to counterbalance Europe's influence. Only two parties – the MIEP on the far right and the MP on the far left, neither of which is represented in Parliament[2] – oppose integration into Western institutions. Now that people have experienced the heavy burden of economic transition, the enthusiastic pro-integration mood of the population has declined somewhat, but, according to a recent poll, fewer than 20 per cent of respondents would vote against integration.

Hungarian voters are rather moderate and centrist. The war in Croatia and Bosnia, as well as the dissolution of Czechoslovakia, negatively affected the international image of Central and Eastern Europe, including Hungary, regardless of the wishes of the Hungarians. Five of Hungary's seven neighbours are new nation-states, struggling with the problems of national identity, state-building and elite-settlement. Still, the emerging nationalisms in the region had little effect on the electoral behaviour of the Hungarians. Having regained their freedom, what Hungarians want is simply a better life.

The present post-communist democracy is characterized not by the rise of nationalism, but rather by the lack of ideas. Neither breakdown nor miracle is the most probable future scenario. More likely is the maintenance of democracy under worsening conditions. The future will be less dramatic and less attractive than predicted: the accommodation and longevity of weak democracies seem likely to occur in Central and Eastern Europe in the future (Greskovits, 1996).

The main problem comes from the simultaneity of changes. The consequences of economic transformation impoverished half of Hungarian society, including most members of the middle class. In 1995 Hungarians suffered a 10 per cent decline in real wages as a result of the government's austerity programme. Such a shocking decline in wages last occurred in 1951. Nevertheless, society remained patient: no strikes, no hunger-strikes, no riots. The Hungarian experience of transformation does not offer, by any means, a less painful 'solution' to simultaneous economic and political transformation, the so-called 'simultaneity problem'. The new democracy is built on the patience of the poor.

Some recent examples of democratization do not exclude the possibility that poverty and democracy, for a while at least, can go hand in hand. Although wealth certainly increases the likelihood of successful democratization, it is not a pre-condition for it. Democracy can be established in poverty, but, in the longer run, poverty can undermine and delegitimize democratic institutions (Przeworski *et al.*, 1996), particularly if elected officials tend to use their terms in office to benefit private interests as well as achieving public goals. The lack of a clear borderline between public and private spheres creates a hotbed of corruption, which further undermines democratic values. The main problem facing Hungarian democracy today is the informal and uncontrolled interpenetration of economy and politics. The process of allocating economic and political goods is under pressure from non-institutionalized interests. Civil society, independent journalists, even the police cannot really counteract this opportunity structure of invisible pressures. The heavy presence of this phenomenon stems from the simultaneity problem.

Now, for many Hungarian citizens, the desire to join Europe in the foreseeable future serves as a substitute for rapid economic development. People still have expectations for democracy, but economic development is one of the most important factors, beyond democratic commitment, in maintaining and deepening democratic legitimacy (Meyer, 1994; Przeworski *et al.*, 1996).

Hungarians are not particularly well informed about the structure and internal conflicts of the EU and they do not know too much about the competing conceptions of the future of the EU. People, tired of the economic burdens, want to see the light at the end of the tunnel. They regard European integration as an important condition for further steps towards a better life.

Notes

1. Csurka later formed a new party, the Hungarian Justice and Life Party (MIEP), which failed to pass the threshold to enter Parliament in 1994.
2. Both are marginal parties, having won only 1.5 and 3 per cent of the vote respectively in the 1994 elections.

9

Slovenia: From Yugoslavia to the Middle of Nowhere?

TONČI KUZMANIĆ

Introduction

A national programme for a united Slovenia was written in 1848 and the first political parties appeared towards the end of the nineteenth century. After World War II Slovenia became one of the six republics of the Socialist Federal Republic of Yugoslavia. It was the most Westernized and most developed part of the country.

After the long Yugoslav crisis more than 88 per cent of voters voted for independence in December 1990. In July 1991 the Yugoslav People's Army terminated its ten-day military involvement in Slovenia, signing the Brioni Declaration. In December 1991 the Slovene constitution was adopted, in January 1992 the European Union (EU) officially recognized Slovenia and in May the country joined the United Nations. In November 1992 the first elections were held. The EU has concluded an association agreement with Slovenia.

Constitutional aspects

In formal terms, there are almost no serious deficiencies in the Slovene constitution (as is true of almost all Slovene legislation) which could cause discrimination in the country's society. In contrast to other former Yugoslav republics, for example, the Slovene constitution starts from the premise that Slovenia is the 'state of Slovene citizens' and not the 'state of the Slovene nation'.

None the less, one of the central problems concerning the Slovene constitution is the introduction of the concept of so-called 'autochthonous national minorities'. The idea dates back to socialist Yugoslavia and the situation immediately after World War II. The concept was established in order to promote a relatively liberal, Western-oriented foreign policy. For Slovenia the concept applied primarily to Italians and Hungarians, through whom the Yugoslav government tried to create channels of communication with the West and to protect Slovene minorities in Italy, Austria and Hungary.

After the inauguration of the Slovene Republic as an independent state, the concept remained in force. In the changed circumstances the once liberal concept of 'autochthonous national minorities' has created its own contradictions. The concept continued to apply to Hungarians and Italians but not to people from other former republics. These people, approximately 200,000 persons, do not officially exist. The point is that the very fact that Italians and Hungarians enjoy a special status opens up the possibility of future conflicts.

During the past ten years or so, there have been numerous human rights groups in Slovenia. Moreover, the process of developing the Slovene state was, in a way, carried out through human rights activities. This tradition led to the creation of the National Council for Human Rights, the main human rights institution in Slovenia. In 1994 the National Assembly dissolved the council and inaugurated the office of human rights ombudsman; its holder reports to the National Assembly. The ombudsman is responsible for protecting human rights and fundamental freedoms in matters involving public authorities. The first Slovene ombudsman was elected in September 1994.

The division of power and judicial reorganization

There are no serious difficulties concerning the separation of powers in Slovenia. Clear distinctions between the judicial, executive and constitutional branches of power function properly. The most serious problem concerns the judicial branch. In particular, market forces are adversely affecting the judicial sphere. An enormous number of attorneys are leaving the state sector and starting their own private enterprises, mainly on the basis of knowledge and connections gained during their previous state employment. The 'Westernization' of Slovene law and judicial practice has resulted in lengthy delays. Thousands and thousands of cases are awaiting hearings.

The reasons behind these processes should be understood on the basis of the deeper transition from the labour-based and -structured law of the previous system to the civil-based law of the current system, accompanied by judicial reorganization. The rapid growth of crime, especially 'economic' crime, exacerbates the problems besetting the judicial branch. Corruption and clientelism are part of the post-socialist climate.

Political parties and political space

The Slovene party system can be described in traditional terms as a sufficiently stable division between three political positions: centre, left and right, where the centre is the largest party. There are eight political parties in the

Slovene Parliament. Three occupy the political centre. Two of them are liberal parties: the Liberal Democracy of Slovenia (LDS, 30 deputies) and the Democratic Party of Slovenia (four deputies). The other is the Slovene National Party (four deputies). The former communist Associated List of Social Democrats (fifteen deputies) occupies the left wing (or semi-left wing) of the Slovene party space. New types of left-wing politics in Slovenia are to be found only among individuals and some groups that are not yet politically organized.

By contrast, the political right is composed of traditional and new political forces. The traditional right is represented by the Slovene Christian Democrats (fifteen deputies) and the Slovene People's Party, formerly the Peasants' Party (twelve deputies). The new (anti-political) right is composed of the Slovene National Right (three deputies) and the Social Democratic Party of Slovenia (four deputies). The Italian and Hungarian 'autochthonous national minorities' each have one representative.

Slovene post-socialist party divisions, like those in other post-socialist systems, are hardly comparable with those found in Western societies. This is illustrated, for example, by the presence of the Social Democratic Party on the political right (Janez Janša is leader of the party). This situation can be attributed to the serious problems regarding the exacting process of transition from the one-party system into the pluralist parliamentary mechanisms of post-socialism.

Ten years ago the situation in Slovenia was much more pluralistic and an enormous number of individual and collective political subjects were debated. Today the Slovene political scene is occupied by political parties which all have more or less hierarchical organizations based on crude discipline and centralization. Slovenian democracy could be described as a sort of 'partitocracy'. Ordinary people, who were partially politically socialized during the 1980s, feel that this is not what they wanted. The reduction of politics and political space to party politics is building up serious anti-political (including anti-parliamentary and anti-democratic) feelings. Moreover, this factor could contribute to the rise of extreme right-wing feelings, which, according to public opinion surveys, are growing.

Government and opposition

The current Slovene government is the third democratically elected government since 1990. The first was the DEMOS[1] coalition led by the Christian Democrat Lojze Peterle. During the past three years there have been various governing combinations of Liberal Democrats (under President Dr Janez Drnovšek) with Christian Democrats and the Associated List of Social Democrats (a grand coalition) or with just the Christian Democrats. The grand coalition was quite stable and pursued neo-liberal policies. The opposition was pushed into the corner on almost all serious political questions. After the Associated List of Social Democrats left the governing coalition in March 1996 the opposition became stronger.

However important the differences between and conflicts among the Slovene political parties, they are always framed by a strong view of the 'national interest'. To put it in Kantian terms, the 'regulative idea' produces a more or less uniform national consensus on almost all key political questions. The recent response to Italian opposition to Slovenia's joining the EU clearly illustrates this national consensus. The president Milan Kučan constitutes the most cohesive Slovene political force.

Perhaps the most important factor concerning Slovenia's political system is the appearance of an elite political technocracy living in the midst of post-socialist privileges. Given the previous egalitarian system and (semi- or even anti-political) values, this could contribute to political instability in the future. The previous communist power elite was mainly based on two revolutionary ideas, the notion of a 'chosen class' and, at least in theory, that of honest, ascetic, morally inspired behaviour.

The post-communist power elite is a grouping without scruples, mainly composed of heterosexual men between 35 and 50 years of age, who are rapidly becoming corrupted. The leading pattern of thinking in Slovene politics centres around 'new values' and mainly proceeds from the equation of politics with the economy and economic management. For leading young Slovene liberals, government is enterprise and enterprise is politics based on *ad infinitum* (self)-instrumentalization. Slovenia, despite its 'smallness', is an excellent example of 'big business' run by one big family (the nation). All this has reduced the reputation of politics, diminished the good name of all individuals interested in politics and especially destroyed the good standing of the political class (politicians as whores) (Jalušič, 1995). Although less acute in Slovenia than in some other post-socialist countries, this 'anti-political syndrome' is closely connected with two additional and comparatively new elements: social inequality/insecurity and poverty (Novak, 1994), which contribute to these dangerous feelings and could present a serious challenge in the future.

Pluralism and tolerance

New challenges to tolerance are connected with the eruption of war in the region, the transformation of citizens from other Yugoslav republics into 'foreigners',[2] and, later, the arrival of refugees. According to some unofficial data, there are several thousand 'foreigners' living in Slovenia without passports or any possibility of getting work (or work permits). Slovene politicians have been tactless about refugees, especially those from Bosnia. In a symptomatic statement, the former Slovene prime minister and foreign minister, Lojze Peterle, having been turned down for the post of foreign minister, spoke of Slovene 'immigrant politics' being even 'worse than that of Bulgaria'!

(Anti-)politics and right-wing extremism

Instead of giving an over-simplified picture of political extremism, I will try to present some elements of the programme of the first chauvinist and racist post-socialist political party in Slovenia, the Slovene National Party (SNS). Although it is already 'domesticated' (it is a parliamentary party), and other political forces and interests – particularly the Slovene National Right led by Sašo Lap – have taken over its radicalism, its programme is still the 'right thing' for almost all of the quite numerous extremists in Slovenia.

The key to understanding the SNS's positions is its fight against citizenship rights for those 'foreigners' who gained Slovene citizenship through their recent residence in Slovenia and the breakup of Yugoslavia. Slovene citizenship, SNS leader Zmago Jelinčič argued, should be an 'honour' and, above all, it should be one that is extremely 'hard to earn'. The principal argument is simple: he or she who 'is not Slovene, should leave Slovenia'!

The main elements of the SNS programme are:

1. cancellation of the existing citizenship law;
2. revocation of the citizenship of all non-Slovenes who gained citizen's rights after 25 December 1990 (the date of the plebiscite);
3. reduction of the number of non-Slovenes in Slovenia by 90 per cent.

The SNS's economic programme is short: the so-called heavy ('black') and machine industries have no future in Slovenia. Almost all those factories, plants, mines and similar installations were 'political ones' (i.e. 'socialist factories') and for that reason ought to be closed. In the SNS's eyes that would achieve several objectives: the labour force from other republics would go home, which would free housing and jobs for young Slovenes; and Slovenia's ecological balance of payments would improve, as the 'political factories' consume about 40 per cent of Slovenia's potential energy. Thus there is a synergy among SNS's biggest enemies: heavy, dirty industry; socialism; and workers from the other former Yugoslav republics.

Two other elements are required to complete the picture of the SNS programme. First, social policy should be for Slovenes and Slovene citizens alone; everyone else is just foreign labour. Second, the SNS opposes integration with the EU, rejecting 'totalitarian dictate of Europe' over Slovenia (Kuzmanić, 1996a).

Information and the media

The transition of Slovene self-managing socialism to post-socialism was achieved primarily through the media. Opposition forces were able to change the system because they won the battle for free and independent media. Free and independent media under the former system actually meant the end of the Party system; the abolition of the former system is itself evidence of a free media. After the 1990 elections the right-wing DEMOS tried to destroy the existing and (more or less) already democratized media and to establish completely new ones. Its targets were primarily the national television and radio networks. Its efforts were not entirely successful, so today the media in Slovenia are a combination of reformed established media and new ones.

Slovene television is divided among several TV networks. National TV (three programmes) is a 'renewed' former TV station within which the split among political parties and interests had already taken place. For the time being it is under the control of the right-wing political lobby, its director being a member of the Slovene People's [peasants'] Party. The new TV stations are more or less commercial. Three are particularly strong, one of which is connected with the Slovene Catholic Church.

Slovene radio is also divided. There are three national radio stations, and several private, mostly commercial, radio stations, including Radio Student, the most important of the alternative Slovene media, and Radio Ognjišče, the Catholic Church's radio station. The strongest newspaper, with a circulation of about 100,000, is *Delo*. Other daily newspapers are *Dnevnik*, *Republika* and *Slovenec*. There are also two influential weeklies, the centre-left *Mladina* and the right-wing *Mag*. There are three or four strong regional daily newspapers in Slovenia (with print runs of nearly 100,000) and several regional TV and radio stations.

Slovene media are not dependent on the former communist forces. However, some media, especially some of the national TV and radio stations, are not truly independent, particularly those financed by the government. As a result, parliamentary parties are trying hard to have some control over these media. The board of the national TV is composed of representatives of political parties in the same proportions in which they are represented in Parliament.

The most important foundation of Slovene media independence is the journalists' trade union. It was among the first independent trade unions in Slovenia and still plays an important role in Slovene media and political space (Kuzmanić, 1996b).

Control of the military

Almost all processes of Slovene independence during the 1980s went through the ideology of anti-militarism, the peace movement and peace activism. According to public opinion surveys, at the end of the 1980s more than 60 per cent of respondents supported the Slovene peace movement in its fight against the military attitudes of the former state! When the Yugoslav People's Army sought to prevent the Slovenes from claiming their independence, pacifism became opposition overnight. The first defence minister and the strongest military person in modern Slovene history, Janez Janša, was a member of the Slovene peace movement! The Slovene military question is one part of wider pro-military–anti-military polemical confrontations, but takes place within the confines of the national consensus (compromise). With conflict so close, in time and space, there are few political individuals ready to defend the once popular idea of demilitarization (Kuzmanić, 1992). Today Slovenia has a relatively strong army under a civilian defence minister. The Slovene Army is under the control of Parliament as well as that of the government and the president, who is commander-in-chief. Perhaps the best indicator of the control over the military is the debates over its budget. From year to year the arguments against military expenditure become louder and louder, and the military's demands for new weapons (the embargo on arms trading is in force) are not always fulfilled.

It is reasonable to expect that the ending of the war in Bosnia would lead to a decline in the social and political role of the Slovene Army. The army is in general politically neo-liberal and favours membership of the North Atlantic Treaty Organization (NATO). Visiting Slovenia in September 1995, the then US Defense Secretary William Perry found Slovenia to be already functioning as a 'friendly state' to the USA and NATO – especially as during World War II Slovene partisans fought 'side by side with Americans', as Mr Perry put it!

The police and security

Although crime has been increasing over the past few years, the people's perception of their safety within the country is still among the highest in Europe. This would imply that the Slovene police and security forces are quite successful. It should also be noted that during the ten-day war with Yugoslavia the police were primarily responsible for defeating the JNA.

In the past five years the police in Slovenia have gone through an extremely turbulent transition: from being an ideological socialist people's militia towards becoming a non-ideological civil police force. Previously, their main concern was about the impact of words and statements on the ideological system. Today it is the protection of private property. As the result of this transition a large number of policemen have left the force. Younger men – mainly trained in the tradition of American street-fighting police – have replaced them.

Business associations and trade unions

The self-management system from which Slovenia emerged was, by definition, a kind of (neo-)corporatist system. The Communist Party, which tried to replace the state with self-managing society, played a leading role. Business associations and trade unions were treated with disdain. The constitutional concept of the enterprise as the 'basic organizations of associated labour' was a revolutionary attempt to abolish the distinction between business associations and trade unions. The post-socialist revolution breaks this setting. In the midst of the most creative reformist forces in the 1980s, numerous trade unions and hundreds of labour activists sought to emancipate themselves from the communist *nomenklatura* (Kuzmanić, 1994). While trade unions have been functioning as independent economic, social and political bodies since the mid-1980s, business associations are only just appearing. They are still more or less connected with the government or other civil associations and thus lack independence. Their weakness and lack of independence are due mainly to the absence of capital and other financial resources and to the absence of capital-based relationships at the level of the society.

Non-governmental organizations and 'fat rats'

The Slovene opposition movement during the 1980s was initiated by implicitly political non-governmental organizations (NGOs), especially new social movements, such as feminists, peace activists, environmentalists and gay rights campaigners (Benderly and Kraft, 1994). Prior to the first democratic elections, Slovenia was, in a way, 'NGO country'. With the emergence of parliamentary democracy the NGO sector waned as most NGO activists joined this or that component of the machinery of parliamentary democracy almost overnight.

Only about 10 per cent of activists remain in their previous social and political roles, either in NGOs or, more likely, in science or journalism. The outbreak of war at the beginning of the 1990s further obstructed the extension of existing NGO activities, but helped to build new ones, especially those providing humanitarian aid, working with refugees or helping raped women, elderly people and children. In this period Slovene NGOs started to receive financial assistance from abroad (private foundations, the EU, etc.), and so-called 'fat rats', former activists who control most of the financial resources coming into Slovenia, began to appear.

One should distinguish between two types of NGOs: those fighting for human rights and broad common interests, and those fighting for ownership rights and narrow, including private, interests. The former type includes the NGOs, already mentioned, dealing with refugees, disabled persons, children, etc. The latter, appearing under various names (such as 'Civil Initiative'), could be referred to as part of the 'enlarged revolution of 1989'. These organizations push for 'radical denationalization'. The more vigorously they argue for denationalization, the more they rail against refugees, 'those from the south', gays and lesbians, and women. Arguments based on human rights and equality in the 1980s have changed into arguments based on private property in the 1990s. The conflict between the *ancien régime* and NGOs, which dominated the 1980s, has turned into a battle among NGOs as well.

None the less, the NGOs' main achievement of the past couple of decades has been the creation of some important alternative institutions: Radio Student in the early 1970s; the Council for Human Rights (in the late 1990s), and later the Ombudsman; the Peace Institute (in the late 1980s); the Metelkova Alternative Culture Centre (in the early 1990s); and a strong feminist movement fighting for abortion and women's rights (at the beginning of the 1980s).

The role of the Church

For various historical reasons, the Slovene Catholic Church is the dominant religious force in Slovenia. It is one of the most vital elements of Slovene private, social, public and political life. More than 75 per cent of the Slovene population are of Catholic descent, although less than a third are religiously active. The other important religious communities include Muslims (mostly from Bosnia-Herzegovina and Kosovo), Orthodox Christians (from Serbia, Montenegro and Macedonia), Protestants (a traditional group in north-eastern Slovenia) and Jews.

To understand the role of the Catholic Church in Slovenia it is important to know that during World War II it was active on the fascist side. It fought against Slovene (and Yugoslav) partisans as well as against the forces of the anti-fascist alliance. As a result the Slovene Catholic Church was excommunicated from socialist society between 1945 and 1990.

The tension between Church and state was exacerbated by bloodshed at the end of World War II. According to some sources, the communists killed several thousand collaborators. These terrible events resurfaced at the beginning of the 1990s when the Catholic Church demanded a central social and political role in post-socialist Slovenia.

Two sides have formed in the ensuing political battle. The pro-Catholic bloc, mainly preaching 'traditional values', is composed of the Christian Democratic Party, the Slovene People's Party, the Slovene Social Democratic Party, Slovene Nationalist Rights, the Slovene Independent Trade Unions, the NGO Civil Initiative and a number of small, non-parliamentary political and civil groups and associations. The anti-Catholic bloc is a combination of marginalized groups, liberals, 'soft' nationalists and former communists, and usually argues in terms of development, freedom and, sporadically, equality. It is composed of the Associated List of Social Democrats, the Slovene National Party, parts of Slovene Liberal Democracy, the two main trade union associations and many NGOs, especially those connected with or led by women and/or feminist activists. In other words, a profound social and political split has taken place in post-socialist Slovenia as the Slovene Catholic Church develops its 'new', post-socialist role.

Local government and the process of centralization

The former Yugoslav self-management system was a highly decentralized anti-political system. It proceeded from Marxist theory concerning the local community. The result was that almost every Slovene town with more than 10–15,000 inhabitants had everything the people living in it needed: factories, schools, kindergartens, churches, hospitals and sometimes even a theatre.

By contrast, centralization appears to be a key 'post-socialist concept' in Slovenia. The emergence of the Slovene state was heavily influenced by theoreticians and influential politicians who were primarily connected ideologically with the French and Bavarian Catholic experiences and systems of thinking and acting. The Napoleonic system was particularly attractive, while the Bavarian model of regulation of the Parliament was exciting for these powerful people. The rather high degree of centralization in Slovenia is already bringing some negative consequences, which their ideological fathers claim were not intended.

The appearance of regional interests and the possibility of regional development are still only rudimentary. There are several regional political parties, two of which have already contested elections without much success. In addition, some remnants of the former self-managing system still function at the local level, especially in bigger towns. For the time being, however, we are witnessing an interesting fusion of the decentralized remnants of the former regime and the new forms of post-socialist centralization.

Mayors in some cities, such as Kranj and Maribor, are able to behave like local kings. They feel so strong that they have even tried to oust central state authorities from 'their' local buildings. In any event, all the 'strong' local people are members of the remarkably centralized political parties, which use them in order to implement their own political interests at the local level.

Although Slovenia has diverse regions in terms of geography, culture, history, language and even climate, it is still a small and compact national community in which national sentiments are stronger than regional interests. The regional differences are not sufficiently strong for it to be plausible that the state might disintegrate.

Anti-communism and the mainstream

If one seeks to understand the past and present in Slovenia, one cannot deduce the post-communist processes from the general scheme of Gorbachev's *glasnost*. In most parts of the former Yugoslavia, but particularly in Slovenia and some urban centres – such as Belgrade, Sarajevo, Zagreb, Rijeka and Split – post-socialist processes began several years before they did in the former Soviet Union. The process of democratization, accompanied by a strong verbal critique of the system, started in the 1980s. The mid-1980s were the time of the liberal left and post-modernist critiques of self-management. The critique of the Yugoslav state implicit in nationalism, chauvinism and racism came only later. The central values of the early style of critique were concentrated around individuality, freedom and political equality. Other forms of anti-communist critique were not so influential or powerful. This was because the liberal and left critique was the first serious critique of the Yugoslav system, and it was this form of critique and vision which influenced Slovene voters. Slovene anti-communist ideology, heavily based on the conflicts of World War II, rose to the surface a few years later when the systematic and structural internal transition of the former system had largely been completed – if not in appearance, at least in content.

It is very important to note that the Slovene system of self-management changed during the 1980s, and not just at the beginning of the 1990s. The change was the result of step-by-step internal modifications, in a 'Gramscian way', and not of dramatic overnight reforms.

Slovene anti-communist ideology and attitudes exist around four main loci: the Catholic Church; right-wing writers and poets; civil initiative groups that advocate radical denationalization; and some extreme political parties.

A paradoxical situation appears to exist in Slovene political life. First, and perhaps most important, the Slovene National Party, during the early 1990s, was the most chauvinist, even racist, party in Slovenia; simultaneously it was pro-choice (in favour of abortion rights) and it built on pro-partisan (anti-Nazi) feelings. Second, perhaps the strongest traditional party in Slovenia, the Slovene People's Party, dropped its anti-communist stance in 1994 and started referring to the 'positive role' of Slovene partisans during World War II. Last but not least, the strongest anti-communist and most extreme right-wing political behaviour and attitudes come from the Slovene Social Democrat Party.

Slovene anti-communism still contains a substantial reservoir of adrenaline and anger, but not in the same way as elsewhere, such as in Croatia, where the ideological conflict between communism and nationalism dominates the state and society as a whole. The national and even nationalist role of the Slovene Communist Party before and during World War II and during the 1970s and 1980s should not be underestimated in present ideological discussions. The symbolical power of nationalism is, in my opinion, not (yet) sufficient to destabilize the present post-socialist political setting centred around the Liberal Democrats. In addition to the symbolic anger, anti-communist ideology and social populism represented by the SDS, there is at least some real nationalist force, for example in the protest votes of the unemployed and among chauvinists and racists. Last but not least, within the next decade Slovenia might be governed by a coalition of Liberal Democrats and Social Democrats – a combination which could be considered liberal right-wing, similar to the government in the Czech Republic today.

European integration?

The Slovene decision to leave the former Yugoslavia was based on the calculation, atmosphere and emotions of rejoining Europe: Slovene independence was equated with non-violence, which was equated with an anti-militarist attitude, which was anti-Yugoslav and therefore anti-Belgrade and anti-Serb (Kuzmanić, 1993). In other words, the disintegration of Yugoslavia meant, for Slovenes, 'escaping from the Balkans'. In this ideological context the East meant totalitarianism, militarism, Stalinism, while the West meant God, democracy, non-violence, freedom. During the 1980s, especially at the end of the decade, 'escaping' from the East was perceived as the same as running directly to the West.

At the same time there were only a few people who really understood what West and East meant. Most people knew almost nothing about the functioning of parliamentary democracy, about freedom in the West, not to speak about the concrete running of diverse subsystems. For millions of people in the East, including Slovenes, the 'reality' of the West was that depicted by Hollywood. This uncritical acceptance of the Hollywood fiction as viewed on TV was the decisive vehicle of the transition. The situation was biblical: it seemed to the people of the East that they finally had the opportunity to escape from hell (self-management, socialism, Yugoslavia) to heaven (capitalism, democracy and the West).

The dreams have come true. Post-socialism and democracy came, but standards of living fell at almost all levels of income. The role of Europe in the war in the former Yugoslavia has been improvised, unstudied and modest. Slovenes, whose anti-Yugoslav feelings and attitudes were strongest and whose sense of self was based on the idea that they are superior to other (former) Yugoslavs, expected concrete help from their 'allies', especially those in Western Europe.

Having developed their own national-ideological, albeit artificial, imprecise, even wishy-washy, self-consciousness, the 'average' Slovene thought that Europeans were simply waiting for their beloved Slovenes to join their democratic and affluent society. When these expectations were not realized, the Slovenes, of course, felt dissatisfied and disappointed. Particularly striking was Italy's extreme political attitude towards Slovenia, which appeared to echo Mussolini's rhetoric and conflictual style.

Slovenes still favour integration into the European institutions – the EU and NATO – but not as strongly as they did during the late 1980s and early 1990s.[3] Instead of emotion, cool calculation has come to the fore.

An unfinished story

Observing the existing European, both Eastern and Western, circumstances from Central and Eastern Europe it is possible to perceive a new and interesting element in the 'game'. There is an uneasy connection between the dream of the West and the reality which emerged in the 1960s. Political strife within Western Europe and tensions between Western Europe, the USA and Japan, and particularly the delay in Central and East European accession to the Western European Union (WEU), do not fit easily with the Slovenes' earlier, idealized vision.

Consequently, that vision, which has existed for at least two centuries, has begun to fade. After the fall of the Berlin Wall, the countries of Central and Eastern Europe suddenly found themselves in risky, if not dangerous, positions. They are forced to survive in the middle of nowhere. They are forced to exist politically between Russia and the West and without any real possibility of 'escaping to America' (the dream of generations ago) or bringing America to them (the ideology of the new social movements in the 1980s).

Although it is extremely hard to predict future events, it seems to me that there are already some signals which indicate potential changes. One is the emergence of a new regional factor: Central and Eastern Europe itself. It has not emerged as a result of a particular ideology or political idea, nor is it the result of the activities of a particular political group or organization; rather it is the troubled outcome of various pressures within and around the region.

In more abstract terms, if we want to understand the intense conflicting processes within the region, we need to develop a new form of thinking that moves beyond dichotomies – East–West, bad–good, theirs–ours – and open the door to a 'third', intermediating, element. 'Running from the East' (the 1989 revolutions onward) is not and should not be equated with 'running (directly) towards the West'. It is already possible to argue for the existence of a political and economic place between 'Western' and 'Eastern' Europe. In other words, Eastern (European) dreams of 'Central and Eastern' Europeans are fading away at the end of the century. This is due in part to Western Europe's improvisation in Croatia and Bosnia and the unsatisfactory response to the wars in the former Yugoslavia. It is also due to serious conflicting arguments with ideology and even prejudices in connection with the process of European integration.

Notes

1. DEMOS was the national–conservative and anti-communist Democratic Opposition of Slovenia, composed, at that time, of seven parties: the Christian Democrats, the Social Democrats, the Peasants' Party, the Slovenian Greens, the Liberal Party, the Democrat Party and the 'Panthers', the party of Slovene pensioners.

2. In colloquial Slovene, the term 'foreigners' designates solely those people from the former Yugoslavia (specially from Bosnia), regardless of whether they have Slovene citizenship or not. Since most immigrants from Serbia, Macedonia, Bosnia, Croatia and Montenegro during the past three decades already have Slovene citizenship, we can understand the never-ending extremist attempt to abolish the law of Slovene citizenship on the grounds that it is 'too liberal'.

3. It seems that the number of pro-European Slovenes is falling slightly. Some recent, unrepresentative approximations show that around 40 per cent of respondents support joining the EU and roughly 70 per cent favour NATO membership, but more than 50 per cent oppose the establishment of NATO military bases in Slovenia (*Nedelo*, 14 April 1996).

10

Romania: From Procedural Democracy to European Integration[1]

ALINA MUNGIU PIPPIDI

Background

Romanian society in December 1989 was the product of fifty years of social engineering and ideological shaping, a society completely penetrated by and dependent on political authority. Almost one-third of Romania's 14 million adults were members of the Communist Party at the time of Ceaușescu's downfall. The exact number of the Securitate's (Ceaușescu's secret police) informers is not known, but inside sources such as General Ion Pacepa have stated that one in seven Romanians worked for the Securitate in one way or another.[2] Almost all private property had been nationalized, leaving only a few islands in the mountains, where the land was considered so unproductive that it was not worth confiscating.

What is important about the Romanian 'Revolution' is that the popular uprising in December 1989 was not preceded by any attempt to liberalize the regime, nor was it organized by any institutional form of opposition or dissent. In November 1989, at the last Communist Party Congress, Romania was still a Stalinist country where all organized resistance had been broken long ago and only a few isolated dissenters dared to raise their voices in protest. The totalitarian project had been successful there more than anywhere else: the state and society had almost become one. Yet in just a couple of days in December 1989 a handful of protesters in Timișoara and Bucharest, a secret deal between the Securitate and the army to let Ceaușescu fall, and Gorbachev's consent were enough to bring down Ceaușescu's regime.

This change was due mostly to circumstantial factors, such as the international context, the popular uprising of a handful of revolutionaries, and the decision of the repressive institutions to replace Ceaușescu. No new elite existed to challenge the old one, and the bulk of the population did not take part in the anti-Ceaușescu movement and were frightened by the violence and the insecurity during the so-called Revolution. Even after the dictator was dead the society was still Ceaușescu's society, as events in 1990 largely proved.

The 1996 elections

It took no less than seven years for the anti-communist opposition to win elections. The significance of its victory in November 1996 only just surpasses in significance the willingness of the post-communist ruling party to give up power after seven years. As analysts pointed out, this was the second time since 1937 that political power has changed hands through the ballot box and the first time that a Romanian head of state has left office other than by dying (naturally or not) or being deposed.

Both the ruling party and the political opposition looked unprepared for such a radical change. In fact, most of the analysts had predicted a victory for the opposition, but a defeat of its presidential candidate, Emil Constantinescu. His success in defeating the third-time runner Ion Iliescu on 17 November was due in part to the good performance of Petre Roman, the former prime minister, who won 20 per cent of the votes in the first round of voting. This high share of the vote led to a deal between Constantinescu's Democratic Convention (DCR) and Roman's Social Democratic Union (USD), which led to the creation of the governing coalition. Roman traded his constituency's votes in the second round of presidential elections for his party's participation in the governing coalition. Less noisily, but quite obviously, the Hungarian Alliance (DAHR) did so as well.

After the elections the winners embarked on a quite unusual exercise in Romanian political life: the negotiation and building of a consociational democracy. National and local government positions were divided among the parties according to the shares they had won in the elections. Allocating the positions proved more difficult within the Democratic Convention, and several days were lost in negotiations between the National Peasant Party and the National Liberal Party. However, owing to the newly elected President Constantinescu's strong presence as an arbiter the negotiations progressed well. One after another, posts of ministers, state secretaries, prefects and deputy prefects were shared between the winners. An important part of the deal was the distribution of the presidencies of the Parliament's two chambers. Roman became president of the Senate, a position which under the 1991 constitution is second in the state hierarchy. Ion Diaconescu, the leader of the National Peasant Party, became president of the Assembly of Deputies.

Proportionality was respected when allocating local government positions as well. In counties with ethnically mixed populations, positions were divided between Romanians and Hungarians. In counties such as Harghita, where there is a Hungarian majority, the prefect is a Hungarian, as are most of the mayors and the local councillors. Except for an incident in Cluj – where the Hungarian deputy prefect's declaration that Hungarian would immediately become the second language in the administration provoked strong disputes – in the rest of Transylvania this important transfer of power to DAHR was accepted without any problems.

The allocation of posts in general started being looked upon more suspiciously after it reached lower levels, such as county governmental agencies. The former government party, the Party for Social Democracy of Romania (PDSR), reduced to a minority in both chambers of Parliament, alleged that the appointment process amounted to political cleansing. The new government inherited a strongly politicized bureaucracy and had to consider whether to dismiss these people or undertake a conversion process (which in fact started immediately). In the event, the rush by former government party members to join the new winning parties was so great that the USD announced that it was suspending new admissions for a while.

On 11 December the Parliament voted in favour of the government proposed by Victor Ciorbea, mayor of Bucharest, and the programme he presented. The programme combined short-term policies meant to address some of the very concrete electoral promises and long-term policies, including the implementation of economic reforms. But the arrival of the International Monetary Fund (IMF) overshadowed these policies and presaged weeks of negotiations to create a shock-therapy programme accompanied by some mild social protection measures.

Since the elections were won with promises to increase child support and pensions for peasants, the government appeared reluctant to forget completely its electoral promises and start a socially devastating economic reform. In a dramatic address to the nation Prime Minister Ciorbea accused the former government of hiding the extent of the economic disaster. He declared that the budget deficit was three times higher than the one previously officially declared, at 13 per cent of gross domestic product (GDP). Ciorbea claimed that the 1996 growth rate of 4.5 per cent was 'unhealthy' and achieved on the back of a growing budget deficit. The inflation rate in 1996 also exceeded the former government's figure, reaching almost 60 per cent.

After 1994, when the macro-stabilization programme was introduced, the government of Nicolae Vacaroiu returned to the old strategy of postponing reforms. As a result, many analysts fear that the national economy faces a fate similar to that of Bulgaria's unless some reforms are attempted promptly. However, the policy of macrostabilization of 1997 was not followed by an approach closer to the real economy. The Ciorbea government, replaced in April 1998 by the Radu Vasile government, was unable to increase the pace of privatization or to close down the loss-making state industries. Squabbles inside the government coalition set the Social Democrats under Petre Roman, who were in favour of keeping large state ownership of the agricultural sector, against the Democratic Convention and the Hungarian Alliance

(DAHR), promoters of land restitution and complete privatization. After the financial assistance for reform, especially for the restructuring of industry, stopped in the spring of 1998, the government of Radu Vasile was in the delicate position of negotiating new programmes with the IMF and the World Bank. Both institutions, however, seem sceptical over the prospect that tough measures of restructuring will and can be carried out by the coalition government. The level of foreign investment in Romania remains low, even after the change of regime in November 1996 and the February 1997 vote of the new majority, allowing foreign investors to buy land for the first time. This symbolic end to seven years of official xenophobia has not brought the expected increase in foreign investment.

The constitutional framework

The post-1989 Romanian regime was eager to establish a legal and legitimate basis. The constitution was ready for a popular vote by December 1991. It was designed during a period of tough, sometimes violent, confrontation between the old and the emerging elites. The referendum was widely seen as a choice between the existing republic and the return of King Michael, but at a deeper level left this issue unresolved.

The next most important issue in the 1991 constitution was the separation of powers. The legacy of the communist government was a fused, over-centralized system which emasculated the judiciary. The 1991 constitution declares that the judiciary is 'independent' but does not, beyond this formal guarantee, provide the means to achieve independence. The judiciary is defined merely as an 'authority', compared to the other 'powers'; and prosecutors are renamed 'magistrates', enjoying a status similar to that of the judges in the newly created Council of the Superior Judiciary. This created a strange discrepancy between the positions of judges and prosecutors: the former are subjected to the disciplinary authority of the council, while the latter, though members of the council, are exempted from its authority, being subordinate to the government. This enables prosecutors to sanction judges by disciplinary means via the council, while the reverse is not true.

The 1991 constitution does, however, provide judges with some means of exercising real power and pressing for democratization. Article 20b specifies that international regulations will prevail over domestic laws in the case of contradictions and Article 150 says that laws and other normative regulations remain valid only to the extent that they do not contravene the constitution.

The third important constitutional issue is the distribution of power between central and local governments. The Constitutional Assembly decided in 1991 to establish the office of prefect, which is to be the local representative of the central government. However, the constitution is ambiguous in defining the limits of the prefect's powers. One consequence was that in the period after 1992 the Department for Local Administration dismissed more than 100 mayors all over the country, most of whom belonged to opposition parties. Following intense protests from the international community, the Senate voted to reduce the power of the prefect. Once this law is finally adopted, prefects will not be able to dismiss mayors directly, but only take them to the courts. The new administrative law will not, however, address the central issue of local government autonomy and financial independence.

A further important constitutional issue concerns government ordinances and the tendency to rule through ordinances rather than laws. Before 1996 the democratic opposition accused the post-Communist parties that formed the government coalition of violating the representative democracy procedures by by-passing Parliament: afterwards, it was their turn to rule via emergency ordinances. The Ciorbea government passed almost all its important bills this way, and Parliament took revenge by rejecting the 22/1997 Ordinance, a major piece of institutional reform meant to bring more autonomy to local communities and establish bilingualism at local government level. The Radu Vasile government promised to avoid using emergency ordinances, but since Parliament kept up its slow ineffective procedures, it soon had to revoke this promise. The advantage of emergency ordinances is that they come into force immediately, even if Parliament doesn't put them on the agenda until a year later. The risk is that after one or two years of enforcement Parliament may eventually reject the bill, as was the case with the 22/1997 Ordinance.

Serious constitutional issues were also at stake in the November 1996 elections. The decision of President Iliescu to run for a third term was strongly attacked by various non-governmental organizations (NGOs) and political parties, among other reasons on the grounds that the constitution allows a person to serve as president for only two mandates (a mandate being defined as a four-year term).

The new government, although long critical of the constitution, has thus far refrained from initiating any amendments. This approach is likely to continue in the near future, as the main purpose of the new regime, confronted with serious economic and social problems, seems to be to maintain political stability. This stability is an argument in Romania's favour for early accession to the North Atlantic Treaty Organization (NATO), and nobody seems eager to provoke national debates around modifications of the constitution. In the future, if, during the process of adopting European legislation, some constitutional modifications are required, they could be made. But for the moment, discussions concerning delicate matters such as the form of government – republic or constitutional monarchy – seem unlikely. The president of the Constitutional Court, interviewed by the author, even declared that European legislation could be adopted without having to modify the 1991 constitution.

The status of the political opposition

The Romanian Communist Party (RCP) vanished during the Revolution. 'Bad' communists were replaced with 'good' communists, most of whom were directly elected by collectives in factories, state institutions, schools and universities. These 'revolutionary' committees were supposed to be provisional, but were transformed into a political party in January 1990 in a cunning move by the 'provisional' President Iliescu.

Within two weeks of Ceauşescu's death Romania again had a party–state, a legitimate one this time, claiming that 'it was we who made the revolution'. It was ruled by a mass party with structures at all levels of government down to the smallest village. This post-communist party, the National Salvation Front (NSF), could not easily be identified with the Communist Party, even if it was led by a few former *apparatchiks*, which is why, in 1990, opinion polls showed that an overwhelming majority did not believe that the NSF and the RCP were one and the same. Later, when the NSF identified itself more and more closely with the communist past, defending the Securitate and important policies of the RCP such as nationalization and collectivization, it lost some voters, but not many.

How could opposition to the provisional government become legitimate in early 1990 when the dominant slogan was 'the Front is all of us'? The dissenters did their best: they resigned from the NSF and denounced its transformation into a political party. As a result, they lost popularity and found themselves identified as foreign agents and enemies of the Romanian people, just as they had under the communist regime.

The government boosted its popularity by reducing prices and working hours. President Iliescu denounced the reborn historical parties and parties in general. He explained in a speech on National Television two weeks after Ceauşescu's fall that parties are outdated even in democratic countries. Later he was forced to admit that the NSF had become a party and to allow other parties into the political game. But he never accepted the idea that an opposition is a political institution indispensable to a liberal democracy. In a speech in June 1990 which was shown on National Television, he famously thanked the miners for having tried to destroy the opposition. He continued to sustain his conspiracy theory about an attempted opposition putsch on 13

June even after serious evidence (including a report by the Parliament) had completely dismissed it as an effort to justify the brutal repression.

President Iliescu persistently blamed the opposition for the economy's poor performance and the failure of reforms. He claimed that foreign aid and capital were not flowing into the country because of opposition criticisms of the problems encountered by the democratization process. Later he proposed a Romanian version of the 'Moncloa convention': that is, the opposition should stop attacking governmental policies, especially economic reforms, and instead support the government and wait patiently for the elections to compete for power. The personal values and opinions of President Iliescu had enormous political influence. He remains a believer in a 'third way', not only for the economy but also for democracy, which he envisages as a sort of political corporatism.

Between the 1992 and 1996 parliamentary elections the Democratic Convention of Romania (DCR) tried eight times to provoke a no-confidence vote against the regime. None of the topics it raised – ranging from the slowness of reform to the deterioration of the conditions of social life to Iliescu's unconstitutional pressure on the Supreme Court – provoked real debate. The government's voting machine simply mobilized its national–communist allies without even discussing the opposition's arguments.

Iliescu's party faces an uncertain destiny as an opposition party. Following seven years of clientelism it has a strong network controlling industry, the privatization process, the state administration and the state television. The new government's weak attempt to dismantle this network was strongly denounced as 'political cleansing'. Iliescu and his colleagues bitterly criticized, even in Strasbourg, the replacement of the general director of the state television service and of the president of the State Privatization Fund. The arrest of Miron Cosma (the miners' leader who beat up Iliescu's opponents in 1990), one of the first made by the new government in a wider anti-corruption campaign, was also denounced as 'political', and Iliescu complained that this anti-corruption campaign is in fact a political witch-hunt.

Independence of the media

One of the first laws adopted by the first post-communist Parliament was on the broadcast media.[3] Broadcasting licences were given to dozens of private radio stations, most funded by Western donations. Competition is fierce – Bucharest alone has more than ten private short-wave radio stations – but, unlike in the print media, competition, along with the effects of a BBC training school, has increased the quality of radio journalism.

Private television has also developed enormously. More than 2 million

Romanians subscribe to cable companies, thereby receiving alternative sources of programming. Local stations are still financially weak and therefore dependent on local business and government networks. Nation-wide stations, broadcasting from Bucharest and via satellite, are more independent. This plurality, however, is more apparent than real. The three private television networks are owned by businessmen who had strong connections with the post-communist parties, which is not surprising given the degree of state control over the business environment. No wonder, then, that the values promoted by some shows on these private stations are closer to national communism – sometimes using characters from Ceaușescu's close entourage – than to Western liberal democratic values.

The situation of the print media is also poor. There is a sharp tendency towards yellow journalism, which is partly the consequence of privatization and partly due to poor distribution. A serious threat to the independence of the media is the legislation on press offences. The new law on state secrecy, already adopted by the Senate, considers almost everything a 'state' or 'company'. An information law is absolutely necessary in a post-totalitarian country where the most basic information needed by journalists and pollsters, such as electoral lists, not to mention more refined things such as state archives, can be obtained only through the mercy of the bureaucracy.

The most delicate issue was and remains National, supposedly public, Television with its two channels. It was repeatedly accused by the opposition of being only the government's television. The news department, it is true, had for seven years maintained the pattern set during the communist period, starting each broadcast with the president's visits to factories and work fields and continuing, hierarchically, with government and Parliament news. While other media showed the government party losing many of its former fiefdoms in the June 1996 elections, National Television presented them as a victory for the government party.

National Television is beset by problems. It is underfinanced, overstaffed and lacks professionalism. The prospects for reform are far from good. Much international support and domestic goodwill will be needed to transform this state television into a real public television service.

Who governs Romania?

Until the 1996 elections, the bureaucrats formed the most important ruling group. No bureaucrat has ever been dismissed for corruption or inefficiency (only directly elected administrators are subject to such treatment).

In 1991 Prime Minister Petre Roman complained that second-rank bureaucrats (he had managed to dismiss those in the first rank) were blocking reforms. After his forced departure from the government the first-rank communist bureaucracy came back into office.

Close to this very influential network of former *apparatchiks*, who enjoyed the personal protection of the former President and Prime Minister, are the 'government's' businessmen. They are businessmen who made their fortune by taking preferential loans and credits from state-run banks and who were the main sponsors of the government's and Iliescu's election campaigns. They are the 'state capitalists'.

The third group are 'entrepreneurial politicians', central and local members of the former government party who have seats on the boards of state banks and on the newly created Boards of Shareholders (AGAs) which control the privatization process. In other words, there is an alliance of politicians, would-be businessmen, future owners of banks and industrial assets, with a common background in the management of state-owned enterprises or in the propaganda structures of the communist regime.

The most important tools used by these groups to ensure their supremacy are the secret services, notably the Romanian Service of Information (RSI), the direct heir of the Securitate. The RSI dismissed 35 per cent of former Securitate officers and appears quite anxious to improve its public image. However, squabbles with the rival information service, UM02115, which is part of the Department of Internal Affairs, occasionally bring to light the truth about both. The 1990 Parliament protected the RSI from civilian control. According to the Law on National Safety, adopted even before the new constitution, the director of the RSI can be dismissed only at the suggestion of the president and by a two-thirds majority in both chambers of Parliament.

A common background as Securitate collaborators is responsible for the cohesion of the ruling groups. Although they are part of the political power structures, their autonomy is limited, as they are accountable to whoever has their Securitate files. In the past six years the only files made public have been those of people who joined the opposition, as was the case of two journalists from the main opposition daily, *Romania libera*.

These different groups share a common interest in a strong state. The bureaucrats want to defend the state in order to ensure their survival; the new 'capitalists' want to keep their monopolies and avoid real competition through a sort of state-favoured company status; and the entrepreneurial politicians need slow, state-controlled privatization in order to make their fortunes.

The new government is encountering serious problems in dealing with these groups. Neither the Ciorbea nor the Vasile government was able to take full control of the vast state apparatus and to put some order in the state banks, the main financial supporters of the 'state capitalists'. Even legal prosecution did not improve the situation, since the government was forced to include in the public debt the large losses of state banks such as Bancorex, BRD and the Agriculture Bank, all important sponsors of the 'state capitalists' and their ventures. Each time the government tried to dismantle the important state monopolies it was stopped short by lack of support even inside the governing coalition, especially from Petre Roman's Social Democrats.

The status of ethnic minorities

The 1991 constitution granted a full set of rights to the three 'historical minorities' left in Romania: Hungarians, Roma (Gypsies) and Germans. None the less, they face serious problems. The first and most important problem is poverty, especially for Roma, who face massive unemployment. One of the immediate consequences of transition has been to worsen the economic problems of minorities. Even if they do not choose the path of organized crime, as it is claimed some Roma groups have done, the minorities are in danger of becoming its main losers.

The second important minority issue is education. Education is still highly centralized, with a uniform network of state schools with a common curriculum and hierarchical teaching methods. Most of the criticisms that the Hungarian minority levels, with good reason, at the government are problems faced by all Romanians. Complete training in German and Hungarian from the primary to high-school levels is adequately supplied, but there is no Hungarian-language state university.

A third problem for minorities is the growing politicization of ethnic issues, especially the Hungarian question. The Constitution gives each minority the right to a reserved seat in the Assembly. Roma, of whom there are more than 400,000 according to the last census, could be better represented, but they usually vote for the government party (the same voting behaviour as shown by poorly educated, low-income Romanians) and not for their ethnic political organizations. Hungarians vote unanimously for their ethnic party, the Hungarian Alliance (DAHR), which holds about 7 per cent of the seats in Parliament. The DAHR is an alliance of parties and NGOs, and is the sole representative of Hungarian interests.

In 1996 a radical group consolidated its position within the DAHR, for the first time giving a political character to its pleas and supplanting the human and minority rights discourse. Consequently, the main political objectives of the DAHR are to obtain personal autonomy, territorial autonomy and internal self-determination. This radicalization was partly due to the total lack of dialogue between the authorities and the Hungarian representatives during the previous six years, and to the association of Romanian nationalist parties with the government after 1993. After its radicalization, however, the DAHR's support dropped from 67 to 53 per cent (*Magropress*, October 1995). The DAHR won its usual share of 7 per cent of the votes in the June 1996 local elections, but in the three major cities in the heart of the Szekely area the mayoral elections were won by Hungarian independents running against the DAHR on less nationalistic, more pragmatic programmes.

After lengthy negotiations Hungary and Romania finally, in September 1996, concluded a treaty in which Hungary accepted Romania's interpretation of the Council of Europe's recommendation, which ruled out territorial autonomy on ethnic grounds. After endless postponements, the conclusion of the agreement and its swift ratification by both national Parliaments came as a total surprise and can be explained only in terms of the governments' electoral calculations. The Romanian mass media unanimously attributed Hungary's sudden acceptance of Romania's interpretation to American pressure and Hungarian eagerness to join NATO.

Within Romania the treaty met internal opposition from Romanian nationalist parties and from the Hungarian Alliance. The Hungarians felt they had been abandoned by their mother-country; Bishop László Tokes strongly criticized the Hungarian government. Even after the final text had been agreed, the DAHR lobbied the Hungarian Parliament for modifications. The treaty, it declared, would not improve the lives of ordinary Hungarians in Romania at all.

The treaty had immediate and positive effects: praise from the international community (the US ambassadors to Hungary and Romania jointly wrote a congratulatory text in the *Washington Post*) and the total disappearance of nationalist themes from electoral rhetoric. The long-worn topic of revisionist Hungarians wanting Transylvania back was finally laid to rest as the treaty asserted that neither country has territorial claims on the other. Popular support from both Romanians and Hungarians living in Romania was also considerable.

The prime beneficiary of the treaty, however, was the DAHR. The conclusion of the treaty facilitated the victory of the opposition in the November 1996 elections, which in turn made possible the DAHR's participation in government. In a rush towards consociational democracy, political power is shared with its allies at both central and local levels according to the exact results of the November elections. 'Moderate' Hungarian leaders have become fashionable again in the DAHR, and despite radicals in the Hungarian diaspora few Hungarian voices in Romania support separatism or criticize DAHR participation in the government. This start for consociational democracy is the best first outcome of the November 1996 elections.

Societal trends in post-communist Romania

At the end of 1989 it was widely assumed that Romania, like most communist societies, had made important steps on the road of social homogenization: the creation of a classless political and economic culture. This thesis was largely invalidated by sociologists in other Central and East European countries, and looks highly dubious even in Romania, where social engineering was particularly pervasive.

The most important group in the towns are ex-peasants or recent urban inhabitants, most of whom work in unprofitable industries, live in new, ghetto-like suburbs and have lost all sense of connection to a social class or any tradition. Other urban categories include blue- and white-collar workers, who retain some urban traditions and values; intellectual elites; and members of the ruling class.

Since 1990 income inequality has become a characteristic of Romanian society. Successive studies conducted for UNESCO by the Institute for the Quality of Life in Bucharest show that two-thirds of Romanians live below the poverty line. Romania is divided between the mass of people living on an average monthly income of $60 to $100 and a small group of *nouveaux riches* who have key positions in the state system, bank accounts in Switzerland and the latest models of Mercedes. This division is aggravated by the extraordinary grip that the state (or, more precisely, key persons of the state) keeps on many economic data. This minimizes the chances an average citizen has to start a business by selling his car; to find a job paid according to his or her qualifications; or to identify a reliable investment fund. By September 1994 there were only 14,000 Romanians registered as private employees. Compared to the indispensable network of connections, merit and initiative stand little chance. The population finds its salvation in the shadow economy, suspected by the Romanian Information Service of amounting to 40 per cent of annual GDP.

From the totalitarian state to the civil society

Communism destroyed all traces of civil society and replaced it with party-controlled nation-wide associations of all kinds, from women's groups to professional and sports organizations. Some of these organizations survived and held new elections after 1989. Unions like CNSRL (the National Confederation of Free Unions) are direct heirs of the communist unions, but have managed to become true representatives of the workers.

The principal problem that besets unions and NGOs of all kinds, in common with parties, is the low level of participation. Polls indicate that the percentage of people belonging to a political party is somewhere between 3 and 8 per cent.

The number of NGOs looks impressive compared to 1989, although urban intellectuals still dominate the NGO sector and most NGOs face chronic financial problems. However, the number of civic activists is growing and their energy and will to continue this unprofitable and at times quite unrewarding experience – marketing democracy in the countryside is not always an encouraging activity – give some hope for the future.

Attitudes and values are slow to change. There is still a strong collectivist mentality and authoritarianism persists. In the past six post-communist years polls show that the public has the greatest confidence in the army, followed by the police, the prosecution service and the RSI. Only the courts rival Parliament in the public's distrust, even though the judiciary has fought hardest since 1990 to become a democratic institution.

There is a growing portion of the population that displays more democratic attitudes. By democrats I mean people who in interviews or polls showed concern for the democratization process, who consider the birth of the multi-party system and of a free press important. Their numbers have increased since 1990. In 1990 only 15 per cent, half of whom were of Hungarian origin, did not vote for Iliescu. In 1992 45 per cent voted for the opposition candidate in the second round. These people are, according to the IMAS Polling Agency, mostly active, young, male, urbanites or inhabitants of Transylvania. Over the past two years polls have also shown a majority in favour of massive privatization, and almost unanimous support for integrating Romania into Western institutions.

Polls show that Romanians and Poles, because of their experiences, have the greatest fear of a possible Russian threat. This, together with the feeling of international isolation due to the bad press the former government received in Western countries, has contributed to an increase in the popular desire to join NATO and the EU. This does not mean that the 80 per cent in favour of European integration know what it implies. It means only that anti-Western and anti-capitalistic attitudes exist mainly when supported or induced by the authorities. Once the official discourse began to favour integration, Romanians could finally express their true desire to belong to Europe. In many of my interviews, people complained that 'We're caught inbetween'; 'We no longer belong anywhere'; 'We were on the bad side before, but at least we were somewhere'; 'We need to find friends'.

Eight years have not been long enough for a radical change to occur in Romania's political culture, especially in the countryside. It was in the best interests of the post-communist ruling class that the Romanians keep their authoritarian and collectivist political attitudes, and they were encouraged to do so.

The new government and European integration

Romania's present problems can be summarized in two main categories. First are those linked to the legacy of the worst totalitarian regime in Central and Eastern Europe: loss of social identity and autonomy, which created a psychological state of helplessness and chronic dependence on the authorities; the poor quality of the political elite; and the dependence on state subsidies of a large segment of the economy. Second are the problems created by the poor management of the transition: the creation of an oligarchy; corruption; pauperization; the persistence of the state sector; the birth and consolidation of private monopolies; the degradation of services due to inexcusable delays in privatization; the absence so far of the political will to create a middle class, owing to reluctance to restore small businesses to their rightful owners or privatize firms; the absence of a new labour market able to cure the unemployment due to industrial restructuring; the degradation of social services resulting from chronic underfinancing due to the wasting of budgetary resources on subsidies to bankrupt industries; the public's growing lack of confidence in politicians and interest in politics; and the appearance of mafia-like networks of smugglers, managers of state-owned enterprises (including banks) and corrupt police officers.

No other Central and East European country has had a political elite as determined to stay in power at any price as Romania. This economic oligarchy, although seriously damaged by the defeat of Iliescu and his party in November 1996, is a constant enemy of trade liberalization and free markets. The new President is heading a national anti-corruption campaign which has already led to the arrest of the famous miners' leader Miron Cosma, among others. But dismantling this network of secret service agents, bankers, bureaucrats and smugglers will be a difficult job, and the struggle for real control of the state apparatus may take months or even years.

Nevertheless, the drives for democracy and to join Europe are strong. The mass media, despite financial problems, managed to become independent on a large scale within only a few years of 1990. Universities have become more and more a part of the European network. The mentality of the workers has become more market-friendly, mainly because of the failure of the 'third way' tried by the Iliescu regime, which reached its limits in 1995. Romanians are willing to accept sacrifices if they see some sense, some direction behind them. By no means is Romania an ungovernable country, nor will it be, despite the serious economic and social hardships it is currently encountering.

I do not, in all fairness, know whether Romania's joining Europe is the only formula for a good future for the Romanians, or, indeed, if it is possible. It is difficult to anticipate what 'Europe' will mean and imply by the time

Romania is ready to join. But it is my strongest belief that 'Europe' is the only strong incentive, for both the political class and the people, to further the democratization of the country. Left out, Romania would follow a pattern of chronic misdevelopment with nationalist–populist internal politics; occasional outbursts of political violence, as in 1990; and perhaps a major, politically engineered, inter-ethnic conflict.

If Romania's economic conditions will not permit it to join the EU in the near future, NATO might provide an intermediary step for integration. The main issue is to avoid isolating the country and further feeding the theme dear to communist and post-communist propaganda: the West's betrayal. Quite a few politicians are ready to take advantage of the situation. But there is also a large, well-educated European population in Romania that hopes Europe will help them to help themselves.

Notes

1. I made extensive use of the Centre for Political Studies and Comparative Analysis's documentary files (including press coverage and documents) and analyses in compiling this chapter. I also used the collection of the monthly *Sfera politicii*, a political science journal, and the Romanian Democracy Barometer, a Soros Foundation venture.
2. In the light of revelations concerning East Germans' collaboration with the STASI (East German secret police), this figure seems highly plausible.
3. Fourteen people went on a hunger strike during the opposition's rally in 1990, demanding the creation of an independent public television service. Some were forcibly hospitalized by force after 40 days on strike.

11

Democratization in Bulgaria: Recent Trends

RUMYANA KOLAROVA

Introduction

Before World War II the Bulgarian political system was not very different from those in other Central and East European countries (CEECs); it could be classified either as an unstable democracy or as a quasi-authoritarian regime. There were periods of parliamentarism and constitutionalism interrupted by wartime states of emergency (1913–19; 1941–4) and military take-overs (in 1923, 1934, 1944). During the very brief periods of democratic government there was only one case of peaceful transfer of power through general elections.

Bulgaria's weak democratic tradition was wiped out by the practices of the communist regime. Through both its initial severe repression and its subsequent mild repressive and clientelistic strategy, the Bulgarian Communist Party managed to destroy all civil associations and practices. Bulgaria's communist politics were strikingly more stable than those of the other CEECs. Between 1948 and 1989 there were no examples of popular unrest or significant dissident movements.

Since the beginning of 1990 the accelerated institutional democratization of Bulgaria has passed through three stages: first, a relatively prolonged round-table negotiation resulting in an agreement to proceed with constitutional amendments designed to allow democratic and fair elections to select a Constituent Assembly; second, a rapid and in some ways pre-emptive constitution-making process; and third, a protracted, and as yet incomplete, period in which legislation on regulating the major democratic institutions is adopted.

In institutional terms the Bulgarian political system seems to be overperforming (one does not find the kind of open violations of constitutional and legal provisions that are observed in some of the other CEECs). On the other hand, the Bulgarian economy and even Bulgarian society itself are visibly degrading owing to ineffective governance. In this chapter I shall outline the positive and negative tendencies in political developments during the past five years.

Positive tendencies since 1991

Institutional system and consolidation of the party system

The established system of government has proved to be stable and capable of channelling political and social conflicts smoothly. Since 1990 there have been three general elections and several changes of government between elections.

After the first general election, the former Communist Party, the Bulgarian Socialist Party (BSP), held the majority of seats. However, the BSP government was replaced by a grand coalition government during the 1990–1 Grand National Assembly. After the 1991 election the Union of Democratic Forces (UDF) established a minority government supported by the Movement for Rights and Freedoms (MRF), the Turkish party. This was subsequently replaced by a loose coalition government of the MRF, BSP and a group of centrist members of Parliament who split off from the UDF. In the 1994 elections the BSP once again won a majority and established a government with the general support of the Bulgarian Business Block (BBB).

Thus, peaceful alternation of government has been clearly established, not only through elections but also through parliamentary procedures which enable the reconfiguration of party coalitions and which have helped to avoid institutional power vacuums. A unique feature of the Bulgarian situation, which arises not so much from the institutional framework as from the traditions and culture of the political elite, is the way in which one and the same majority is able to elect a new Cabinet in cases of governmental crisis. In 1992 the coalition between the UDF and MRF was incapable of doing this and consequently fell. Currently the economy's disastrous performance fosters expectations that when the stable BSP majority reaches the end of its mandate it will try to elect another, new Cabinet. If, as is possible but not likely, the majority splits, the 1992 practice of 'restructuring of the parliamentary majority' in cases of severe Cabinet crisis may be adopted again.

Two major political parties – the BSP and UDF – dominate the Bulgarian party system. They are opposed along a 'transitional' cleavage: the main divide between their party platforms and their voters' attitudes is of an 'ideological' nature (pro-communist/anti-communist). The classic socio-economic cleavages do not yet divide parties and voters. Of course, within both the BSP and UDF there are tendencies to develop as catch-all parties, but future unproductive splits might also occur in what now seems to be a very stable party system.

Despite the large number of parties participating in the general and local elections and the proportional electoral rules, the Bulgarian Parliament has never suffered from over-fragmentation. There are, in fact, signs of consolidation in the party system. There were four party factions in the 1990 Parliament, three in the 1991 Parliament, and five in the current (1994) Parliament. 'Secondary' fragmentation (within parties) due to weak party discipline, again typical in Central and Eastern Europe, was experienced in 1991 but was overcome in 1994 since electoral results in the second and third general elections clearly showed that splinter groups could rarely pass the 4 per cent threshold necessary to gain representation. Even in the 1995 local elections only a couple of non-parliamentary parties managed to have representatives elected to just a few municipal councils. The only splinter group that succeeded in passing the 4 per cent threshold was the coalition People's Union (PU). It was able to do so because its member parties proved to be loyal partners despite their strategic disagreements.

It is clear that stable electoral regulations have helped avoid the danger of recurring partisan changes in the electoral regulations (typical of inter-war Bulgaria). General elections have been held three times (1990, 1991, 1994) and local elections twice (1991, 1995). During the first (founding) elections for a Constituent Assembly with 400 seats, a mixed electoral system was adopted (half of the mandates were elected in single-member districts and half by proportional representation with seats allocated according to the D'Hondt system). Since 1991 general elections have been held according to the provisions of the proportional half of the 1990 electoral law.

The 1995 change in the local election law preserved the electoral formula and introduced a key improvement, the abolition of coloured ballot sheets. Coloured ballot sheets were one of the essential peculiarities of Bulgarian electoral law and voter behaviour. Colour happens to be a traditional means of identifying political parties (violet is the colour of the conservatives, green of the liberals, red of the communists and orange of the agrarians). Initially, at the beginning of the century, coloured ballot sheets were used in order to help illiterate voters make their choices, but currently, coloured ballots discriminate against small parties. As there are only four basic colours, only four parties can have a genuine coloured ballot sheet; the rest have white with coloured strips. The colours are distributed by the Central Election Committee and are usually the subject of heated debate. Coloured ballot sheets were abolished for the 1995 local elections, and in May 1996 the Parliament abolished them in presidential elections. Hence it looks likely that there will be no coloured ballot sheets in the next general election.

Governing by consensus

Since 1990 there have been no serious public threats to the democratic order by any political party or former communist state structure, and no significant acts of violence. The initial liberalization – as in Poland, Hungary,

Czechoslovakia and East Germany – was introduced by the incumbent communist elite, and the first steps were negotiated at national roundtable talks, held in January–May 1990.

After winning more than 50 per cent of the seats in the Constituent Assembly the BSP tried to promote a consensus policy of shared responsibility, demanding a grand coalition government. The BSP was also the leading party within the two-thirds majority that worked out the new constitution. The presidential elections have shown the ability of the political elite and the general public to promote a head of state committed to democracy and oriented towards consensus-building, bargaining and tolerance. The former president, Zhelyu Zhelev, was first elected as the result of a consensus-seeking procedure by 400 Constituent Assembly deputies and re-elected in the 1992 direct presidential elections with the support of the UDF, MRF and other centre and centre-right parties. The presidential elections of 27 October and 3 November 1996 have once again proved that the institution of the president, although relatively weak, helps to promote consensus. The current parliamentary opposition had to go through a slow and painful process of consolidation in order to win the direct presidential elections and preserve its legitimacy as a viable alternative to the governing post-communist party.

The absence of militant nationalism

Bulgaria has long been a nation-state and has always been a unitary state. The dramatic changes in Central and Eastern Europe demonstrate that during post-totalitarian transitions constitutional arrangements of the federative form are the most vulnerable. The devolution of the socialist federative state could be described as a replacement of the dismantled 'prison of nations' by 'provincial or county goals of minorities'. In former federations – Czechoslovakia, the Soviet Union and Yugoslavia – militant nationalism and the 'ethnification of politics' emerged in response to changes in the constitutional provisions regulating the form of state, its sovereignty and its territory. This was not the case in Bulgaria.

Bulgaria's communist regime never considered a federal arrangement or any other kind of autonomy as a possible solution to the problems of the Turkish ethnic minority. On the contrary, immediately before the 1989 liberalization it repressively targeted the Turkish minority. With the notable exception of Romania, this was quite unusual in Central and Eastern Europe in the 1980s. In both Bulgaria and Romania the regimes tried to gain wider public support by promoting nationalistic policies and campaigning for ethnic assimilation.

In post-communist Bulgaria, changes to the constitutional provisions regulating human rights became the most pressing and indispensable issue. These changes were a kind of litmus test for the transition from authoritarian to democratic governance and determined the key role that the Turkish minority's political organization, the Movement for Rights and Freedoms (MRF), was to play in the process of democratization.

The main issue was to integrate the Turkish minority through political participation and to prevent the consolidation of extremist nationalist associations. Although the constitution includes provisions banning parties based on ethnic and religious lines, explicitly discriminatory articles are absent because the Bulgarian constitution avoids the term 'minority'. Current political practice and the strategies of the parliamentary parties are characterized by the lack of militant nationalism, and the MFR has been represented in the Parliament and in local government since the 1990 elections. The MRF was even a member of the governing coalition from 1991 to 1994. Hence we can find only a mild form of nationalism, owing in part to the fact that anti-Turkish feelings have their most influential expression in some of the local party allies of the BSP, such as the Fatherland Party of Labour, and their demands are additionally refracted by BSP policy.

The separation of powers

Ever since the establishment of democracy, the Bulgarian Parliament has had a single chamber. Before World War II, the constitutionality of legislation was never discussed, and only two laws were overturned because they were unconstitutional. Today the main check on the power of the Parliament is provided by the Constitutional Court, the functions of which have been compared to those of a second parliamentary chamber. The parliamentary opposition has been the main petitioner to the Court and the number of decisions for unconstitutionality is quite high. For example, during 1991–2, when there was a stable coalition government composed of the UDF (110 seats) and MRF (24 seats) with the BSP (106 seats) as the only opposition party and the main petitioner to the Court, six of the 21 cases involving parliamentary conflicts were resolved against the ruling majority. Since the beginning of 1995 there has been a stable BSP majority in the Parliament and the main petitioners have been UDF, PU and MRF deputies, and six of eleven appeals concerning the unconstitutionality of parliamentary acts were upheld.

The prosecutor general is the other active appellant to the Court and has an even better record for winning appeals. Five of the six parliamentary Acts appealed against the prosecutor general were judged to be unconstitutional. The president, whose veto is very weak, has also appealed against some legislative texts.

The judiciary also enjoys a considerable autonomy despite attempts by virtually all parliamentary majorities to undermine it. All the Parliament's attempts to influence the recruitment of magistrates have been blocked by the Constitutional Court. The judiciary has played a crucial role in reconciling the post-electoral tensions provoked by the victory of the MRF candidate for mayor in Kardzhali. Twice, in 1991 and in 1995, the election results were appealed against to the Court by the losers (the BSP and its local allies), and twice the Court has affirmed the legality of the results.

The judiciary, however, is the branch of government that lacks a properly developed structure. This creates inefficiency, which in turn creates a severe and persistent legitimation crisis.

Local government

The 1991 constitution contains a separate chapter regulating the autonomy of local government in general terms. In September 1991 the Parliament passed the Law on Local Government, which specified and implemented the constitutional provisions. This law gave the municipalities responsibility for health care, education, social services and local infrastructure, including roads, water supply and sewerage.

The democratization of local government in Bulgaria started with a delay of a year and a half. The first local elections were held in October 1991, simultaneously with the second free general elections. The victory of the non-communist coalition UDF was much more decisive at the local level since the mayors are directly elected. The most recent local elections, in November 1995, reproduced the BSP's overwhelming 1994 victory. The opposition preserved its mayors and majorities in only the three largest cities, including the capital, Sofia, and about 30 towns.

The municipal budgets are also decentralized, both to meet the requirements of democratization and because of the insolvency of the state. The practice of raising funds for municipal budgets through privatization of local assets has been established. It has been accompanied by numerous cases of embezzlement and corruption, which have provoked conflicts, between the mayors and the municipal councils, that have been brought before the Constitutional Court. This indicates that there are some institutional checks against the *partitocrazia*, which is much stronger at the local level. Since 1995 much attention has been paid to conflicts between the regional governors, appointed by the BSP government, and the municipal authorities, dominated by the opposition.

Non-governmental organizations

The non-governmental organizations (NGOs) in Bulgaria seem to be flourishing. The first boom occurred from September 1991 to April 1992, after the adoption of a special law introducing a tax- and duty-free regime for the economic activities of all political parties, foundations and students' co-operatives provided a rationale for establishing numerous NGOs. The second wave of NGO development is related to international (mainly West European and American) funding.

The activities of the NGOs are broadly covered by the media and significantly contribute to the development of civil society networks. They are very active in the spheres of education, ethnic minorities and the environment. The only legal restrictions concern non-traditional religious/denominational groups.

Negative tendencies since 1991

Even consolidated democracies confront and experience serious challenges and problems. I shall leave aside such problems and challenges, and focus on the tendencies that have appeared during the past five years that are hampering the process of democratization.

The position of ethnic minorities

There are two destructive tendencies regarding ethnic minorities. The first is the exceedingly high level of chronic unemployment among members of the Turkish minority, who are predominantly employed in tobacco production. This has led to their mass emigration to Turkey, although emigration is currently being restricted by the Turkish government. The second is the dramatic pauperization of the Roma minority, which has no exit option and is steadily being marginalized. Roma live in more or less isolated suburbs. Their life expectancies, child mortality rates, crime rates and literacy rates are much worse than the national average and are deteriorating.

Economic hardship and privatization manqué

The aggravation of the economic situation and the escalating crime rate hamper democratization. The Group on East–South Systems Transformation has pointed out that it is quite difficult and arbitrary to define some substantial characteristics of democratic institutions. It offers instrumental criteria for establishing sustainable democracy, arguing that 'democracy is sustainable, when its institutional framework promotes normatively desirable and politically desired objectives, such as freedom from arbitrary violence and material security'.

Unfortunately, six years after the first democratic elections, the Bulgarian government is still unable to provide these two desired objectives. This failure is to a large extent due to the slow, sometimes stalled, process of privatization. The privatization strategy chosen in 1991–2 was to promote market privatization only in industry and to restore property in agriculture to the previous owners (restitution). The latter was essentially a substitute for mass privatization. The 1993–4 coalition government of Prime Minister Ljuben Berov proclaimed the restructuring of the economy and mass privatization as its priorities, but its initiative was blocked, although the required normative basis was enacted. Even though the current cabinet under Prime Minister Zhan Videnov has a majority, it has still failed to implement the necessary steps.

Economic policy in general has been inefficient. The legislative vacuum in vital spheres of the economy has become notorious. There are no true market agents, and the major financial institutions are speculative, unstable and dependent on the state. Economic analyses also provide indisputable proof that instead of privatization there is a process of decapitalization, with profitable industrial assets being sold off.

The *partitocrazia* is particularly powerful in the economic sphere. The complex and intertwined network of corporate interests and pressure groups within the governing party is the major cause of the blocking of economic reform. This has led to two very painful waves of inflation: in 1994, when the inflation rate hit 120 per cent, and in 1996, when it is expected to exceed 150 per cent.

Criminalization of the economy and society

Since 1994 there have been repeated examples of unprecedented and unpunished mafia wars or public executions of policemen or members of private security agencies. Indisputably there is a considerable degree of criminalization of the economy, which is particularly visible in financial services and tourism. The assassination of former Prime Minister Andrei Lukanov, a key political and financial figure after 1990, was another dramatic example of the uncontrolled criminalization of all spheres of social life.

Two major legacies of the communist regime contribute to the inability of successive Bulgarian governments to deal with the problems of economic reform and internal security: the weak state and the well-developed clientelistic networks at both the national and local levels.

Increasing political polarization

As described in various analyses by different authors, it often happens that during the initial stage of the peaceful liberalization of an authoritarian regime there are two groups that promote changes: the reformers within the incumbent elite and the moderates within the ascending elite. They generate the basis for the future consensus and set the rules for the future interactions between the major political agencies.

As elsewhere in Central and Eastern Europe, after the electoral defeat of the former Communist Party Bulgaria's ascending elite opted for a radical, non-co-operative policy towards the incumbents. The radicals, not the moderates, dominated the decision-making process in the 1992 UDF government. The result was not only a loss of support and the return of the left, but also a split within the governing coalition UDF and two years of unproductive government. The BSP experienced a similar radicalization after its spectacular victory in the 1994 general elections. The hard-liners began to dominate the decision-making in the government.

During the past five years the governing parties in Bulgaria have tended to radicalize their platforms instead of making them more consensus oriented. It seems that those who promoted the liberalization of the communist regime and laid down the institutional basis of democracy never enjoyed recognition and quickly lost legitimacy. The unproductive polarization of the major political parties has very destructive consequences.

One of these consequences is the recurring legislative agenda. There are several laws, regulating key elements of the newly established democratic state authorities or key economic spheres, that have been repeatedly revisited. Every new majority in the Parliament has tried to introduce changes to the Law on Restitution of Landed Property and the laws regulating the autonomy of the judiciary. The Constitutional Court has overridden some of the amendments, but the fact that parliamentary majorities repeatedly vote for the same unconstitutional amendments has led to deadlock. Obviously the confrontation between BSP and UDF refers not only to party programmes and policy strategies, but also to basic legislative acts regulating government procedures and constituting the emerging system of democratic institutions.

The ensuing deadlock creates legislative vacuums in vital spheres of public life. Although deputies have repeatedly submitted crucial bills, six years after the beginning of the Bulgarian transition and five years after the adoption of the new constitution, laws on the Supreme Administrative Court, on the Supreme Court of Cassation and on Public Service have still not been enacted. Two other essential laws – the Law on Bank Failure/Bankruptcy (June 1996) and the Law on National Radio and Television (July 1996) – were passed only recently.

This legislative vacuum is even more striking since the transitional and concluding provisions of the constitution explicitly require passage of precisely these laws within a three-year period. Irreconcilable differences between the two major political parties do not provide a sufficient and reasonable explanation; a more plausible explanation would refer to the fact that when these spheres are not regulated, the parliamentary majority or the executive can exercise substantial control over them.

The media

The current mechanism of media regulation gives the legislature direct control over the national electronic media. According to 'temporary provisions' passed by the Parliament in 1990, the activities of the National Radio and Television are controlled and sanctioned by the Parliamentary Committee on Radio and Television. The committee in fact acts as a branch of the executive and guarantees full control of the majority over the activities of the National Radio and Television, and the national news agency. Every new majority elects new directors of the national electronic media.

Partisan control of the administration

There have been three substantial waves of change at all levels of state administration (in 1992, 1993–4 and 1995) related to changes in government. This reflects the practice of maintaining partisan control of the administration. Under a special amendment to the Labour Code ('Kapualiev's amendment'), middle and senior managers in the administration and state enterprises can be fired at short notice without particular justification. Thus 500 directors of state enterprises were replaced during the most recent wave of partisan replacements. This amendment has been annulled, but only after the new BSP majority had made the necessary replacements.

As the Law on the Civil Service has not yet been adopted, there is still no reliable legal constraint on partisan recruitment to the administration. The new Law on National Radio and Television also gives the parliamentary majority and the Cabinet a dominant role in the appointment of the members of the governing bodies of the public electronic media.

Inconsistent strategies in foreign policy

All over the region, the return of post-communist parties has led to a revitalization of political and economic contacts with Russia, but in Bulgaria this tendency has developed almost to the extreme, if not in actual political behaviour, then at least in public discourse. What is more, the current majority promotes a foreign policy under which relations with the European Union (EU) and the North Atlantic Treaty Organization (NATO) are to be developed within the context of Bulgarian–Russian relations.

The most controversial issue concerns Bulgarian membership of NATO. Factions within the BSP publicly express cautious to negative attitudes towards membership and support the idea that Russia should play a special role in the stabilization of the Balkans.

The parliamentary opposition parties and the President oppose the BSP's negative attitude towards NATO. The paradoxical outcome is that the conflict over membership of NATO strengthens support for integration with the EU, although all BSP experts seem to be well aware that closer integration with the EU would hardly be possible without integration with NATO.

The results of the 1996 presidential election

Regardless of these socially destructive negative tendencies, the results of the 1996 presidential election and concomitant political developments signal the vitality of Bulgaria's democratic institutions and of its emerging civil society.

Petar Stoyanov of the UDF won an overwhelming victory. On the level both of the political elite and of the public, highly ideologized politicians of both extreme left and right have indisputably lost credibility. The first and the most explicit change in the strategy of the major political forces is the search for consensus regarding the setting of priorities in domestic and foreign policies. This is viewed by both the governing socialist party and the opposition as an inevitable first step, since the BSP controls the majority in the current Parliament, elected with a term lasting until 1998, while the opposition has the support of the majority of the public. This just might result in a democratic way out of the political deadlock: either irresolvable cabinet crisis will lead to early elections in which a broad centre-right coalition government following a non-ideological approach to policy might be elected; or a new socialist Cabinet and an Austrian-type consociational democracy could be established. Given the immaturity of the Bulgarian democracy, the first seems to be the easier and less painful solution.

Conclusion

We may conclude that Bulgaria is over-performing where formal, normative institutional criteria are applied, but the democratic regime is in an extremely critical situation in terms of real outputs from the political and economic process. If Bulgarian democracy is still to be consolidated and stabilized, it must confront two serious challenges. First, it must build a consensus concerning the priorities of domestic and foreign policies as well as on substantial aspects of the legislative regulation of key state institutions. Second, it must address the country's poor economic performance.

12

Conclusion: Towards a European Democratic Space

MARY KALDOR AND IVAN VEJVODA

In this book we have drawn a distinction between formal and substantive democracy. Formal democracy refers to the institutions and procedures of democracy. Substantive democracy refers to political equality, to the distribution of power, to a political culture of democratic participation. Substantive democracy is the situation in which the individual citizen is able to influence decisions that affect his or her life, in which political institutions are responsive to the demands of citizens.

In the introduction we argued that in all ten of the Central and East European countries (CEECs) that have applied to join the European Union (EU) the prerequisites of formal democracy have been largely, if not completely, achieved. But this is not the case for substantive democracy. Different countries exhibit different weaknesses. These can include, to varying degrees, a tendency for political parties to extend control over different spheres of social life in ways that limit political participation; a tendency for the government to influence the electronic media; a politicized and clientelistic administration; racism and xenophobia, which can provide a basis for populism; and a widespread sense of personal insecurity owing to rising crime, inadequate law enforcement and an underdeveloped judiciary.

What all the CEECs lack is an active citizenry able to check these tendencies. There are, in several countries, numerous non-governmental organizations (NGOs), but, at the same time, participation in formal political institutions is low. Membership of political parties is low; voter turnout in elections has tended to decline; apathy, disillusionment and cynicism are widely reported.

The implication of our distinction between formal and substantive democracy is that a differentiated strategy that would address the weaknesses of substantive democracy in individual cases is required. Such a strategy is possible only in a context where it is possible to identify those weaknesses because concerned individuals and groups draw attention to them and have forms of access to the relevant decision-making institutions. In this chapter we argue that one of the most relevant of these institutions is the EU, and we put forward the notion of a European Democratic Space as an arena in which the primary mission of the EU is viewed as the deepening of democracy not only among potential new entrants but within the EU itself.

Democracy and 'globalization'

The weakness of political engagement is partly due to the legacy of totalitarianism: the enduring suspicion of parties, politicians, bureaucrats. But as András Bozóki points out in Chapter 8, it also has to do with the so-called simultaneity problem; that is to say, the fact that the transition from totalitarianism to democracy is taking place at the same time as the transition from a planned autarkic economy to an open market system, and the transition from a Soviet-dominated international framework. The breakup of the Council for Mutual Economic Assistance (Comecon), the disintegration of states, and the processes of liberalization, macro-economic stabilization and privatization have all contributed to dramatic falls in income and to growing social and economic inequalities, which, in turn, contribute to dissatisfaction with the political class.

Transition can be viewed as an opening up to the world economy and to global political arrangements, as one aspect of the various complex contemporary phenomena that are often lumped together under the rubric of 'globalization'. In this context, the space for manoeuvre of national governments is more and more limited. All mainstream political parties are committed to transition policies, and this may explain why it is so difficult for any individual party to offer a distinctive programme to the electorate and why it is so difficult for a party in power to respond to popular demands. In such a constrained framework there is a tendency for governments to push forward with difficult economic decisions on the basis of a presumed formal democratic legitimacy but without consultations or democratic participation (Arato, 1993).

It is generally assumed that the transition to a market economy is a necessary condition for democracy. It is certainly true that, quite apart from its economic advantages over central planning, private ownership and individual economic initiative are necessary, if only to provide space in society that is outside state control, to ensure the existence of financially autonomous institutions which can criticize and check abuses of state power. Transition, however, has often involved more than this; it has been associated with a neo-liberal ideology in which an extreme version of the free market has been imposed from above in societies in which public (as opposed to either private or state) institutions are inadequately developed. Not only has this led to the problems described above, but also it has engendered a growing sense that societies are being created in which egoism and self-interest are valued above all else. Pushing through policies of this kind, even in the well-intentioned belief that this will benefit society in the long run, can easily encourage the persistence of limited forms of democracy – 'low-intensity' democracy, semi-democracy, democratic despotism – in which the participation of the citizenry is greatly diminished or reduced to a limited number of occasions. In an important recent article, George Soros (1997) argued that the greatest threat to the 'open society' nowadays is a neo-liberal ideology.

Until 1989 the citizens of the CEECs were exposed to politics only as purely instrumental and manipulative action on the part of the rulers. The danger is that they come to experience transition strategies in a similar way. There is a sense that transition strategies stem from a collusion between the national authorities and 'global' institutions such as the International Monetary Fund (IMF), the World Bank and even the EU. Politics could again come to be experienced as external, instrumental and manipulative; as an act of distant institutions. In contrast to those societies where democracy is more deeply embedded, there is a real danger of a loss of citizen confidence in democracy *tout court*.

In several countries the largest political parties are the former communist parties. They have abandoned socialism and are now committed proponents of transition strategies. Even though they may express more concern for social issues in election campaigns than other parties, when in power their capacity to deliver is no greater than that of their opponents. Since they remain the 'left' parties, the political spectrum has shifted rightwards. Those parties which seek a distinctive stance are therefore likely to emphasize national or religious identity. The latter seems to offer a moral sense of community that is absent in the cruel new world of transition.

A thread which runs through all the chapters in this book is the absence of emancipatory ideas; in particular, the need for an inclusive, forward-looking political project that could offer a more hopeful future than either the routine transition strategies experienced up to now or the backward-looking nostalgic appeals to nationalism. As Marcin Król concludes in Chapter 5, 'What . . . really endangers democracy is not a weak nationalism but the lack of a common project. Individualist and utilitarian attitudes – which are not dangerous when accompanied by a solid moral vision of society – seem to be overwhelming.'

This set of problems has its parallels in the West. The constraints of so-called globalization have produced a consensus at elite levels around market ideas, deregulation and liberalization and about the need, at the very least, to reform the welfare state. The socialist and social democratic parties, even if they have not changed their names, have, like their former communist counterparts in the East, largely joined this consensus. The convergence criteria of the Maastricht Treaty impose a constraint on political choice for EU member states that is at least akin to the discipline of transition strategies.

It could be argued that in the context of globalization it is very difficult to achieve substantive democracy at a national level, or, more precisely, only at a national level. The lives of the individual citizen are profoundly influenced by decisions taken at many different levels: the European, the global, the national, the regional and the local. Yet the focus of democratic politics remains the national level.

If by substantive democracy we mean the ability of citizens to influence decisions that affect their lives, then democratic politics has to focus on all the levels at which significant decisions are taken. In this context, the European level is of great importance. It may be that it is only through a measure of political integration that substantive democracy can be consolidated, in the case of Central and Eastern Europe, and reinvigorated, in the case of Western Europe. The question is whether political integration could offer an alternative forward-looking project and, if so, what this might imply for the whole European enterprise.

The return to Europe

One of the key demands of the 1989 revolutions was to 'return to Europe'. For those citizens who participated in the revolutions, the return to Europe meant not only the democracy and prosperity enjoyed by the West European countries during the post-war period but also a commitment to what were regarded as 'European values': democracy, civil society, citizenship, individualism, reason, enlightenment. Subsequently, the 'return to Europe' was translated in practical terms into membership of European institutions, especially the EU. But the reality of the EU as an institution and of the process of joining it are very different from the idea proclaimed in 1989.

The goals of the founders of the EU were not so very different from the goals of the 1989 revolutionaries. When Monnet and Schuman launched the European Coal and Steel Community (ECSC) in 1950, their strategy was to use very practical means to secure peace and democracy on the continent of Europe and, as was stated in the preamble to the treaty, 'to create real solidarity'.[1] This technique of finding intergovernmental compromises on concrete forms of co-operation, which has characterized the EU and its predecessors, the European Communities, has produced a peculiar animal. As many scholars have pointed out, the EU is also a *sui generis* polity (Keohane and Hoffman, 1991; Jachtenfuchs, 1995). It is neither a typical intergovernmental international institution nor a new European state, even though it possesses significant elements of supranationality.

On the one hand, it has evolved through grand compromises from above. This has tended to lead to an emphasis on the marketplace (the common market, the single market, economic and monetary union (EMU)), especially in the past two decades, because this is the area where agreement is easiest to reach. On the other hand, it has also evolved through incremental processes of functional integration resulting from those compromises that have become embedded in both formal and informal institutions; for example, the Commission itself, sectoral networks, the activities of the European Court of Justice, the plethora of regulations governing environmental and social standards, etc.

What has been missing, by and large, from these processes is the underlying involvement of European democratic politics. The grand compromises result from the political relationships between governments, which may be responsive to their individual domestic constituencies but are, first and foremost, elite-level bargains. The functional processes of integration give rise to a politics of special interests and generate what some have described as 'issue networks' (Petersen, 1995).

What is lacking, however, is a Europe-wide political debate in which European institutions are directly responsive to European citizens and in which the goals of the EU can be articulated through a bottom-up process. Hence the loftier European goals can easily be swamped in the politics of intergovernmentalism and special interests. The deals that nurture the European animal in its current stage of evolution need not necessarily be congruent with the kind of European animal that could contribute to the original goals.

When people refer to the 'democratic deficit' what they usually mean is a deficit in formal terms. Nation-states have surrendered part of their sovereignty to European institutions which do not meet the formal criteria for democracy. Elements of sovereignty that used to belong to accountable parliaments have been abrogated in favour of institutions in which decisions are initiated by an appointed agency, the Commission, often in consultation with functional networks, and finalized in the relatively secretive environment of the Council of Ministers. The role of the European Parliament, compared with that of national parliaments, is severely restricted (Dinan, 1994).

Undoubtedly, formal democratic reform is of utmost importance, but when we talk about the absence of a European domestic politics, we are also talking about the 'democratic deficit' in substantive terms. We are talking both about the lack of forms of access for critical individuals and groups at a European level and about the absence of a sense of civic belonging at a European level. We are referring to the fact that there is no Europe-wide debate about the future of Europe, except perhaps at elite levels; rather, the debates are conducted within individual states and are largely about what Europe means in each national context.

The relationship between the EU and the CEECs has largely followed a similar pattern, with functional links established as a result of inter-governmental agreements. The commitment to eventual membership, conditional on certain (qualitative) economic and political criteria, was made at the Copenhagen European Council in June 1993 (Sedelmeier, 1994). At the Madrid Summit in December 1995 the European Council asked the Commission to prepare opinions on the CEECs' applications, to be ready shortly after the conclusion of the Intergovernmental Conference (IGC). It expressed the hope that the 'preliminary stages' of accession negotiations would take place six months after the end of the IGC. Associa-tion agreements ('Europe Agreements') were signed with ten CEECs between 1991 and 1996. Although these agreements expressed lofty goals and include provisions for a 'political dialogue', they were basically commitments to open trade asymmetrically over a ten-year period. There were some concessions to special interests, as expressed in the limited concessions made by the EU in the so-called sensitive sectors, and in the provisions for contingent protection for both the EU and the CEECs (Rollo and Smith, 1993). In addition, as part of the EU's 'pre-accession strategy', the Commis-sion presented a 'White Paper on the preparation of the associated countries of Central and Eastern Europe for the Community's internal market' (Smith *et al.*, 1996). By and large, the CEECs have responded positively and have started on its implementation. Alongside these intergovernmental arrange-ments, a programme of technical assistance has been initiated through a variety of programmes, especially the PHARE/TACIS assistance pro-gramme,[2] through which a range of concrete links are being created.[3]

Many commentators have drawn attention to the implications of enlarge-ment for the evolution of the European animal. The addition of ten more members would require some changes in decision-making procedures. The current arrangements for decision-making in the Council of Ministers and the College of Commissioners would become unwieldy with up to 27 member states. Moreover, there are serious implications for the EU's budget and emphasis on the market. Given the low level of gross domestic product (GDP) of the aspiring members and the undeveloped structure of CEEC agriculture, enlargement would mean a very substantial increase in the Common Agricultural Policy's (CAP) budget as well as in structural funds, at least in the framework of present arrangements.[4] Given the constraints of EMU, it is doubtful whether the present EU members would be willing or able to countenance such increases.

It is often argued that, in any case, both the CAP and the structural funds have to be reformed. Moreover, since the CEEC governments are anxious to be accepted as members, they would be willing to accept lower levels of financial assistance as a share of income than is currently the case, for example, for Greece or Portugal.

Looked at from the point of view of the citizens of the CEECs, however, it could be argued that further trade liberalization might well widen the social and economic divergence between East and West; the EU already has a sizeable trade surplus with the CEECs. In such a context, even an increase in the EU budget, calculated on the basis of present norms, might not be sufficient to compensate for the ensuing stresses and strains of economic integration. The consequences could be higher unemployment and greater poverty, and more disillusionment with and distance from decision-makers, with worrying implications for the stability not only of the CEECs but of the EU itself.

As Helen Wallace (1997) points out, the EMU project is currently testing the extent of elite-level solidarity among the existing members of the EU, calling into question how far even the present model can be extended:

> In an EU where economic regulation is easier to agree than social redistribu-
> tion, where monetary rigour is more valued than generosity in public
> expenditure, and where labour market immobility contends with pressures on
> competitiveness ... forms of local segmentation and political affiliation may
> produce centrifugal consequences to set against the pressures for centripetal
> policy integration. (p. 227)

The most important condition for successful enlargement to the East could be the development of what former Commission President Jacques Delors called 'active solidarity' between EU citizens and citizens of the CEECs, as distinct from elite co-operation only.[5] This is what we mean when we put forward the concept of a European Democratic Space. We mean that individual Europeans see themselves as part of a common endeavour which could be defined in terms of the deepening of democracy. We mean a commitment to formal and substantive democracy among all member states of the EU and among the CEECs as a concrete primary goal of the EU, for citizens as well as for elites. In effect, we are proposing a political movement for democracy. The most positive finding of this study has been the energy and initiative to be found throughout the CEECs at a local level. Individuals have sought ways to change their situations through forming NGOs, setting up small businesses or getting involved in local politics. Often they make links with similar individuals and groups in Western Europe, thus acting as harbingers of a possible European civil society. The problem is that these efforts are often frustrated by the overall economic and political climate, by centralizing tendencies at national levels and by financial constraints. A political movement for democracy would need to be able to mobilize these local efforts and provide a public political expression of their concerns at the European level.

The problem is how to provide a context in which such a movement can exist; how to create a medium through which a European-wide political debate can be conducted. The national segmentation of the public sphere is the perennial obstacle to moving beyond the current configuration of intergovernmentalism and functionalism. In the rest of this concluding chapter, we reflect on the notion of democratic space and on the way in which the national segmentation of politics currently represents a constraint, not only on European integration, but more importantly on the process of democratization across Europe.

A European Democratic Space

Europe is still divided, even though the Cold War is over. Central and Eastern Europe is no longer part of the East, but it has not joined the West either. The future of this historically troubled part of the world may well be the most salient issue for the whole continent. If Central and Eastern Europe is excluded from the European project, the continent will be divided again. If Central and Eastern Europe is included in the European project on present terms, then it could well import its troubles to the western part of the continent, exacerbating already existing tendencies for distant political engineering to act as a substitute for democracy and for the growth of extremist exclusivist movements.

Both Western and Central and Eastern Europe bear heavy responsibility for stability and peace on the continent. This is why their citizenries need to be engaged in the forthcoming processes of enlargement, which also entails the need for the imagination and invention of a shared democratic space. By this we mean a space in which ordinary people, through mutual discussions and joint actions, appear to each other as citizens in an attempt to reach decisions that concern everyone. This is no simple task when the disparities between these two parts of Europe are still great. But it is just these disparities that spell out the urgency to undertake clear steps at all levels to venture into the uncharted territories of a modern common democratic polity.

The temptation of the *arcana imperii*, of invisible power, both in nation-states and at the European level is still great. The more or less explicit desire to employ primarily a means of political engineering as a way of attaining the goals of democracy and the market inhibits the civic energies of those willing to self-organize from below. A democratic space implies that power is not circumscribed within a bureaucratic organ or an individual. The mere existence of this space is a precondition for the appearance of a common Europe. It is by participating in such a space, by becoming visible on the public stage, that individuals can apprehend each other as equals (Lefort, 1988).

The tensions arising between the conflicting tendencies of the will to contract or expand democratic space have accompanied political modernity since its inception. These processes have been both complex and ambiguous (Woloch, 1994). Andrew Arato (1993) has convincingly shown that when, in these first post-1989 years, there were periods of contraction of democratic space, restrictions of democracy or attempts at semi-secret arrangements, democratic responses were (contrary to many expectations) often immediate and manifest through various forms of pressure, denunciation and opposition. This led to the insight that a shift of the 'locus of democratisation to civil society . . . is a better way of solving the problem of the relationship between the two transitions': political and economic (Arato, 1993, p. 645). In other words, the public sphere is the only possible arena in which the simultaneity problem can be resolved. It is only by fostering social and political imagination, by using enabling strategies, by strengthening the processes apparent in the spaces in which civic energies have been stifled during the long communist decades that politics, as a key element in the dynamics of change, can be redignified and thus become specifically rational for the citizens of the CEECs.

The interdependence of all parts of the continent calls for great prudence as well as boldness, and for a multiplication and permanent openness of all channels of political, economic, social and cultural communication. The democratic space thus requires a public sphere where informed discussion and reasoned agreement can take place. The public sphere in which critical debate on issues of general interest is institutionally guaranteed has historically played a crucial role in mediating between state and civil society.

Early civil society theorists were preoccupied with how to reconcile the demands of individualism in a secular polity with a shared sense of public responsibility, of the importance of participation in the public sphere. For thinkers like Adam Ferguson, the notion of civil society was underpinned by moral sentiment, by civilized attitudes towards fellow-citizens, which were not so very different from Delors's notion of 'active solidarity'. Such attitudes were contrasted with the more cynical conception of private self-interest put forward by later utilitarians and with statist or communitarian attitudes that tended to accompany socialist ideas (Seligman, 1992).

In Central and Eastern Europe, the public sphere, in so far as it ever existed, was eliminated during the communist period. In the West, it can be argued that with the development of welfare state democracy in the second part of this century there has been a decline in the role of the public sphere. Jürgen Habermas (1989) suggests that the public sphere has been transformed into an arena of competition between conflicting interests in which various groups and agencies meet to negotiate and compromise at a distance from the public view. In so far as there still exists a shared outlet for debate on questions of public importance, it tends to be nationally bounded by language, education, patterns of ownership of media, traditional party loyalties and so on. Whether one can envisage a reconstitution of such a public sphere in a wholly new setting is a question which forms part of the search for a formula which could lead to the invention of a European Democratic Space and is, therefore, of great importance to both Western and Central and Eastern Europe.

Could the concept of a European Democratic Space constitute the missing political project? Could it offer an alternative to both the egoistic privatized ideology of the market and the exclusive communitarianism of the nation? On the one hand, what is required is an active strategy for enhancing democracy in Central and Eastern Europe, for enabling and encouraging those bottom-up initiatives that can be observed throughout Central and Eastern Europe in which individuals and groups are trying to organize their lives through community development, local democracy, and cultural, educational and humanitarian activities. Such a strategy would focus on those features of substantive democracy that are weakest; for example, fostering alternative sources of information, especially in local areas; supporting local media; encouraging dialogue with minorities; stimulating debate about the distribution of tax revenue between different levels of governance; developing training programmes for public service; and strengthening private and public security.

A beginning has been made through initiatives such as the PHARE Democracy Programme. The problem is that these efforts are, as yet, insufficient for a variety of reasons: insufficient resources; a constraining economic and political environment; and the absence of mechanisms for evaluating initiatives and increasing their user-friendly character. While, undoubtedly, piecemeal improvements can be made, what is needed is, in a sense, a permanent political lobby for these kinds of activities, a public expression of bottom-up democratic initiatives that can jump-start a sense of 'active solidarity' in both moral and material terms.

Hence what is required, on the other hand, is the construction of a European public sphere in which critical voices from different parts of Europe and at all levels of society have access to policy-making and can help to define the 'democracy mission'. Essentially this means the development of networks of 'active solidarity', interdependencies for the democratic practice of justice, networks based on ideas rather than issues. Such networks would need to involve a range of social actors in co-operative and transnational forms of discourse. Pan-European networks already exist as a result both of the 'structured dialogue' and of various academic and cultural exchanges, but they tend to be confined to elites. The question is how to reach out beyond elite networks to, for example, local community organizations, women's groups and young people.

The electronic media are one important arena. Ideas need to be developed about the possibilities for accessible shared media debates or regular European TV news time. Consultations with NGOs, assistance for young people wanting to take part in a 'democracy mission', local partnerships or women's links are also avenues that should be explored.

The aim is the institutionalization of pan-European opportunities to raise key concerns about the process of democratization in a sustained and public way. To take one example, there is today a lively youth culture in Europe in which the values of anti-racism, anti-xenophobia, anti-homophobia and transnational solidarity are expressed in music, dance and theatre. Are there ways in which these widespread and strongly felt sentiments, which are currently associated with a tendency towards anti-political attitudes, can be translated into a pan-European activism?

These two aspects of the European Democratic Space – an active democracy mission and the construction of a European public sphere – are mutually reinforcing. Public debate is needed to generate the policies aimed at support for individual citizens, to stimulate 'active solidarity'.

At the same time, substantive policies, practical expressions of 'active solidarity', are needed on a large scale to show that public participation is worthwhile. A strengthening of democratic institutions at a national level is impossible unless it is also accompanied by an increased responsiveness and accountability of both continental and local institutions to their citizens. Thus, the dynamic interaction between policy and participation and between local and European levels of governance will buttress the way ahead. In the struggle to form democratic polities and viable, efficient economies in the CEECs the ordinary citizen must not be the last item on the agenda after all other issues have been settled and all foreign creditors have been paid off.

The citizens of the CEECs emerged from the long years of communist rule with high expectations for a better life. This is the energy they still possess that will help them to endure the many hardships that still lie ahead. The challenge they confront is likewise a challenge for the EU – a challenge to transform itself as both sides of Europe encounter each other with the common goal of confronting the new millennium. If political courage falters in Europe, then the very real fear of the reappearance of old evils will stalk among us once more.

Notes

1. Preamble, *Treaty Establishing the European Coal and Steel Community*, Paris, 18 April 1951.
2. At the insistence of the European Parliament, a 'Democracy Programme' was included in PHARE.
3. For the background to the EU's policy see Sedelmeier and Wallace (1996); for the background to enlargement see Grabbe and Hughes (1997), and Baldwin (1996).
4. For calculations about the costs of enlargement see Grabbe and Hughes (1997), Baldwin (1996) and Baldwin *et al.* (1997).
5. The notion of 'active solidarity' was influenced by Emanuel Mounier and was distinct from both self-interested individualism and the socialist project. This was essential to Delors's conception of a 'European model' in which Europe stands for a 'humane combination of institutions and ideas which could stimulate market success while simultaneously promoting social solidarities designed to ameliorate the harshness of market relations' (Ross, 1995, p. 4).

Further Reading

Arato, A. (1993), *From Neo-Marxism to Democratic Theory* (Armonk, NY: M. E. Sharpe).

Arato, A. and Fehér, F. (eds) (1991), *Crisis and Reform in Eastern Europe* (New Brunswick, NJ: Transaction Press).

Ash, T. G. (1990), *The Magic Lantern: The Revolution of '89 Witnessed in Warsaw, Budapest, Berlin and Prague* (New York, NY: Random House).

Ash, T. G. (1990), *The Uses of Adversity: Essays on the Fate of Central Europe* (New York, NY: Vintage).

Aslund, A. (ed.) (1992), *Market Socialism and the Restoration of Capitalism* (Cambridge: Cambridge University Press).

Baldersheim, H., Illner, M. and Offerdal, A. (eds) (1996), *Local Democracy and the Process of Transformation in East-Central Europe* (Boulder, CO: Westview Press).

Baloyra, E. A. (ed.) (1987), *Comparing New Democracies: Transition and Consolidation in Mediterranean Europe and the Southern Cone* (Boulder, CO: Westview Press).

Barany, Z. and Vinton, L. (1990), 'Breakthrough to democracy: elections in Poland and Hungary', *Studies in Comparative Communism*, 23(2), Summer, 196–212.

Batt, J. (1988), *Economic Reform and Political Change in Eastern Europe* (Basingstoke: Macmillan).

Batt, J. (1991), *East Central Europe from Reform to Transformation* (London: Pinter).

Berglund, S. and Aarebot, F. H. (1997), *The Political History of Eastern Europe in the 20th Century: The Struggle between Democracy and Dictatorship* (Cheltenham: Edward Elgar).

Berglund, S. and Dellenbrant, J. A. (eds) (1994), *The New Democracies in Eastern Europe: Party-Systems and Political Cleavages* (Aldershot: Edward Elgar).

Beyme, K. von (1993), 'Regime transition and recruitment of elites in Eastern Europe', *Governance*, 6(3), 409–25.

Beyme, K. von (1997), *Transitions to Democracy in Eastern Europe* (Basingstoke: Macmillan; New York: St Martin's Press).

Bourdieu, P. and Coleman, J. S. (eds) (1991), *Social Theory in a Changing Society* (Boulder, CO: Westview Press).

Bozóki, A. *et al.* (eds) (1992), *Post-Communist Transition: Emerging Pluralism in Hungary* (London: Pinter).

Brogan, P. (ed.) (1990), *The Captive Nations* (New York, NY: Avon Books).

Bryant, C. G. A. and Mokrzycki, E. (eds) (1994), *The New Great Transformation: Change and Continuity in East-Central Europe* (London: Routledge).

Calinescu, M. and Tismaneanu, V. (1991), 'The 1989 revolution and Romania's future', *Problems of Communism*, 45, January–April, 42–59.

Chirot, D. (1989), *The Origin of Backwardness in Eastern Europe* (Berkeley, CA: University of California Press).

Chirot, D. (ed.) (1991), *The Crisis of Leninism and the Decline of the Left: The Revolutions of 1989* (Seattle, WA: University of Washington Press).

Cohen, J. and Arato, A. (1992), *Civil Society and Political Theory* (Cambridge, MA: MIT Press).

Crawford, B. and Lijphart, A. (eds) (1997), *Liberalisation and Leninist Strategies: Comparative Perspectives on Democratic Transitions* (Berkeley, CA: International Area Studies).

Dahl, R. (1961), *Who Governs?* (New Haven, CT: Yale University Press).

Dahl, R. (1991), *Democracy and Its Critics* (New Haven, CT: Yale University Press).

Dahrendorf, R. (1990), 'Transitions: politics, economics and liberty', *Washington Quarterly*, 13, 133–42.

Dawisha, K. (1988), *Eastern Europe, Gorbachev and Reform* (Cambridge: Cambridge University Press).

Dawisha, K. and Parrott, B. (eds) (1997), *The Consolidation of Democracy in East-Central Europe* (Cambridge: Cambridge University Press).

Deacon, B. (ed.) (1992), *Social Policy, Social Justice and Citizenship in Eastern Europe* (Aldershot: Avebury).

Deacon, B. *et al.* (1992), *The New Eastern Europe: Social Policy, Past, Present, Future* (London: Sage).

Dentich, B. (ed.) (1979), *Legitimation of Regimes* (London: Sage).

Di Palma, G. (1991), 'Legitimation from the top to civil society: politico-cultural change in Eastern Europe', *World Politics*, 44, 49–80.

Diamond, L. (1989), 'Beyond authoritarianism and totalitariansim: strategies for democratization', *Washington Quarterly*, Winter, 141–60.

Diamond, L. (ed.) (1997), *Consolidating the Third Wave Democracies* (Baltimore: Johns Hopkins University Press).

Drachkovitch, M. M. (1982) (ed.), *East Central Europe: Yesterday–Today–Tomorrow* (Stanford, CA: Hoover Institute Press).

Duncan, G. (ed.) (1983), *Democratic Theory and Practice* (Cambridge: Cambridge University Press).

Duncan, G. and Lukes, S. (1963), 'The new democracy', *Political Studies*, 11(2), 156–77.

Duverger, M. (1964), *Political Parties* (London: Methuen).

Dvořáková, V. and Voráček, E. (1993), *The Legacy of the Past as a Factor in the Transformation Process in Postcommunist Countries of Central Europe* (Prague).

East, R. (1992), *Revolutions in Eastern Europe* (London: Pinter).

Echikson, W. (1990), *Lighting the Night: Revolution in Eastern Europe* (New York: William Morrow).

Einhorn, B. (1993), *Cinderella Goes to Market: Citizenship, Gender and Women's Movements in East Central Europe* (London: Verso).

Eisenstadt, S. N. (1992), 'The breakdown of communist regimes', *Daedalus*, 121(2), Spring, 21–41.

Ekiert, G. (1991), 'Democratization processes in East Central Europe: theoretical reconsiderations', *British Journal of Political Science*, 21(3), July, 285–313.

'Electoral statistics and public opinion data' (1993), *East European Politics and Societies*, 7(3), Fall, 555–76.

Elster, J. (1996), *The Round Table Talks and the Breakdown of Communism* (Chicago: University of Chicago Press).

Etzioni-Halévy, E. (1992), 'The autonomy of elites and transitions from non-democratic regimes: the cases of the Soviet Union and Poland', *Research in Political Sociology*, 6, 257–76.

Farrell, R. B. (ed.) (1970), *Political Leadership in Eastern Europe and the Soviet Union* (Chicago: Aldine).

Fehér, F. and Heller, A. (1990), *From Yalta to Glasnost: Dismantling Stalin's Empire* (Oxford: Basil Blackwell).

Fehér, F., Heller, A. and Markus, G. (1983), *Dictatorship over Needs* (Oxford: Basil Blackwell).

Fejtö, F. (1971), *A History of the People's Democracies* (London: Pall Mall).

Frentzel-Zagorska, J. (1990), 'Civil society in Poland and Hungary', *Soviet Studies*, 42(4), 759–77.

Friedrich, C. and Brzezinski, Z. (1956), *Totalitarian Dictatorship and Autocracy* (Cambridge, MA: Harvard University Press).

Funk, N. and Mueller, M. (1993), *Gender Politics and Post-Communism: Reflections from Eastern Europe and the Former Soviet Union* (London: Routledge).

Garber, L. and Bjorlund, E. (eds) (1992), *The New Democratic Frontier* (Washington, DC: National Democratic Institute for International Affairs).

Gati, C. (1974), *The Politics of Modernization in Eastern Europe* (New York: Praeger).

Glenny, M. (1993), *The Rebirth of History: Eastern Europe in the Age of Democracy*, 2nd edn (London: Penguin).

Goldfarb, J. (1989), *Beyond Glasnost: The Post-totalitarian Mind* (Chicago: University of Chicago Press).

Goldfarb, J. (1990), 'Post-totalitarian politics: ideology ends again', *Social Research*, 57(3), Fall, 533–56.

Graubard, S. R. (ed.) (1991), *Eastern Europe . . . Central Europe . . . Europe* (Boulder, CO: Westview Press).

Gyáni, G. (1993), 'Political uses of tradition in post-communist East Central Europe', *Social Research*, 60(4), Winter, 893–913.

Habermas, J. (1975), *Legitimation Crisis* (Boston: Beacon Press).

Habermas, J. (1990), 'What does socialism mean today? The rectifying revolution', *New Left Review*, 183, September–October, 3–21.

Hall, S., Held, D. and McGrew, T. (eds) (1992), *Modernity and Its Futures* (Cambridge: Polity Press).

Hammond, T. T. (ed.) (1975), *The Anatomy of Communist Takeovers* (New Haven, CT: Yale University Press).

Harrison, R. (1993), *Democracy* (London: Routledge).

Hawkes, N. (ed.) (1990), *Tearing down the Curtain: The People's Revolution in Eastern Europe* (London: Hodder & Stoughton).

Held, D. (1987), *Models of Democracy* (Cambridge: Polity Press).

Held, D. (1993), *Prospects for Democracy: North, South, East, West* (Cambridge: Polity Press).

Held, D. and Pollitt, C. (eds) (1986), *New Forms of Democracy* (London: Sage).

Held, J. (ed.) (1992), *The Columbia History of Eastern Europe in the Twentieth Century* (New York: Columbia University Press).

Held, J. (ed.) (1997), *Democracy and Right-Wing Politics in Eastern Europe in the 1990s* (Boulder, CO: East European Monographs; New York: distributed by Columbia University Press).

Hesse, J. J. (ed.) (1993), *Administrative Transformation in Central and Eastern Europe* (Oxford: Blackwell).

Higley, J. and Pakulski, J. (1992), 'Revolution and elite transformation in Eastern Europe', *Australian Journal of Political Science*, 27, 104–19.

Hill, R. and Zielonka, J. (1992), *Restructuring Eastern Europe* (Aldershot: Edward Elgar).

Hockenos, P. (1993), *Free to Hate: The Rise of the Right in Post-communist Eastern Europe* (London: Routledge).

Holmes, L. (1986), *Politics in the Communist World* (Oxford: Clarendon Press).

Holmes, L. (1997), *Post-communism: An Introduction* (Cambridge: Polity Press).

Horak, S. M. (1985), *Eastern European National Minorities, 1919–1980: A Handbook* (Littleton, CO: Libraries Unlimited).

Huntington, S. P. (1968), *Political Order in Changing Societies* (New Haven, CT: Yale University Press).

Huntington, S. P. (1984), 'Will more countries become democratic?', *Political Science Quarterly*, 99, 193–218.

Huntington, S. P. (1991–2), 'How countries democratize', *Political Science Quarterly*, 106(4), Winter, 579–616.

Hutchings, R. L. (1990), ' "Leadership drift" in the communist systems of the Soviet Union and Eastern Europe', *Studies in Comparative Communism*, 22, 5–9.

Ignatieff, M. (1993), *Blood and Belonging* (New York: Farrar, Straus & Giroux).

János, A. C. (1991), 'Social science, communism, and the dynamics of political change', *World Politics*, 44(1), October, 81–112.

Jedlicki, J. (1990), 'The revolutions of 1989: the unbearable burden of history', *Problems of Communism*, 39, July–August, 39–48.

Jelavich, B. (1983), *History of the Balkans* (Cambridge: Cambridge University Press).

Jones, A. (ed.) (1992), *Research on the Soviet Union and Eastern Europe* (London: JAI Press).

Judt, T. (1990), 'The rediscovery of Central Europe', *Daedalus*, Winter, 23–54.

Kariel, H. S. (1970), *Frontiers of Democratic Theory* (New York: Random House).

Karl, T. and Schmitter, P. C. (1991), 'Modes of transition in Latin America, southern Europe and eastern Europe', *International Political Science Journal*, 128, May, 269–84.

Karvanen, L. and Sundberg, J. (eds) (1991), *Social Democracy in Transition: Northern, Southern and Eastern Europe* (Aldershot: Dartmouth).

Katzenstein, P., Lowi, T. and Tarrow, S. (eds) (1990), *Comparative Theory and Political Experience* (Ithaca, NY: Cornell University Press).

Keane, J. (ed.) (1985), *The Power of the Powerless: Citizens against the State in Central Eastern Europe* (London: Hutchinson).

Keane, J. (1987), 'The modern democratic revolution', *Chicago Review*, 35(4), 4–19.

Keane, J. (1988), *Democracy and Civil Society* (London: Verso).

Kesselman, M. and Krieger, J. (eds) (1992), *European Politics in Transition* (Lexington, KY: D. C. Heath).

Kim, I. and Žáček, J. S. (eds) (1991), *Reform and Transformation in Communist Systems* (New York: Paragon House).

Király, B. K. and Bozóki, A. (eds) (1995), *Lawful Revolution in Hungary, 1989–94* (Boulder, CO: Social Science Monographs).

Kiss, E. (1992), 'Democracy without parties?', *Dissent*, 1, 226–31.

Kitschelt, H. (1992), 'The formation of party-systems in East Central Europe', *Politics and Society*, 20(1), March, 7–50.

Konrád, G. (1983), *Antipolitics* (San Diego, CA: Harcourt Brace Jovanovich).

Konrád, G. and Szelényi, I. (1979), *Intellectuals on the Road to Class Power* (New York: Harcourt Brace Jovanovich).

Kovacs, J. M. (ed.) (1994), *Transition to Capitalism? The Communist Legacy in Eastern Europe* (London: Transaction Publishers).

Kumar, K. (1992), 'The 1989 revolutions and the idea of Europe', *Political Studies*, 40(3), September, 439–61.

Kuran, T. (1991), 'Now out of never: the element of surprise in the East European revolution of 1989', *World Politics*, 44, 7–48.

Laclau, E. (1990), *New Reflections on the Revolution of Our Time* (London: Verso).

Lefort, C. (1986), *The Political Forms of Modern Society: Bureaucracy, Democracy, Totalitarianism* (Cambridge, MA: MIT Press).

Levine, A. (1981), *Liberal Democracy: A Critique of Its Theory* (New York: Columbia University Press).

Lewis, P. G. (1990), 'Democratization in Eastern Europe', *Coexistence*, 27.

Lewis, P. G. (ed.) (1992), *Democracy and Civil Society in Eastern Europe* (Basingstoke: Macmillan).

Lijphart, A. (1977), *Democracy in Plural Societies: A Comparative Exploration* (New Haven, CT: Yale University Press).

Lijphart, A. (1991), 'Consociational choices for new democracies', *Journal of Democracy*, 2(3).

Lijphart, A. (ed.) (1992), *Parliamentary versus Presidential Government* (Oxford: Oxford University Press).

Linz, J. (1990), 'Transitions to democracy', *Washington Quarterly*, 13, Summer, 143–64.

Linz, J. and Stepan, A. (1996), *Problems of Democratic Transition and Consolidation: Eastern Europe, Southern Europe and South America* (Baltimore: Johns Hopkins University Press).

Littlejohn, G., Smart, G. and Wakeford, B. (eds) (1978), *Power and the State* (London: Croom Helm).

Magocsi, P. R. (1993), *Historical Atlas of East Central Europe* (Seattle: University of Washington Press).

Mainwaring, S., O'Donnell, G. and Valenzuela, J. S. (eds) (1992), *Issues in Democratic Consolidation* (Notre Dame, IN: University of Notre Dame Press).

Mandelbaum, M. (ed.) (1996), *Postcommunism: Four Perspectives* (New York: Council on Foreign Relations Press).

Marks, G. and Diamond, L. (eds) (1992), *Reexamining Democracy: Essays in Honor of S. M. Lipset* (Newbury Park, NY: Sage).

Mason, D. S. (1992), *Revolution in East Central Europe: The Rise and Fall of Communism and the Cold War* (Boulder, CO: Westview Press).

Meštrović, S. G. (1993), *The Road from Paradise: Prospects for Democracy in Eastern Europe* (Lexington, KY: University of Kentucky Press).

Meyer, G. (ed.) (1993), *Die politischen Kulturen Ostmitteleuropas im Umbruch* (Tübingen: Francke Verlag).

Michnik, A. (1985), *Letters from Prison and Other Essays* (Berkeley: University of California Press).

Michta, A. and Prizel, I. (eds) (1992), *Post-communist Eastern Europe: Crisis and Reform* (New York: St Martin's Press).

Miszlivetz, F. (1991), 'The unfinished revolutions of 1989: the decline of the nation state', *Social Research*, 58(4), Winter, 781–804.

Miszlivetz, F. and Jensen, J. (eds) (1993), *Paradoxes of Transition* (Szombathely: Savaria University Press).

Moghadam, V. M. (ed.) (1993), *Democratic Reform and the Position of Women in Transitional Economies* (Oxford: Clarendon Press).

Nee, V. and Stark, D. (eds) (1989), *Remaking the Economic Institutions of Socialism: China and Eastern Europe* (Stanford, CA: Stanford University Press).

O'Donnell, G., Schmitter, P. C. and Whitehead, L. (eds) (1986), *Transitions from Authoritarian Rule*, 4 vols (Baltimore: Johns Hopkins University Press).

Offe, C. (1991), 'Capitalism by democratic design? Democratic theory facing the triple transition in East Central Europe', *Social Research*, 58(4), Winter, 865–92.

Offe, C. (1997), *Varieties of Transition: The East European and East German Experience* (Cambridge, MA: MIT Press).

Pakulski, J. (1990), 'Eastern Europe and "legitimacy crisis"', *Australian Journal of Political Science*, 25, 272–88.

Palmer, A. W. (1970), *The Lands Between: A History of East Central Europe since the Congress of Vienna* (New York: Macmillan).

Parry, G. and Moran, M. (eds) (1993), *Democracy and Democratization* (London: Routledge).

Pinder, J. (1991), *The European Community and Eastern Europe* (London: Pinter).

Poznanski, G. (ed.) (1992), *Constructing Capitalism: Reemergence of Civil Society and Liberal Economy in the Post-communist World* (Boulder, CO: Westview).

Pridham, G. (1990), *Securing Democracy* (London: Routledge).

Pridham, G. and Lewis, P. G. (eds) (1996), *Stabilizing Fragile Democracies: Comparing New Party Systems in Southern and Eastern Europe* (London: Routledge).

Prins, G. (ed.) (1990), *Spring in Winter: The 1989 Revolutions* (Manchester: Manchester University Press).

Przeworski, A. (1991), *Democracy and the Market: Political and Economic Reforms in Eastern Europe and Latin America* (Cambridge: Cambridge University Press).

Przeworski, A. (1991), 'The "East" becomes the "South"? The "autumn of the people" and the future of Eastern Europe', *Political Science and Politics*, 24(1), March, 20–4.

Przeworski, A. (ed.) (1995) *Sustainable Democracy* (Cambridge: Cambridge University Press).

Rady, M. (1992), *Romania in Turmoil* (London: I. B. Tauris).

Ramet, S. (ed.) (1992), *Adaptation of Communist and Post-communist Systems* (Boulder, CO: Westview Press).

Ramet, S. P. (1991), *Social Currents in Eastern Europe: The Sources and Meaning of the Great Transformation* (Durham, NC: Duke University Press).

Ramet, S. P. (ed.) (1994), *Rocking the State: Rock Music and Politics in Eastern Europe and Russia* (Boulder, CO: Westview Press).

Ramet, S. P. (1997), *Whose Democracy? Nationalism, Religion and the Doctrine of Collective Rights in Post-'89 Eastern Europe* (Lanham, MD: Rowman & Littlefield).

Raskovska-Harmstone, T. (ed.) (1984), *Communism in Eastern Europe* (Bloomington: University of Indiana Press).

Rau, Z. (ed.) (1991), *The Reemergence of Civil Society in Eastern Europe and the Soviet Union* (Boulder, CO: Westview Press).

Rieder, I. (1991), *Feminism and Eastern Europe* (Dublin: Attic Press).

Rigby, T. H. and Fehér, F. (eds) (1982), *Political Legitimation in Communist States* (New York: St Martin's Press).

Roberts, B. (ed.) (1990), *The New Democracies: Global Change and US Policy* (Cambridge, MA: MIT Press).

Rootes, C. and Davis, H. (eds) (1994), *Social Change and Political Transformation* (London: UCL Press).

Rose, R. (1991), *Between State and Market: Key Indicators of Transition in Eastern Europe* (Glasgow: Centre for the Study of Public Policy).

Rosenberg, T. (1996), *The Haunted Land: Facing Europe's Ghosts after Communism* (New York: Random House/Vintage).

Roskin, M. G. (1991), *The Rebirth of East Europe* (Englewood Cliffs, NJ: Prentice-Hall).

Rothschild, J. (1989), *Return to Diversity: A Political History of East Central Europe since World War II* (Oxford: Oxford University Press).

Rüb, F. W. (1993), 'Designing political systems in East European transitions: a comparative study of Bulgaria, Czechoslovakia and Hungary', Papers on East European Constitution Building, No. 3 (Bremen: ZERP).

Rueschemeyer, M. (1994), *Women in the Politics of Post-communist Eastern Europe* (Armonk, NY: M. E. Sharpe).

Rupnik, J. (1989), *The Other Europe: The Rise and Fall of Communism in East-Central Europe* (New York: Schocken Books).

Rustow, D. (1970), 'Transitions to democracy: toward a dynamic model', *Comparative Politics*, 2(3), 337–63.

Rustow, D. (1990), 'Democracy: a global revolution?', *Foreign Affairs*, 64, Fall, 75–91.

Sakwa, R. (1990), *Gorbachev and His Reforms, 1985–1990* (Englewood Cliffs, NJ: Prentice-Hall).

Saunders, C. T. (ed.) (1992), *Economics and Politics of Transition* (Basingstoke: Macmillan).

Schöpflin, G. (1991), 'Obstacles to liberalism in post-communist polities', *East European Politics and Societies*, 5(1), Winter, 189–94.

Schöpflin, G. (1991), 'Post-communism: constructing new democracies in Central Europe', *International Affairs*, 67(2), April, 235–50.

Schöpflin, G. (1993), *Politics in Eastern Europe 1945–1992* (Oxford: Basil Blackwell).

Schöpflin, G. and Wood, N. (eds) (1989), *In Search of Central Europe* (Cambridge: Polity Press).

Schumpeter, J. A. (1950), *Capitalism, Socialism and Democracy* (New York: Harper & Row).

Schwartz, H. (1991), 'Constitutional developments in East Central Europe', *Journal of International Affairs*, 45, Summer, 71–89.

Selbourne, D. (1990), *Death of the Dark Hero: Eastern Europe, 1987–90* (London: Jonathan Cape).

Seldon, A. (1994), *What Is Democracy?* (Oxford: Blackwell).

Share, D. (1987), 'Transitions to democracy and transitions through transactions', *Comparative Political Studies*, 19, 525–48.

Sheffer, G. (ed.) (1993), *Innovative Leadership in International Politics* (Albany, NY: State University of New York Press).

Skilling, G. H. (1989), *Samizdat and an Independent Society in Central and Eastern Europe* (Oxford: Macmillan).

Staniszkis, J. (1984), *Poland's Self-Limiting Revolution* (Princeton, NJ: Princeton University Press).

Staniszkis, J. (1989), 'The dynamics of breakthrough in Eastern Europe', *Soviet Studies*, 41, 560–74.

Staniszkis, J. (1991), *The Dynamics of Breakthrough in Eastern Europe: The Polish Experience* (Berkeley: University of California Press).

Stokes, G. (ed.) (1991), *From Stalinism to Pluralism: A Documentary History of Eastern Europe since 1945* (New York: Oxford University Press).

Stokes, G. (1995), *The Walls Came Tumbling Down* (New York: Oxford University Press).

Sussman, L. R. (1989), 'The information revolution', *Encounter*, 73(4), November, 60–5.

Swain, N. and Swain, G. (1993), *Eastern Europe since 1945* (London: Macmillan).

Sword, K. (ed.) (1991), *The Times Guide to Eastern Europe* (London: Times Books).

Szacki, J. (1995), *Liberalism after Communism* (Budapest: Central European University Press).

Szajkowski, B. (ed.) (1991), *New Political Parties of Eastern Europe and the Soviet Union* (London: Longman).

Szelényi, I. (1990), 'Alternative futures for Eastern Europe: the case of Hungary', *East European Politics and Societies*, 4(2), Spring, 231–54.

Szilágyi, I. (ed.) (1991), *Transition and Changes in Europe in the 80s and 90s* (Veszprém: University of Veszprém).

Szoboszlai, G. (1991), *Democracy and Political Transformation: Theories and East-Central European Realities* (Budapest: Hungarian Political Science Association).

Szoboszlai, G. (ed.) (1992), *Flying Blind: Emerging Democracies in East-Central Europe* (Budapest: Hungarian Political Science Association).

Sztompka, P. (1991), 'The intangibles and imponderables of the transition to democracy', *Studies in Comparative Communism*, 24(3), September, 295–311.

Taras, R. (ed.) (1992), *Handbook of Political Science Research on the USSR and Eastern Europe* (Westport, CT: Greenwood Press).

Taras, R. (1997), *Postcommunist Presidents* (Cambridge: Cambridge University Press).

Tismaneanu, V. (ed.) (1990), *In Search of Civil Society: Independent Peace Movements in the Soviet Bloc* (London: Routledge).

Tismaneanu, V. (1992), *Reinventing Politics: Eastern Europe from Stalin to Havel* (New York: The Free Press).

Tökés, R. L. (ed.) (1979), *Opposition in Eastern Europe* (Baltimore: Johns Hopkins University Press).

Tökés, R. L. (1990), 'Hungary's new political elites: adaptation and change, 1989–90', *Problems of Communism*, 39, November–December, 44–65.

Tökés, R. L. (1996), *Hungary's Negotiated Revolution* (Cambridge: Cambridge University Press).

Touraine, A. (1991), 'What does democracy mean today?', *International Social Science Journal*, 128, 259–68.

Verdery, K. (1996), *What Socialism Was and What Comes Next?* (Princeton, NJ: Princeton University Press).

Volten, P. (ed.) (1990), *Uncertain Futures: Eastern Europe and Democracy* (New York: Institute for East–West Security Studies).

Volten, P. (ed.) (1992), *Bound to Change: Consolidating Democracy in Eastern Europe* (Boulder, CO: Westview Press).

Walter, E. G. (1988), *The Other Europe* (Syracuse, NY: Syracuse University Press).

Wandycz, P. S. (1992), *The Price of Freedom: A History of East Central Europe from the Middle Ages to the Present* (New York: Routledge).

Weilemann, P. R. and Brunner, G. (eds) (1991), *Upheavals against the Plan: The Challenge of Reform in East Central Europe* (New York: St Martin's Press).

Wesolowski, W. (1990), 'Transitions from authoritarianism to democracy', *Social Research*, 57(2), 435–61.

White, S. (ed.) (1991), *Handbook on Reconstruction in Eastern Europe and the Soviet Union* (Harlow: Longman).

White, S., Batt, J. and Lewis, P. G. (1993), *Developments in East European Politics* (Durham, NC: Duke University Press).

White, S., Gardner, J., Schöpflin, G. and Saich, T. (1990), *Communist and Post-Communist Poltical Systems* (New York: St Martin's Press).

Whitefield, S. (ed.) (1993), *The New Institutional Architecture of Eastern Europe* (Basingstoke: Macmillan).

Zeman, Z. A. B. (1991), *The Making and Breaking of Communist Europe* (Oxford: Blackwell).

Bibliography

Adolfs, S. (1990), 'Die Entwicklung der Republik Latvia', in B. Meissner (ed.) *Die baltischen Nationen: Estland, Lettland, Litauen* (Cologne: Markus Verlag).

Agh, A. (1994), 'The revival of mixed traditions: democracy and authoritarian renewal in East Central Europe', Budapest Papers on Democratic Transition No. 92 (Budapest: Hungarian Center for Democracy Studies Foundation).

Agh, A. (1995), 'The emergence of democratic parliamentarism in Hungary', in B. K. Király and A. Bozóki (eds) *Lawful Revolution in Hungary, 1989–94* (Boulder, CO: Social Science Monographs).

Almond, G. A. and Verba, S. (eds) (1990), *Civic Culture Revisited* (London: Sage).

Arato, A. (1993), 'Interpreting 1989', *Social Research*, 60(3), Fall, 609–46.

Arendt, H. (1973), *The Origins of Totalitarianism* (New York: Harcourt Brace Jovanovich).

Baker, K. M. (ed.) (1994), *The French Revolution and the Creation of Modern Political Culture: The Terror*, Vol. 4 (Oxford: Pergamon-Elsevier Science).

Baldwin, R. (1996), *Towards an Integrated Europe* (London: Centre for Economic Policy Research).

Baldwin, R., François, J. and Portes, R. (1997), 'The costs and benefits of eastern enlargement', *Economic Policy*, 24, 125–76.

Banac, I. (ed.) (1992), *Eastern Europe in Revolution* (Ithaca, NY: Cornell University Press).

Barnovský, M. (ed.) (1995), *Od diktatúry k diktatúre: Slovensko v rokoch 1945–1953* (Bratislava: Veda).

Bělohradský, V. (1992), *Kapitalismus a občanské ctnosti* (Prague: Československý spisovatel).

Benderly, J. and Kraft, E. (eds) (1994), *Independent Slovenia* (New York: St Martin's Press).

Bibó, I. [1945] (1991 edn), 'The crisis of Hungarian democracy', in *Democracy, Revolution, Self-Determination* (selected writings, edited by Károly Nagy) (Boulder, CO: Social Science Monographs).

Bogdanor, V. (1990), 'Founding elections and regime change', *Electoral Studies*, 9(4).

Borger, J. (1996), 'He was a communist with the Midas touch, now he is Sofia's first "illustrious corpse" ', *Observer* (London), 27 October.

Bozóki, A. (1993), 'Hungary's road to systemic change: the opposition roundtable', *East European Politics and Societies*, 7(2), Spring, 276–308.

Bozóki, A. (ed.) (1994), *Democratic Legitimacy in Post-communist Societies* (Budapest: T-Twins).

Bozóki, A. (1995), 'Censorship in the 1980s', *The Hungarian Quarterly*, 36(3), Autumn, 100–10.

Bozóki, A. (1996), 'Building democracy: institutional transformation in Hungary', in S. S. Nagel.

Brown, A. (ed.) (1984), *Political Culture and Communist Studies* (London, Macmillan).

Bruszt, L. (1990), '1989: the negotiated revolution in Hungary', *Social Research*, 57(2), 365–87.

Bullain, N. (1996), 'A nonprofit szektor alapfogalmai, jellemzöi és fö dilemmái Magyarországon', JuDr thesis, Eötvös University, Budapest.

Bunce, V. (1996), 'The return of the left and the future of democracy in Central and Eastern Europe', paper presented at the Annual Meeting of the Council for European Studies, Chicago, 14–17 March.

Bútora, M. (1995), 'Some foreign policy implications of early elections in Slovakia', in S. Szomolanyi and G. Mesežnikov (eds) *Slovakia: Parliamentary Elections 1994. Causes – Consequences – Prospects* (Bratislava: Slovak Political Science Association).

Bútora, M. and Hunčík, P. (eds) (1997), *Global Report on Slovakia: Comprehensive Analyses from 1995 and Trends from 1996* (Bratislava: Nadácia Sándora Máraiho).

Bútora, M., Koštálová, K., Demeš, P. and Bútorová, Z. (1997), 'Nonprofit sector and volunteerism in Slovakia', in M. Bútora and P. Hunčík (eds) *Global Report on Slovakia: Comprehensive Analyses from 1995 and Trends from 1996* (Bratislava: Nadácia Sándora Máraiho).

Bútorová, Z., Gyárfášová, O. and Kúska, M. (1996), *Current Problems of Slovakia on the Verge of 1995–1996* (Bratislava: FOCUS).

Conradt, D. P. (1990), 'Changing German political culture', in G. A. Almond and S. Verba (eds) *Civic Culture Revisited* (London: Sage).

Csizmadia, E. (1995), *A magyar demokratikus ellenzék.* (Budapest: T-Twins).

Czech Helsinki Committee (1996), *Report on the State of Human Rights in the Czech Republic in 1995* (Prague: Czech Helsinki Committee).

Dahl, R. (1968), *Political Oppositions in Western Democracies* (New Haven, CT: Yale University Press).

Dahl, R. (1982), *Dilemmas of Pluralist Democracy* (New Haven, CT: Yale University Press).

Dahrendorf, R. (1990), *Reflections on the Revolution in Europe* (London: Chatto & Windus).

Di Palma, G. (1990), *To Craft Democracies: An Essay on Democratic Transitions*, (Berkeley: University of California Press).

Di Palma, G. (1991), 'Why democracy can work in Eastern Europe', *Journal of Democracy*, 2(1), Winter, 21–9.

Dinan, D. (1994), *Ever Closer Union? An Introduction to the European Community* (London: Macmillan).

Dostál, O. (1997), in M. Bútora and P. Hunčík (eds), *Global Report on Slovakia: Comprehensive Analyses from 1995 and Trends from 1996* (Bratislava: Nadácia Sándora Máraiho).

Dworkin, R. (1996), *Freedom's Law: The Moral Reading of the American Constitution* (Oxford: Oxford University Press).

Eberstadt, N. (1993), 'Eastern Europe's disturbing health crisis', *Wall Street Journal*, 30 September.

Einhorn, B., Kaldor, M. and Kavan, Z. (eds) (1996), *Citizenship and Democratic Control in Contemporary Europe* (Aldershot: Edward Elgar).

Elster, J. (1993), 'The necessity and impossibility of simultaneous economic and political reform', in Greenberg *et al.* (eds) *Constitutionalism and Democracy* (Oxford: Oxford University Press).

Elster, J. and Rune, S. (eds) (1993), *Constitutionalism and Democracy* (Cambridge: Cambridge University Press).

European Bank for Reconstruction and Development (1995), *Transition Report 1995* (London: EBRD).

Fisher, S. (1996), 'Mečiar retains control of the political scene', *Transition*, 2(16), 127–46.

Gaidys, V. (1996), *Praeities, dabarties ir ateities verinimas Baltijos Šalyse, 1993–95* (published in English as 'Attitudes toward the Past, Present and Future in the Baltic States in 1993–1995', *Journal for Mental Changes*, 2(1), 25–36).

Gaisbacher *et al.* (eds) (1992), *Krieg in Europa: Analysen aus dem ehemaligen Jugoslawien* (Frankfurt am Main: Sandkorn).

Gati, G. (1996), 'The mirage of democracy', *Transition*, 2(6), 22 March.

Gindl, E. (1997), 'Media', in M. Bútora and P. Hunčík (eds) *Global Report on Slovakia: Comprehensive Analyses from 1995 and Trends from 1996* (Bratislava: Nadácia Sándora Máraiho).

Girnius, S. (1995), 'Ahead of the censors, but feeling the economic strain in the Baltic states', *Transition*, 1(18).

Gouldner, A. (1979), *The Future of Intellectuals and the Rise of the New Class* (New York: Seabury Press).

Grabbe, H. and Hughes, K. (1997), *Eastward Enlargement of the European Union* (London: Royal Institute for International Affairs).

Greskovits, B. (1996), 'Good-bye breakdown prophecies, hello poor democracies: on failed predictions and eastern transformation realities', paper presented at the Annual Meeting of the Council for European Studies, Chicago, 14–17 March.

Gyárfášová, O. (1996), 'Media', in Z. Bútorová, O. Gyárfášová and M. Kúska, *Current Problems of Slovakia on the Verge of 1995–1996* (Bratislava: FOCUS).

Habermas, J. (1989), *The Structural Transformation of the Public Sphere: An Inquiry into a Category of Bourgeois Society* (Cambridge, MA: MIT Press).

Habermas, J. (1996), *Between Facts and Norms: Contributions to a Discourse Theory of Law and Democracy* (Cambridge, MA: MIT Press).

Halmai, G. (1995), 'The constitutional court', in B. K. Király and A. Bozóki (eds) *Lawful Revolution in Hungary, 1989–94* (Boulder, CO: Social Science Monographs).

Hankiss, E. (1990), *East European Alternatives* (Oxford: Clarendon Press).

Havel, V. (1992), *Summer Meditations* (London, Faber & Faber).

Heller, A. (1988), 'On formal democracy', in J. Keane (ed.) *Civil Society and the State* (London: Verso).

Higley, J., Kullberg, J. and Pakulski, J. (1996), 'The persistence of postcommunist elites', *Journal of Democracy*, 7(2), 133–47.

Holländer, P. and Valko, E. (1993), 'Zmeny v právnom systéme', in *Slovensko: Kroky k Európskemu spoločenstvu. Scenár socialnopolitických súvislostí* (Bratislava: Sociologický ústav SAV).

Holmes, S. (1995), 'Cultural legacies or state collapse? Probing the post-communist dilemma', lecture delivered at Collegium Budapest, 17 October.

Hrabko, J. (1996), 'Posolstvo občanom', *SME*, 9 September.

Huntington, S. P. (1993), *The Third Wave of Democratization* (Norman, OK: University of Oklahoma Press).

Inkens, E. (1996), 'The "let-sprout" democracy III', *Diena*, 30 January.

Jachtenfuchs, M. (1995), 'Theoretical perspectives on European governance', *European Law Journal*, 1(2).

Jalušič, V. (1995), 'Politics as a whore', paper presented to the conference 'The Politics of Antipolitics', Vienna Dialogue on Democracy, Vienna.

Jenkins, R. M. (1992), 'Society and regime transition in East Central Europe', in G. Szoboszlai (ed.) *Flying Blind: Emerging Democracies in East Central Europe* (Budapest: HPSA), 115–46.

Jowitt, K. (1991), 'The new world disorder', *Journal of Democracy*, 2(1), Winter, 11–20.

Jowitt, K. (1992), 'The Leninist legacy', in I. Banac (ed.) *Eastern Europe in Revolution* (Ithaca, NY: Cornell University Press).

Juris, A. *et al.* (1995), 'Privatization in Slovakia. Present problems and questions', MESA 10 (Bratislava: MESA).

Keane, J. (ed.) (1988), *Civil Society and the State* (London: Verso).

Keohane, R. O. and Hoffman, S. (1991), 'Institutional change in Europe in the 1980s', in R. O. Keohane and S. Hoffman (eds) *The New European Community: Decision-Making and Institutional Change* (Boulder, CO: Westview Press).

Kester, G. and Pinaud, H. (eds) (1994), *Trade Unions and Democratic Participation: A Scenario for the Twenty-First Century* (Paris: ISS/LERPSO).

Kettle, S. (1996), 'Slovakia's one-man band: profile of Prime Minister Vladimir Mečiar', *Transition*, 2(17).

Király, B. K. and Bozóki, A. (eds) (1995), *Lawful Revolution in Hungary, 1989–94* (Boulder, CO: Social Science Monographs).

Kirch, M. and Kirch, A. (1995), 'Search for security in Estonia: new identity architecture', *Security Dialogue*, 26(4).

Kitschelt, H. (1995), 'Formation of party cleavages in post-communist democracies', *Party Politics*, 1(4), 447–72.

Klaus, V. (1991), *Nemám rád katastrofické scénáře* (Ostrava: Sagit).

Klaus, V. (1993), *Rok málo či mnoho v dějinách země* (Prague: Repro-Media).

Kováč, M. (1995), 'Náš život je silné prepolitizovaný', *Národna obroda*, 12 December.

Kraft, E., Vodopivec, M. and Cvikl, M. (1994), 'On its own: the economy of independent Slovenia', in J. Benderly and E. Kraft (eds) *Independent Slovenia* (New York: St Martin's Press).

Kraigher, T. (1994), *Prebivalstvo in zaposlenost v Sloveniji na prehodu iz osemdesetih v devetdeseta leta in ocene tendenc razvoja do leta 2000* (Ljubljana: ZRMK).

Krivý, V. (1996), 'Kryštalizácia základných politických zoskupení vo vzťahu k stiepeniu slovenskej spoločnosti', *Sociologia*, 28(2), 127–46.

Kumar, A. (1995), 'Evropska unija in Slovenija', in F. Stiblar *et al.* (eds) *Splosni pogoji za gospodarski razvoj* (Ljubljana: ZRMK).

Kuzmanić, T. (1992), 'Entmilitarisierung im ehemaligen Jugoslawien', in Gaisbacher *et al.* (eds) *Krieg in Europa: Analysen aus dem ehemaligen Jugoslawien* (Frankfurt am Main: Sandkorn).

Kuzmanić, T. (1993), 'Stalinism as the problem of methodology', in T. Kuzmanič and A. Truger, *Yugoslavia, War*, 2nd edn (Peace Institute, Ljubljana, Slovenia, and Study Centre for Peace and Conflict Resolution, Schlaining, Austria).

Kuzmanić, T. (1994), 'Strikes, trade unions, and Slovene independence, v. independent Slovenia', in J. Benderly and E. Kraft (eds) *Independent Slovenia* (New York: St Martin's Press).

Kuzmanić, T. (1996a), '(Anti)political extremism in Slovenia 1990–1995', paper presented to the Conference on Political Extremism and Violence against Foreigners and Other Marginals, Peace Institute, Ljubljana, March.

Kuzmanić, T. (1996b), 'Slovene journalists' trade unions in the nineties: opinion poll research', manuscript, Ljubljana.

Kuzmanić, T. and Truger, A. (1993), *Yugoslavia, War*, 2nd edn (Peace Institute, Ljubljana, Slovenia, and Study Centre for Peace and Conflict Resolution, Schlaining, Austria).

Lefort, C. (1988), *Democracy and Political Theory* (Minneapolis, MN: University of Minnesota Press).

Lefort, C. (1991), *L'invention démocratique: les limites de la domination totalitaire* (Paris: Fayard).

Leško, M. (1996), *Mečiar a mečiarizmus* (Bratislava: VMV).

Lijphart, A. (1984), *Democracies: Patterns of Majoritarian and Consensus Government in Twenty-One Countries* (New Haven, CT: Yale University Press).

Linz, J. J. (1978), *The Break-down of Democratic Regimes. Crisis, Breakdown, and Reequilibration* (Baltimore, MD: Johns Hopkins University Press).

Lipset, S. M. and Rokkan, S. (1968), 'Cleavage structures, party systems and voter alignments: an introduction', in S. M. Lipset and S. Rokkan, *Party Systems and Voter Alignments: A Cross-National Perspective* (New York: The Free Press).

Lipták, Ľ. (1992), 'Slovensko medzi dvoma vojnami', in R. Marsina, V. Čičaj, D. Kováč and Ľ. Lipták, *Slovenské dejiny* (Bratislava: Vydavateľstvo Matice Slovenskej).

Lipták, Ľ. (1995), 'Vonkajšie a vnútorné faktory formovania politických systémov na Slovensku', in M. Barnovský (ed.), *Od diktatúry k diktatúre: Slovensko v rokoch 1945–1953* (Bratislava: Veda).

Marx, K. [1843] (1975), 'On the Jewish question', in *Early Writings* (New York: Vintage Books).

Meissner, B. (ed.) (1990), *Die baltischen Nationen: Estland, Lettland, Litauen* (Cologne: Markus Verlag).

Mesežnikov, G. (1995), 'The parliamentary elections 1994: a confirmation of the split of the party system in Slovakia', in S. Szomolanyi and G. Mesežnikov (eds) *Slovakia: Parliamentary Elections 1994. Causes – Consequences – Prospects* (Bratislava: Slovak Political Science Association).

Meyer, G. (1994), 'Democratic legitimacy in post-communist societies: concept and problems', in A. Bozóki (ed.) *Democratic Legitimacy in Post-communist Societies* (Budapest: T-Twins).

Mezs, I. (1996), 'Does Latvia really suppress minorities?', *Diena*, 9 February.

Mikloš, I. (1997), 'Privatization', in M. Bútora and P. Hunčík (eds) *Global Report on Slovakia: Comprehensive Analyses from 1995 and Trends from 1996* (Bratislava: Nadácia Sándora Máraiho).

Milanovic, B. (1994), 'A cost of transition: 50 million now poor and growing inequality', *Transition*, 5(8), 1–4.

Millar, J. R. and Wolchik, S. L. (eds) (1994), *The Social Legacy of Communism* (Cambridge: Cambridge University Press).

Mungiu, A. (1996), *Die Rumanen nach '89* (Friederich Ebert Stiftung-Intergraph).

MVK (1996), *Multimedia Survey – January 1996* (Bratislava: MVK, Slovak Radio).

Nagel, S. S., Crotty, W. and Scarritt, J. (eds) (1996), *Political Reform and Developing Nations* (Greenwich, CT: JAI Press).

Noorköiv, R. and Annus, T. (1994), 'Estonia on the road to market economy: changes in the social sphere' (Tallinn: Ministry of Social Affairs).

Novák, M. (1994), *Dober dan Revščina* (Ljubljana: Socialna Zbornica Slovenije).

O'Donnell, G. (1994), 'Delegative democracy', *Journal of Democracy*, 5(1), 55–69.

O'Donnell, G. and Schmitter, P. C. (1989), *Transitions from Authoritarian Rule: Tentative Conclusions about Uncertain Democracies* (Baltimore, MD: Johns Hopkins University Press).

Orwell, G. (1957), *Selected Essays* (Baltimore).

Palko, V. (1996), 'Will Parliament make sweeping changes this session? No, and Slovakia's EU, NATO bids suffer', *Slovak Spectator*, 28 August–10 September.

Paul, D. W. (1984), 'Czechoslovakia's political culture reconsidered', in A. Brown (ed.) *Political Culture and Communist Studies* (London: Macmillan).

Petersen, J. (1995), 'Decision-making in the European Union: towards a framework for analysis', *Journal of European Public Policy*, 2(1).

Pokol, B. (1994), *A magyar parlamentarizmus* (Budapest: Cserépfalvi).

Preuss, U. (1993), 'Constitutional aspects of the making of democracy in the post-communist societies of East Europe', Diskussionspapier 2/93 (Bremen: Zentrum für Europäische Rechtspolitik).

Prusák, J. (1995), 'Štát po troch rokoch a v treťom roku existencie', *Národná obroda*, 30 December.

Przeworski, A., Alvarez, M. M., Chebab, J. A. and Limengineto, F. P. (1996), 'What makes democracies endure?', *Journal of Democracy*, 7(1), January, 39–55.

Radičová, I. (ed.) (1995), *Pre ľudí a o ľuďoch: otázky formovania sociálnej politiky na Slovensku* (Bratislava: SPACE).

Rollo, J. and Smith, A. (1993), 'The political economy of Eastern European trade with the European Community: why so sensitive?', *Economic Policy*, 16, April, 139–81.

Ross, G. (1995), *Jacques Delors and European Integration* (Oxford: Oxford University Press).

Rueschmeyer, D., Stephens, E. H. and Stephens, J. D. (1992), *Capitalist Development and Democracy* (Cambridge: Polity Press).

Sartori, G. (1962), *Democratic Theory* (Detroit, MI: Wayne State University Press).

Scheppele, K. L. (1995), 'Women's rights in Eastern Europe', *East European Constitutional Review*, 4(1), Winter, 66–9.

Schmitter, P. C. (1992), 'The consolidation of democracy and representation of social groups', *American Behavioral Scientist*, 35, 422–49.

Schmitter, P. C. and Karl, T. L. (1991), 'What democracy is . . . and is not?' *Journal of Democracy*, 2(3), Summer, 75–88.

Schöpflin, G. (1994), 'Post-communism: the problems of democratic construction', *Daedalus*, Summer, 127–41.

SDIP (1994), Strengthening Democratic Institutions Project: 'The Citizenship and Alien Law Controversies in Estonia and Latvia', John F. Kennedy School of Government, Harvard University, Cambridge, MA, April.

Sedelmeier, U. (1994), 'The European Union's Association Policy towards Central and Eastern Europe: Political and Economic Rationales in Conflict', SEI Working Paper No. 7 (Falmer: Sussex European Institute).

Sedelmeier, U. and Wallace, H. (1996), 'Policies towards Central and Eastern Europe', in H. Wallace and W. Wallace (eds) *Policy-Making in the European Union*, 3rd edn (Oxford: Oxford University Press).

Seligman, A. (1992), *The Idea of Civil Society* (Princeton, NJ: Princeton University Press).

Simko, I. (1996), *Kriticke miesta Ustavy Slovenskej Republiky c. 460/1992 Zb.* (Bratislava: Klub Windsor).

Slab, B. (1994), 'Humanita je vec vsetkych obcanov', *Parlamentny kurier*, 10.

Slovenia for Everyone (1995), 'Politics, economy and other useful information' (Ljubljana: Government Public Relations and Media Office).

Smith, A., Holmes, P., Sedelmeier, U., Smith, E., Wallace, H. and Young, A. R. (1996), 'The European Union and Central and Eastern Europe: pre-accession strategies', SEI Working Paper No. 15 (Falmer, Sussex European Institute).

Smith, G. (ed.) (1994), *The Baltic States: The National Self-Determination of Estonia, Latvia, Lithuania* (New York: St Martin's Press).

Smith, G., Aasland, A. and Mole, R. (1994), 'Statehood, ethnic relations and citizenship', in G. Smith (ed.) *The Baltic States: The National Self-Determination of Estonia, Latvia, Lithuania* (New York: St Martin's Press).

Soros, G. (1997), 'Capital crimes', *Guardian*, 18 January.

Stark, D. (1990), 'Privatization in Hungary: from plan to market or from plan to clan?', *East European Politics and Societies*, 4(3), 351–92.

Stark, D. (1996), 'Recombinant property in East European capitalism', *American Journal of Sociology*, 101(4), January, 993–1027.

Steen, A. (1994), 'Recirculation and expulsion: the new elites in the Baltic states', Forskningsntat 09/94, Institute for Statsvitenskap, Department of Political Science, Copenhagen.

Stiblar, F. (1995), 'Vpliv razvoja mednarodnega ekonomskega okolja na slovensko gospodarstvo', in F. Stiblar *et al.* (eds) *Splosni pogoji za gospodarski razvoj* (Ljubljana: ZRMK).

Stiblar, F. *et al.* (eds) (1995), *Splosni pogoji za gospodarski razvoj* (Ljubljana: ZRMK).

Stubbs, P. (1996), 'Nationalism, globalization and civil society in Croatia and Slovenia', *Research in Social Movements and Change*, 19.

Sunstein, C. R. (1995), 'Rights after communism: introduction', *East European Constitutional Review*, 4(1), Winter, 61–2.

Szabó, M. (1992), 'The taxi driver demonstration in Hungary: social protest and policy change', in G. Szoboszlai (ed.) *Flying Blind: Emerging Democracies in East Central Europe* (Budapest: HPSA).

Szelényi, I. (1988), *Socialist Entrepreneurs: Embourgeoisement in Rural Hungary* (Madison, WI: University of Wisconsin Press).

Szoboszlai, G. (ed.) (1992), *Flying Blind: Emerging Democracies in East Central Europe* (Budapest: HPSA).

Szöcs, L. (1996), 'The present of an old idea: thoughts on the chances of civil society after communism: the Hungarian experience', MA thesis (Budapest: Central European University).

Szomolanyi, S. (1995), 'Does Slovakia deviate from the central European variant of transition?', in S. Szomolanyi and G. Mesežnikov (eds) *Slovakia: Parliamentary Elections 1994. Causes – Consequences – Prospects* (Bratislava: Slovak Political Science Association).

Szomolanyi, S. (1996), 'Report 1996 on Slovakia's capacity for the EU integration', manuscript, Bratislava.

Szomolanyi, S. and Mesežnikov, G. (eds) (1995), *Slovakia: Parliamentary Elections 1994. Causes – Consequences – Prospects* (Bratislava: Slovak Political Science Association).

Tamás, G. M. (1994), 'A disquisition on civil society', *Social Research*, 61(2), Summer, 205–22.

Tocqueville, A. de (1981), *De la démocratie en Amérique*, Vol. II (Paris: Garnier-Flammarion).

Vejvoda, I. (1996), 'Apolitisme et postcommunisme', *Tumultes*, 8, September, 195–206.

Wallace, H. (1997), 'Pan-European integration: a real or imagined community?', *Government and Opposition*, 32(2), 215–33.

Wallace, H. and Wallace, W. (eds) (1996), *Policy-Making in the European Union*, 3rd edn (Oxford: Oxford University Press).

Wheaton, B. and Kavan, Z. (1992), *The Velvet Revolution: Czechoslovakia 1989–1991* (Boulder, CO: Westview Press).

Wolek, A. (1996), 'Symbolic politics in Central Europe after 1989: right-wing agenda in Czech Republic, Hungary, and Poland', MA thesis (Budapest: Central European University).

Woleková, H. (1995), 'Alternatívna sociálna politika', in I. Radičová (ed.), *Pre lúdí a o ludoch: otázky formovania sociálnej politiky na Slovensku* (Bratislava: SPACE).

Woloch, I. (1994), 'The contraction and expansion of democratic space', in K. M. Baker (ed.), *The French Revolution and the Creation of Modern Political Culture: The Terror*, Vol. 4 (Oxford: Pergamon-Elsevier Science).

Index